Spirituality beyond Borders

Spirituality beyond Borders

JustHope's Nicaraguan Solidarity

Kathleen McCallie

PICKWICK *Publications* • Eugene, Oregon

SPIRITUALITY BEYOND BORDERS
JustHope's Nicaraguan Solidarity

Copyright © 2024 Kathleen McCallie. All rights reserved. Except for brief quotations in critical publications or reviews, no part of this book may be reproduced in any manner without prior written permission from the publisher. Write: Permissions, Wipf and Stock Publishers, 199 W. 8th Ave., Suite 3, Eugene, OR 97401.

Pickwick Publications
An Imprint of Wipf and Stock Publishers
199 W. 8th Ave., Suite 3
Eugene, OR 97401

www.wipfandstock.com

PAPERBACK ISBN: 978-1-6667-8243-1
HARDCOVER ISBN: 978-1-6667-8244-8
EBOOK ISBN: 978-1-6667-8245-5

Cataloguing-in-Publication data:

Names: McCallie, Kathleen D., author.

Title: Spirituality beyond borders : JustHope's Nicaraguan solidarity / Kathleen D. McCallie.

Description: Eugene, OR: Pickwick Publications, 2024.| Includes bibliographical references and index.

Identifiers: ISBN 978-1-6667-8243-1 (paperback). | ISBN 978-1-6667-8244-8 (hardcover). | ISBN 978-1-6667-8245-5 (ebook).

Subjects: LSCH: Liberation theology. | Spirituality. | Social justice. | JustHope.

Classification: BR625.N5 M36 2024 (print). | BR625 (epub).

VERSION NUMBER 06/11/24

Permission for the use of song lyrics for "Cristo de Palacagüina" and "Hijos de Maíz" comes courtesy of Carlos Mejía Godoy.

Permission to reprint "Mission," by Sr. Joan Uhlen comes courtesy of the Maryknoll Sisters.

"Cardboard Houses": Words and Music by Cliff B. Worsham and Javier Bolea of RBTS WIN (c) 2009, Reproduced by permission of Third Side Music.

All proceeds from the sale of this book will be donated to JustHope.

Dedicated to the children of Chacraseca

Contents

Preface | ix
Acknowledgments | xiii
Introduction | xvii

1. Liberation Theology with JustHope | 1
2. Preparations for Border Crossing | 16
3. Holy Ground: Ethnography of a Partnership | 38
4. Solidarity in Dignified Work | 61
5. Sustainability in Educational Programs | 95
6. Collaboration in Health Care | 124
7. Model Farm Mutuality | 154
8. Locally Led Construction | 187
9. Gringo Day | 198
10. Three Priests and a Woman Pastor: Chacraseca and JustHope | 214
11. Liberation Theologies, Spirituality, and Social Epistemology | 238
12. Updates: Political Uprising and Then COVID | 260

Appendix | 267
Bibliography | 279
Index | 287

Preface

THE PHENOMENON OF THE faith in action described in this book offers a winsome way of reimagining communities of spiritual seeking and practice that transcends borders. Founded in 2007 with roots in the turbulent Latin America of the 1960s and 70s, the non-profit organization JustHope was born out of transnational partnerships created to foster encounters of reconciliatory work and transformative justice. Based in Tulsa, Oklahoma, JustHope develops long-term partnerships between groups in the U.S. and Nicaraguan communities.[1] For example, a nursing school in Kansas might send a team of a dozen volunteers for a week every year for a minimum of three years to offer free medical care in rural Nicaragua. A congregation in Ohio might organize a partner team to travel for a week each summer and build one house each year. The development work in Nicaragua is led and directed by Nicaraguans; it is funded and engaged by volunteers from the U.S. committed to long-term justice-seeking relationships. JustHope invites encounters with spiritual and theological questions. Traveling to Nicaragua to work for justice and solidarity is not a journey toward a self-fulfillment type spirituality. The path is likely to be heartbreaking as well as joyous. This is an important story when Christianity in North America is changing. The JustHope model also yields examples for experiential learning, intercultural encounter, and spiritual formation that are relevant to Christian education. Ethics and work for justice are inseparable from this type of spirituality informed by liberation theology.[2] I witness and document the JustHope experience as a pathway to advance both discipleship and motivation to

1. http://www.justhope.org.
2. Ruether, *To Change the World*, 19.

better understand and change global economic, political, theological, and ethical systems through liberation.

Therefore, this interdisciplinary study centers ethics and social justice. I acknowledge that although mutuality is a JustHope value, an inherent inequality exists as the starting point of partnerships described here. If this book's method fully represented the solidarity and radical equality of JustHope's values, it would be co-authored by a Nicaraguan and would allow equal voice from that perspective. Perhaps, in the future, such a book will be possible. In contrast, this book is addressed primarily to North Americans and aims to correct the mistaken idea that JustHope partners travel to help Nicaraguans. I have worked to include and amplify Nicaraguan voices; transcribed interviews translated from Spanish are some of the most valuable passages of this book. Some partners have the ability to fly across national borders while others suffer grinding poverty, malnutrition, and oppressive conditions. Some theorists claim there is no way to interact across these economic divides without causing more harm than good. However, an isolationist approach of staying home does not reduce harm either.

JustHope partners learn to avoid slipping into paternalism and older views of helping the poor. We strive to recognize our own interests and admit our own needs. Mutuality demands that North Americans need partnerships as much as Nicaraguans do. At times, then, it can seem as if this writing uses the encounters with Nicaraguans as a means for spiritual growth. However, we all need justice and equality, so redistribution of resources coupled with learning to collaborate and share wisdom are the primary goals. Would-be partners seek honest, transparent, conscious steps toward learning to live in radically new ways in recognition of true interdependence. JustHope offers opportunity to discover obstacles within ourselves to living sustainably in community. This is a challenging journey that requires spiritual growth and transformation. North Americans need help, too.

JustHope recognizes a dialectical relationship between unjust social systems and unhealthy spirituality. The legacy of colonialism results in economic and political systems that make people poor in places like Nicaragua but also results in spiritual bankruptcy and moral disease in places like the United States. Anthropologist Alcida Ramos coined the term "imperialist nostalgia" to denote a type of white supremacist, neocolonial longing for a time before conquest of imagined indigenous communities who are essentialized as being closer to nature and free of white guilt.[3] The history of Christian missions was entwined with colonial horrors and Eurocentric global expansion. Transnational and intercultural relations continue to struggle to root out implicit bias and cultural imperialism. Obsequious tendencies to romanticize revolution, essentialize the poor, and perpetuate paternalistic patterns of dependency through charity abound in religious and poverty tourism. JustHope strives to eschew those types of models and embody solidarity ethics instead.[4] My subject position as a U.S. citizen, a white woman academic from Oklahoma, a pastor in the United Church of Christ, and a volunteer JustHope partner simultaneously limits and facilitates my work.

Organizations that link North Americans and Nicaraguans in partnerships for development, international exchange, and solidarity have fallen on hard times since the political crisis in 2018 when hundreds of Nicaraguans died protesting their own government. COVID-19 thwarted efforts for organizations to resume travel and restore programs during 2020–22. Like many such groups, JustHope sought to regroup and eventually to restructure in response. In 2023, JustHope is exploring reorganization with the center of operations in Nicaragua. This book documents JustHope before the tumultuous changes over the past five years. Perhaps the insights learned over thirty years of work can benefit those who continue the struggle for justice and hope.

3. Ramos, "Pulp Fictions of Indigenism," 373.
4. Peters, *Solidarity Ethics*.

Acknowledgments

I THANK FRIENDS AND colleagues in Nicaragua, especially Elba, Julio, Donã Nimia, Francis, Abimiel, Juan Pablo, Martin, Octavio, Carolina, Stephanie Raquel, and others who have inspired, corrected, challenged, and embraced me through true community. For sharing meaningful work, collaborative learning, good food, great music, dancing, solidarity, and the struggle for justice, I am thankful. I have been blessed to spend time with beloved musicians Katia and Salvador Cardinal, both in Nicaragua and Oklahoma when they toured in concert. Their stories and leadership in the movements for a free Nicaragua continue to inspire me. I thank Carlos Mejía Godoy whom I met at Casa Benjamin Linder in Managua in the early 1990s. Hearing him perform at Nicaraguan nightclubs and the National Theater over the years taught me much about the history and passion embodied in the poetic genius and mastery of his music. I am honored that he granted permission to share his lyrics in this book. Thanks to Juan Pedro Gaffney for his poetic translation and inspiration through Coro Hispano. I am also indebted to Sharon Hoffstetler and the staff of Witness for Peace, whose programs and resources have shaped my learning in Nicaragua.

The opportunity to meet and to learn from Father Uriel and Father Donald enhanced my study and spiritual formation. From the early 1990s, Father Miguel d'Escoto shared pastoral care, prophetic teaching, and political analysis with me, teams of volunteers, students, and members of my family. I appreciate generous ways he welcomed us in his home and granted me lengthy interviews and candid expressions of his faith and work. His wisdom, joy, hospitality, and love for Nicaragua have shaped my own deepest commitments. I am especially thankful for conversations during the last years of his life.

Leslie Penrose and her ministry has enriched and inspired my life since the 1980s. Her spiritual depths, relational wisdom, and courageous integrity birthed creative communities that continue to spread seeds of transformative justice. Her husband, Steve, shared this joy and journey as another essential partner and worker. A number of servant leaders who formed and reformed JustHope through the years served on the board and contributed financial resources as well as love and time to continue the partnerships. I especially thank Brad Mulholland, David Hoot, Ted Campbell, Steve Penrose, Lynn Bradley, Michael Quintan, Tim Collins, Beatrice Perez, Austin Linsley, Andrea Glen, and Kevin Howe. LiErin Probasco's leadership has been important to our board, and her excellent dissertation and publications enhanced my own research. I have led numerous teams over the years who have granted me permission to write about our shared experiences. I am thankful for all those who have contributed their time, talent, and treasure. Special thanks to Marcela Delgado, Donna Greene, and Catherine Buck for their work on our storytelling project collecting oral histories and interviews. Donna's work transcribing recordings was invaluable. The conversations the four of us shared enriched my comprehension and insight. Mindy McGarrah Sharp has been a JustHope board member, a faculty colleague, and a continuing friend and mentor. I am grateful for her wise counsel, research, friendship, and support.

This project has benefited from financial and intellectual support from Phillips Theological Seminary. My sabbatical from teaching provided time to complete this work. Many fine students formed the collaborative learning process in immersion study courses to Nicaragua. I thank those who offered willingness and permission to share these stories. My faculty colleagues continue to enrich my education and teaching. Special thanks to Joe Bessler, Ellen Blue, and Lisa Davison for encouragement and support. Numerous graduate students returned to Nicaragua and became engaged JustHope partners after our classes. Paul Ellis Jackson and Donna Greene continue to connect and serve as partners. I thank Alexis Englebrecht Villefane for reading and commenting on an early draft.

Michele Eodice provided consultation and guidance early in the publication process. I thank K. C. Hanson, Jeremy Funk, and Wipf and Stock Publishers for editorial support. Thanks to the Maryknoll Sisters who granted permission to utilize Sister Joan's writing. Thanks to T. M.

Scruggs for ways his own research enriched my understanding and the ways he assisted in reconnecting with Carlos Mejía Godoy. I thank Zoë Sherinian for reading and discussing early drafts. I value her research on liberation theology and conversations about shared experience in Nicaragua. Stephanie Arel read early sections; I am thankful for her encouragement. I owe Toni Imbler a debt of gratitude for her expert help preparing the manuscript.

My father, Marcus Boyd Shook, shared my love for Nicaragua and traveled with me many times. Manos Juntas, his nonprofit organization, taught me important lessons about partnership. I am thankful for his support and commitment to my research, learning, and ministry. Without his work I would not have gained access to various Nicaraguan leaders. My mother, Sue Shook, gifted me with resilience and encouragement. I thank my sister, Jen Shook, for countless conversations about political theory, art, and intercultural dynamics. She graciously read improved drafts. I thank my daughter, Moriah Bailey Stephenson, who sharpened my thought by discussions of global justice movements, academic ethics, and intercultural competency. Traveling in Nicaragua with daughters, sisters, father, and close friends yielded learning and relational power for social justice transformation. Peggy Johnson shared the journey returning with me to Nicaragua and to revisiting spiritual questions over the years. I thank her for reading an early draft and inspiring me to press on. For all my family of blood and choice, I am thankful for encouragement on this endeavor.

This book would not be possible without the editorial work of Katie Reichert. Her talent, intellect, and friendship bring me hope for the future. Special thanks to Sandy Shapoval for comments. I am grateful to Amy Oden for academic mentoring, provocative discussions, and encouragement in the writing process. I thank Susan Ross for the wise editing, spiritual direction, and guidance. I appreciate companionship and conversations with Jeni Markham Clewell over many years in Nicaragua and Oklahoma. These sacred friendships embody the grace and mystery of the power that keeps us in the struggle for peace, hope, and justice.

All proceeds from the sale of this book go to JustHope.

Introduction

WHY TRAVEL TO NICARAGUA rather than focus on poverty and injustice within North American communities? Does this type of service learning or volunteer partnership do more harm than good? Is JustHope a form of neocolonial poverty tourism? What systemic barriers have we internalized within ourselves as North Americans that we must dismantle in order to collaborate in authentic solidarity? The goal of this book is to explore and sharpen questions like these. As an organization, JustHope wants partners to forge community and justice through mutuality. Unfortunately, the emphasis on the transformations of ourselves as partners who travel could give the impression that we are using Nicaraguans for our own spiritual growth or consciousness raising. Taking this as a serious problem, JustHope works to identify conditions necessary for long term collaboration. JustHope partners share experiences that can be catalysts for change through liberation from unjust ways. The goals include working for systemic economic and social change.

As a theological educator, pastor, and scholar, I never escape the existential burden of my own journey toward becoming a better partner in the work of social justice. Therefore, my own search for transformation and wisdom cannot be excised from my study and teaching of ethics. In this book, I attest to the intersection of social movements, academic disciplines, spiritual formation, and the personal/political quests of companions whose influence shaped my thought and practice. Bonnie J. Miller-McLemore identified Christian practical wisdom as "a kind of theological knowing that arises within practice and makes good practice possible."[1] I frame this monograph as a thick description of a seminary

---

1. Miller-McLemore, "Disciplining," 175.

intercultural immersion course that explores JustHope partnerships as a vehicle to encounter liberation theology praxis in Nicaragua. My hope is that readers who engage this study find challenge, inspiration, and succor for their own journeys of spiritual transformation.

Some readers will be interested in pastoral theology, but the intersections with liberatory praxis in multiple disciplines are integral to theological education and the work of JustHope. In order to understand a group of seminary students, one must know that the paradigm shifts within Christianity continue to deconstruct and interrogate faith and discipleship formation. Although I teach at a seminary, I do not think that following the ways of Jesus includes trying to get people to believe certain metaphysical claims. Jesus invoked his followers to make *disciples*, that is to make students or learners. I want students to embrace a lifelong commitment to becoming more teachable, more open to relationship, more curious about mysteries of justice and kindness. Furthermore, what counts as knowledge is an integral part of the questions that frame this study. I encourage students to interrogate the Eurocentric, individualistic notions of academic learning. I draw on critical pedagogy of Paulo Freire and others in postcolonial and subaltern studies of community organizing and development. By centering Nicaraguan voices and learning from the local community leaders there, we continue to take steps towards unmasking U.S. hegemony and recognizing the imperious Western gaze.

The group of students described in this book is typical of those studying pastoral leadership in mainline, progressive seminaries in the early twenty-first century in the United States. I understand my role as their professor to be a companion with them in the learning community of our class, since I myself have a long way to go in mastering my own practice of spiritual wisdom. Discourses of transnational feminist ethics, development ethics, and liberative pedagogy all inform my teaching and research. For example, Diego de Merich notes how immersion learning experiences are sought within international development programs that may intend to ascribe accountability to subaltern voices but sometimes merely function as "one-off interaction."[2] Instead, interdisciplinary study facilitates practical wisdom and provides theoretical tools for this type of theological education through explorations of ethics and liberation theology, as developed in base communities in Central America and feminist liberation theology. JustHope's model requires thorough reflection

---

2. Merich, "Empathy in Pursuit of a Caring Ethic," 102.

and ongoing dialogue, integrating the best practices of social ethics and liberative praxis.

By beginning each chapter with description of action, followed by critical inquiry and reflection, my goal is to present an example of praxis. Put another way, I aim for my methods and writing to be consistent with values of liberation theology. Praxis is collaborative analysis of shared experience and collective action with the goal of understanding and changing ourselves and the world. For these reasons, by recounting details of our trip, I invite the reader to engage the experience as deeply as possible to contextualize the intellectual inquiry. Understanding must be manifest in action. As Isasi-Diaz argues, "reflective action grounded in community" must be part of praxis. She writes:

> Our insistence on praxis does not put reason and intellect aside . . . On the contrary, those who struggle to survive are the very ones who can question the rationality of the oppressors, who themselves are not capable of understanding this basic truth: that in the long run, only what benefits all of humanity will really benefit them.[3]

I offer this picture of a small group learning by engaging a local Nicaraguan community as an example of shared praxis. We learn and construct meaning in relationship. Thus, as a participant observer, my research utilizes mixed methods, including ethnography as pastoral practice and social epistemology. It must be noted that this book reflects research and praxis in western Nicaragua and does not attempt to represent cultural concerns and dynamics of the communities in the eastern regions of Nicaragua. Scholars and activists in eastern Nicaragua point out that often studies ignore the important linguistic, cultural, and material differences between communities within the nation. JustHope has worked primarily in the western region, and this study is limited in that way. Embodied praxis is local and, thus, geographically specific.

I have been traveling to Nicaragua with service learning and mission teams since 1994 and have shared this type of journey with hundreds of volunteers. With their informed consent, I used the actual names of some of the Nicaraguans quoted in this monograph. The North American partners and students described here are composites rather than actual individuals. Although the dialogue and reflections are direct words of actual people used with their permission, I have changed names, identities, and

---

3. Isasi-Díaz, *In the Struggle*, 170.

details to tell this story. Over the years, I have conducted in-depth interviews with Nicaraguans, including multiple interviews with priests and activists who have been central leaders in the revolutionary movement flowering in the 1970s. In addition to interviews with JustHope partners in Nicaragua, I have focused on textual analysis of the documents that record the history of Chacraseca, including the letters and journal of Sister Joan Uhlen (1923–2019), a Maryknoll woman religious who was instrumental in organizing that base community. I immersed myself in the art, music, politics, and culture of Nicaragua while gathering information in focus groups, in formal interviews, and in informal conversations. Read alongside these discourses, liberation feminist theology and ethics fuels the journey of spiritual formation for justice and wisdom.

By offering glimpses of what a trip is like for JustHope partners, I hope to expand this learning to those who may never travel to Nicaragua. Group participants pose questions about the history of the organization, the structural relationship between leaders in Nicaragua and leaders in the United States, the history of the base community, and the programs, guidelines, and values of JustHope. Some find spiritual nurture and religious inspiration, but all experience the challenge to grow in compassion and more humane relationships accountable to sustainable global community. Participants discover new depths of self-understanding and longing to think carefully about nationalism, critical race theory, economic class analysis, and history. I hope readers may learn and grow as well.

The structure of this monograph mirrors the itinerary of a JustHope team's visit. After offering a framework for delving into liberation theology as a resource for spiritual formation and providing an introduction to JustHope as an organization, I present glimpses of a partner trip. Chapters 1 and 2 highlight team building, orientation, and preparation for travel. Chapter 3 explores initial culture shock and first impressions as North Americans arrive in Nicaragua and begin to absorb the culture and history. The next four chapters develop reflections on the core values of JustHope: solidarity, collaboration, mutuality, and sustainability. These chapters also describe days when the team is in Chacraseca learning about JustHope programs like social enterprise, education, health care, and housing. A typical schedule for a team links one of the core values with a program area for each day. Although critical engagement with theoretical issues occurs throughout each day and entwines all encounters, readers will find invitations to reflect on racism, classism, sexism, and cultural constructions in descriptions of evening reflection times.

Chapter 7 includes an extensive critique of the concept of peasant identity that remains prevalent in numerous academic disciplines and global discourses. Chapter 8 focuses on housing construction, designated a priority by the leaders in Chacraseca. The need for basic housing intersects with health, education, work, and quality of life. Chapter 9 showcases a visit to artisans who make pottery in a tradition documented for centuries in Nicaragua.

As the team of partners prepares to depart for home, they encounter more tastes of local culture. Leslie Penrose facilitates intentional reflections on the transition back to the U.S. In chapter 10, I present a record of interviews and conversations with Father Miguel d'Escoto, Father Urial Molina, Father Donald Mendoza, and Rev. Leslie Penrose. Their own spiritual journeys, theological ponderings, and activism inspire and shape this story. I have found that travelers must absorb the intercultural encounters before they fully appreciate these reflections. Chapter 11 includes a synthesis of liberation theology and the ongoing struggle for theological developments in postcolonial and global justice networks. The collaborative epistemology that JustHope fosters provides a model for intercultural partnership and learning that offers hope for justice.

I conclude this book with updates concerning the work of JustHope after the Nicaraguan political crisis in 2018 and the COVID-19 pandemic's effects in the following years. The romance of the Nicaraguan revolution captivated hopeful fans from around the world, and JustHope partners share enthusiasm for those visionary dreams. Some became ardent defenders of the Sandinista National Liberation Front party (FSLN) and Daniel Ortega, the public face of the party. Others noted the rapid fragmentation of the movement into various competing political parties that criticize Ortega and the FSLN.

1

Liberation Theology with JustHope

A PHOTOGRAPHER WOULD HAVE struggled to capture the scene, unable to convey the excitement and tension in the sweltering, moist air. We were seated in a circle of white, plastic chairs shaded by a verdant canopy of lofty trees, emerald tones in contrast to the packed, dark, tropical soil. Sounds of birds and active farm life surrounded us in every direction, pungent scents wafted on the slight breeze, and a few scrawny chickens ambled in and out of our circle as we talked. Nicaraguan leaders had arranged seating so that our team of North American visitors alternated with local neighbors. We were twenty-six people reaching out to connect across divides of language, politics, economic chasms, national origins. Shy kids brought around a case of cold, sweaty glass bottles of soda for everyone. I gripped the cold bottle and noticed a drop of perspiration rolling down my neck.

Elba, a local leader who works on the JustHope staff, started the meeting with an invitation to work toward solidarity. She said, "Because of JustHope, I visited the United States. Now I ask you to consider why you have come to Nicaragua." This was precisely the question that framed our journey and agitated us even after we returned home. The body language of each member of the circle signaled earnest hope and investment in this interchange. Elba's unapologetic assertion of dignity and equality reminded me of words of Lilla Watson and the Aboriginal activists' group from Queensland in the 1970s, "If you have come to help me, you are wasting your time, but if you have come because your liberation is bound up with mine, then let us work together."[1] Elba knows she has something valuable to teach. Her critique of U.S. culture and religion never fails to deepen my understanding and faith. I was thankful this group of JustHope partners had the opportunity to experience her leadership.

We introduced ourselves one by one, Nicaraguans and North Americans, sharing about our aspirations for partnership. Waiting for the translators to interpret each statement provided time to reflect and absorb the encounter. Faltering attempts at conversation ranged from discussion of ongoing projects like housing, health care, education, and micro-credit banks to desire to bridge differences and move toward a more just, equitable world. We were stretching toward something new, reaching for deeper honesty and authentic collaboration. Some of the statements bluntly displayed the historical and economic injustices that divide us. Elba and other Nicaraguans asked honest questions regarding the inhumanity of U.S. policy in Central America. There were several awkward silences that were marks of authentic conversation. Nicaraguans also expressed sincere warmth and appreciation, reaffirming their invitation to partnership. It was a good step toward mutuality and trust.

Later that evening as we processed the meeting, I asked our group from the U.S. what stood out most from the day. Laura, a pastor from Tulsa, said, "It was a hard day. What stands out most was a statement Elba made during our sharing circle. Elba said, 'In Chacraseca, we can help you become human.' I guess I was offended. I don't appreciate the insinuation that our society is inhumane. I am spending my money and my vacation time to come here and try to learn to be helpful. Did anyone else feel frustrated by that?"[2] Feeling thankful for Laura's honesty and vulnerability, I appreciated her willingness to name a sentiment that many JustHope partners explore.

Letty Russell's book *Becoming Human* offers a warning against paternalism and an invitation to liberation. She writes, "Growth in our humanity takes place as we learn to be helpers by being helped."[3] Not many North Americans think they need help from Nicaraguans, and many would reject the suggestion that we need help becoming human. JustHope's mission is neither charity nor religious proselytizing. The goal

1. Lilla Watson, quoted in MZ.Many Names, "Attributing Words," para. 1.

2. This comment and other statements from participants are written from memory and attributed to subjects whose real names are not recorded.

3. Russell, *Becoming Human*, 104.

is as much to transform North Americans and oppressive global systems as it is to change conditions in Nicaragua. However, the focus is not on what North Americans can gain from Nicaraguans either. Much of what passes for international aid or attempts at caring partnership is harmful rather than helpful. If attempts at mutuality and solidarity are not going to perpetuate more harm, North Americans must work to recognize and root out the imperious, alienating gaze that infects our culture.[4] JustHope aims for justice-seeking education.

This encounter with Elba and others depicts the experience of a group of JustHope partners. JustHope was born of encounters between U.S. faith-based activists invited by Nicaraguans with revolutionary grassroots agendas and missionary connections. In this way it was like many nongovernmental organizations working for a new world through solidarity.[5] Although some JustHope teams are medical volunteers or church groups, others are teams of students from a college or university class. Laura was part of a team that was a class of seminary students who spent ten days in Nicaragua in 2016. This book details their itinerary and theological reflection as an illustration of the JustHope model of partnership. I have four learning objectives for students, and all JustHope partners explore these issues. First, I hope students grasp a critique of imperialism and neocolonialism by learning about the history of U.S. relations with Nicaragua. We become critical students of political history and policy. Second, I hope they come away with a new appreciation for collaborative learning and international partnership for a better future. Third, I hope students will increasingly recognize an alternative to the value system that drives capitalism by experiencing possibilities of the environmentally sustainable life liberated from materialism and greed. Fourth, I hope students accept the never-ending work of cultivating prayerfulness, checking ego, and honoring diversity. JustHope offers encounters with learning that is spiritual formation.

JustHope arose from the growing faith and spiritual integrity of Leslie Penrose, a pastor in the United Church of Christ from Tulsa, Oklahoma. She founded JustHope in 2007, but her work in Nicaragua began in the 1980s. She was mentored by Sister Joan Uhlen, Father Miguel d'Escoto, and Nicaraguan leaders in base communities. Her journey was guided by teaching and ministry of priests like Father Uriel Molina and

---

4. McFague, "Loving Eye vs. the Arrogant Eye," 186.
5. Weber, *Visions of Solidarity*, 102.

Father Donald Mendoza whose leadership developed the community in Chacraseca. In addition to academic thinkers and teachers of liberation theology, these pastoral leaders shape this narrative. I drew on their insights and courageous faith throughout this study.

My students revere Leslie Penrose and appreciated the opportunity to learn with her through JustHope. She began to study liberation theology and the praxis during the sanctuary movement of the 1980s in the United States. By deepening relationships with refugees from Central America, she followed her calling to a tour with the Global Center for Education in the 1980s. After witnessing the violent, war-torn scenes of death and destruction in Honduras, Guatemala, and El Salvador, that trip ended with time in Nicaragua. She fell in love with Nicaragua and found new direction for her ministry on that trip.

Leslie's description of the deconstruction and transformation of her worldview and theology provides pathways for others longing for richer spiritual practice. Her enthusiasm for engagement in Nicaragua has continued to grow over decades since that time. Her ability to share the vision and power of her encounters there built the organization, JustHope, and attracted hundreds of North American partners to get involved.

I also learned from the students in this 2016 class as well as other companions in the journey of partnering with JustHope. Although I have changed names and identity markers of the students depicted in this book, all the encounters described, questions posed, and insights expressed represent actual participants. Many of the conversations included here and statements presented are drawn from written correspondence and reflections used with permission. I have field notes, interviews, and correspondence with partners representing numerous classes and teams. I synthesized and reorganized dialogue and description, but we shared these actual experiences. The JustHope staff and leaders in Chacraseca also stand as pillars of this story.

As a nonprofit organization that works to build relationships between partners in the United States and in Nicaragua, JustHope changes lives. Yet, even the most ardent supporters of JustHope ponder the question: would it be better to just send the money it costs to travel rather than spend the funds necessary to make this trip? JustHope is funded through trip fees, grants, and donations from congregations and individuals. The cost of airline tickets and ground transportation are charged to participants, but travelers pay additional fees that fund the staff and projects. Partners who make the trip to Nicaragua with JustHope are investing in the organization's mission and redistributing resources from the U.S. to communities in Nicaragua.

JustHope partners need to be vigilant in unmasking and acknowledging the colonial roots of international development and humanitarian aid. As Jocelyn Sutton Franklin writes, "'Aid' often does more harm than good, whether due to oversight, greed, or the momentum of the global wealth and power disparity."[6] So, JustHope partners must sincerely engage complex questions. Why do North American partners travel to Nicaragua? The motives vary. The first time I heard about JustHope, it sounded as if the organization was doing good work. Volunteers wanted to help. However, as Elmer Zellya, a Nicaraguan leader said, "Doing a good thing does not always mean you are doing good."[7] With roots in church missions and international humanitarian aid models, JustHope attempts a new model. Partners are asked to commit to long-term relationship. Rather than visiting once and never returning, those who travel with JustHope plan to engage for at least three years.

We continue to ponder the question: would the money it takes to travel be better spent in direct donations for development in Nicaragua?[8] Environmental justice issues demand that we review the consequences of air travel on our climate footprints. Although there are no glib or final answers to these relevant questions, I argue that the JustHope model has the most integrity when it calls partners to seek justice through anti-imperialist, postcolonial, anti-racist and anti-sexist commitments to transformation. Those are spiritual commitments. Our teachers and spiritual directors are partners in the struggle to change the world.[9]

North Americans require new perspectives on the impact and consequences of our impulse to assist those who have been made poor. In his book *Disabling Professions* Ivan Illich claims that those who understand themselves as helpers must reconsider. He writes, "Whatever benefits they might provide can only be assessed after we recognize them as essentially self-interested systems with inherently disabling effects."[10] The risk of fostering dependency or relationships that are not mutual is high. When we patronize others through charity, we dehumanize others and ourselves if we mistake our motives. Willingness to undergo the

6. Franklin, "Danger of the Extended Hand," 1.
7. Interview with Leslie Penrose, June 2016. Transcribed by Donna Greene.
8. Probasco, "More Good Than Harm."
9. Casaldáliga, *Political Holiness*.
10. Illich, *Disabling Professions*, 91.

profound challenges to self-understanding and identity that this type of partnership requires is deeply personal and can be painful. For this reason, JustHope participants need to bond as a team and prepare to go deep while holding each other accountable for critical self-examination and support. In many ways, traveling with JustHope is an opportunity for self-discovery and spiritual development.

These frames for study and collaboration are rooted in liberation theology.[11] JustHope's spiritual and faith praxis of liberation theology demand both bold action and continuous reflection in pursuit of solidarity, mutuality, true partnership, and innovative collaboration. Living in community with these values requires ongoing spiritual practice. I insist that spirituality is an endeavor to embody ethical, inherently valuable ways of living consistent with justice and compassion. Thus, spirituality cannot have integrity apart from theological and ethical discourse. Liberation theologies of Latin America as articulated by Leonardo Boff, Jon Sobrino, and Gustavo Gutiérrez developed simultaneously with feminist liberationist thought. These conversations shaped my journey and learning.

To share spiritual care and formation involves undergoing self-examination and change. Transnational partnerships are both the method and the context of spiritual and ethical development in pursuit of a better world. Nicaragua has attracted social activists from around the globe who are drawn to the inspiring leadership of those collaborating for a more just society. Those whose economic and political privilege allows them to travel to Nicaragua find there a fertile theater for this work. We find inspiration for community and human possibility, as John Brentlinger's title, *The Best of What We Are*, names. Brentlinger, like other scholars, found intriguing potential and hope in the courage and idealism of the Nicaraguan people's struggle for liberation from imperialism. Nicaragua is a place where people collaboratively explore how to be more fully human in the best sense. Through JustHope in Nicaragua, we encounter leaders in the struggle for revolutionary courage and conviction who call us to be better than the materialistic, militaristic, imperialistic culture that Christianity in the United States usually inspires us to be. This invitation to undergo the journey of becoming new in community action aligns with feminist liberation theology.[12]

11. Boff, *Church*. For more on liberation theology, see also Sobrino, *Spirituality for Liberation*; Gonzaléz and Gonzaléz, *Pulpit and the Oppressed*; Gutiérrez, *Theology of Liberation*.

12. Hunt, *Feminist Liberation Theology*.

Liberation theologians offered a new perspective, suggesting that rather than think of faith in terms of a model of sin/grace/redemption, or guilt/sacrifice/forgiveness, or sickness/healing/wholeness, the Christ event had more power when understood as a model of bondage/liberation/new creation. Read in light of that framework, Scripture teaches principles such as:

1. God is on the side of those made poor by social, economic, and political systems like neoliberalism and patriarchy.
2. Jesus taught that his followers must change material conditions and work for social justice, so the way of Jesus is never merely private or internal.
3. Greed and desire for material riches enslave people and turn them away from God.
4. Power should be shared collectively and equally, so that all people can collaborate to improve the lives of all.
5. Faith includes a journey of struggling to become new creation as individuals and communities.
6. The faith journey synthesizes action for justice and continuous, transformational reflection (praxis).

This approach has logical consequences for Christian ethics. I agree with Ivan Petrella's argument that liberation theology unmasks privilege in ways that call for new kinds of theology and a new epistemology. For instance, Petrella thinks that liberation theology calls for dismantling unexamined economic privilege.[13] Similarly, womanist liberation theologian Emilie Townes calls for unmasking uninterrogated whiteness. Both types of liberation are urgent. At the same time, the work of Latin American liberation theologians needs the revision of thinkers like Marcella Althaus-Reid who notes their inadequate attention to gender and sexuality justice.[14] Western theology has gotten off track because of the general affluence and privilege of those who shaped it.

Feminist liberation theology has not always been adequately attentive to white supremacy. Latin American liberation theology was not always committed enough to rooting out sexism and heteronormativity. Liberation is a process of becoming human that demands ongoing

13. Petrella, *Beyond Liberation Theology*, 142.
14. Althaus-Reid, *Indecent Theology*.

learning. Ecumenical and interfaith mutual respect must replace triumphalist or exclusive theology. Liberation theology pushed "the transition from a triumphant church to a church based on service to the poor."[15] There is no hegemony of one, flawless, right perspective about the divine. Therefore, Christians should protect freedom of belief, thought, and worship. Furthermore, Christians must work for political equality regardless of race, gender, sexuality, nationality.

Moral accountability and duty do not change at national borders, so Christians should question nationalist and civic policy. Finally, Christians must regulate or replace neoliberal capitalism. For the sake of future generations, the planet, and our global neighbors, we should unmask and dethrone consumerism and materialism. What is more, since all persons need communities for reflection and mutuality, Christians should offer conversation rather than push for dogmatic forms of conversion. Rather than thinking of transformation as conversion to religious affirmation of faith, the transformation JustHope seeks involves decolonization and redistribution of resources toward genuine collaboration toward equality.

Sister Joan Uhlen, whose ministry played a crucial role in the Nicaraguan community of Chacraseca, embodied this liberation theology. She taught us that we cannot love others unless we know them. To follow Jesus requires living in community, working side by side, listening, and receiving as well as giving. She urged us to open ourselves to a deeply relational way of knowing and being. At the same time, she helped shape new understandings of Christian mission. She lived and worked in Chacraseca for seventeen years, beginning in 1988, building dreams and organizing Christian community with the leaders of that community. While working in Chacraseca, she wrote:

---

15. Gugelot, "Jesuit Way of Being Global?," 1048.

MISSION

Being called, sent and received.
Who has called us?
God, who calls us each by name;
Who awakens us, shakes us from
Our lethargy of satisfaction with
The now, the how.
Who bears us on eagle's wings
So that we do not tire too soon
In the search for what it is
That our God wants of us.

Who sends us?
Maryknoll, blest word for mission,
For struggle, for conflict, for contradiction,
For pain, for death . . .
Blest word for peace, for justice,
For equality, for dignity, for life, for joy,
For resurrection.

Who will receive us?
The poor, the marginated, the roofless,
The rootless, the restless, the searchers,
The peaceful, the peacemakers,
The rebellious, the forlorn,
The lonely, the forgotten, the lovers.

What can we do?
We can be: peacemakers—
Peace-receivers, enablers,
Mutual gift-sharers, workers, listeners,
Tear gatherers, spirit-filled reflectors,
Message bearers, proclaimers, prophetic voices,
Confronters, healers, receivers, walking companions,
Be-ers, agitators, nurturers,
Gospel-seekers and sowers,
Peace seekers, prayer-centerers,
And Christ-sharers.[16]

As a "spirit-filled reflector," Sister Joan embodied, studied, and practiced the liberation theology that connected feminist theory in the

---

16. Joan C. Uhlen, "Mission." Unpublished poem.

United States and Central American liberation theology as it emerged. She witnessed and documented her experience in Nicaragua during the Contra War and the unsavory impact of the U.S. military intervention. JustHope was forged in this praxis, through mutual encounters between Sister Joan and the founder of JustHope, Leslie Penrose, who worked in collaboration with Nicaraguan community leaders in ways that attracted new partners who shared the work. Both Nicaraguan leaders and partners from the U.S. testify to spiritual formation they experienced through Sister Joan's leadership and spiritual direction.

Robust spiritual formation happens best in community, but Western culture often favors self-sufficiency and individualism rather than engagement. Learning to operate collaboratively with others can challenge North Americans. Through transnational partnership, we may stretch and reform to learn mutuality and cooperative praxis. Social epistemology is a growing field of study in philosophy of knowledge that explores ways relationships and community are required for knowing. Conversations with feminist epistemology and postcolonial epistemology offer steps toward safeguarding against blindly operating from an unconscious bias or viewpoint that is sometimes referred to as "the white gaze" or "the western gaze."

The second wave feminist term "male gaze" names a relational phenomenon that prevents full collaboration and mutual flourishing. Likewise, the term "western gaze" identifies a systematic problem in transnational partnerships aiming for social justice. In this book, I use the term imperious gaze, to make clear that domineering stance is not bounded by gender, racial, or cultural identity. Implicit bias, unexamined assumptions, and preconceptions about values are all examples of ways that knowing is thwarted by inept attempts at learning. The Eurocentric assumption of cultural supremacy often drives a paternalistic approach in attempts at transnational partnerships because of the presumption of superior knowledge. Spiritual formation includes transformation in thinking and acting to correct this bias. Participating in close community can facilitate spiritual development when white supremacy is dismantled.

Many North Americans are unimpressed with churches' competitive marketing and recruiting efforts to attract new members. There are numerous problems with the idea that the mission of the church is to convert the world to become the winning Christian team. Too often a privileged, civic form of popular Christianity insists that the heart of Christianity should be kept separate from economic and political questions. In contrast, new models of mission are informed by global, intercultural, and liberationist awareness. Dialogue that transcends national borders as well as identity politics sparks new imaginaries and interest in reimagining theology. Many North Americans who have experienced JustHope partnerships describe deeply satisfying spiritual renewal as a result.

In contrast to older models of mission, the first and last goal of Christian practical wisdom should be relationships that honor the sacred worth, dignity, and equal respect of all lives. If we understand the church as the body of Christ, then it makes sense that we are saved through community. "Mission today has entered a new paradigm, as missiologists David Bosch, Andrew Walls, Lesslie Newbigin, and many others have well documented."[17] So, identifying barriers to deep relationships is important work for those called to build community. We seek conversations rather than conversions. Friendship is the model, and listening an essential tool. As Mary Hunt writes, "Theologizing, as understood by liberationists, is the organic and communal process of sharing insights, stories, and reflections of questions of ultimate meaning and value." Befriending one another is no easy task; it requires fierce tenderness.[18] True friendship is an embodiment of spiritual formation and a practice of Christian practical wisdom.

JustHope partners continue to craft new ways of befriending and building community across borders. This also requires actions to transform political, social, and economic systems. For example, pastoral theologian Melinda A. McGarrah Sharp urges resistance to and active dismantling of neocolonial injustices. Even unconscious privilege and patterns of supremacy often perpetuate harm in attempts at intercultural community. She wrote, "This colonial impulse crosses borders without respect for healthy boundaries, pulling other people into the power, voice, creative potential, and capital of the oppressor through mechanisms of dehumanization."[19] Seminary education must include critical race theory and attention to various forms of white supremacy as well as movements to dismantle privilege.

Removing obstacles to respectful relationships can unite secular humanitarian efforts and Christian mission understood as partnership. A

---

17. Bonnie Sue Lewis, "Learning to Listen," in Lloyd-Sidle and Lewis, *Teaching Mission in a Global Context*, 132.

18. Hunt, *Fierce Tenderness*, 61.

19. McGarrah Sharp, *Creating Resistances*, 147. See also McGarrah Sharp, *Misunderstanding Stories*.

coffee and bee keeping program of Catholic Relief Services in Matagalpa, Nicaragua offers one example of this new type of mission that connects "international humanitarian relief, development, and social justice organization."[20] Some church groups practice liberationist models. Harold J. Recinos calls for scrutiny and new levels of awareness in "immersion techniques for ecclesial communities designed to facilitate global encounter."[21] I argue that JustHope offers another example. However, JustHope partners need vigilance in the practice of critical self-examination and mutual reflection to avoid slipping back to sentimental or patronizing charity models. We must avoid do-gooder tourism, poverty tourism, and forms of educational travel where privileged students unwittingly perpetuate legacies of colonialism. JustHope asks partners to avoid defaulting to "tourist mode" even when the encounter may get emotionally difficult. I asked students to think carefully about voyeuristic aspects of exoticizing or sentimentalizing poverty.[22]

JustHope partnerships cannot be replicated by reading books about liberation theology. My teaching aims to facilitate encounters with the art, music, history, and present action that embody this theology. For example, we explore the lyrics and music of the popular liberation theology written by Nicaraguan singer Carlos Mejía Godoy. Each day during our travels, we reflected on songs that are part of La Misa Campesina, or Folk Mass, that embody the praxis of liberation theology. Such examples of artistic expressions illustrate themes of liberation theology, including economic injustice, poverty, greed, community, and the struggle for justice that is both internal and external. JustHope partners learn to love the folk music and dance which are still taught and cherished in base communities like Chacraseca and La Flor. Through these beloved songs, partners share the spirituality, courage, and strength of liberation theology.

Ann Hidalgo analyzed the importance of the folk mass liturgy in her essay, "Ponte A Nuestro Lado! Be On Our Side! The Challenge of the Central American Liberation Theology Masses." To face the challenge posed by liberation theology is to hear the call to take sides and take stands. Noting the pastoral leadership of Father Miguel d'Escoto and others, Hidalgo writes, "The Masses envision a future of transformation, equality, justice, peace, and joy, and they endeavor to incarnate it in the

---

20. Korgan, *Solidarity Will Transform the World*, 151.
21. Recinos, *Jesus Weeps*, 115.
22. Sumka et al., *Working Side by Side*, 422.

present through the struggle and song of the community."[23] Our class reflected on the movement of liberation theology with its potent influence in the historical changes in church and society despite the small minority of pastoral leaders who fully embraced its revolutionary message. This theology can transform and enliven spirituality, but it can also perplex and disturb unexamined presuppositions.

Like some other JustHope teams, my class of 2016 visited a parish in Managua where illustrations of liberation praxis glow in the vibrant colors of the artwork on the walls of a church. We witnessed the extraordinary murals of Iglesia Santa María de los Ángeles, where Father Uriel Molina began forming the movement of base communities in the 1980s.[24] Although the murals, designed and painted by Italian artist Sergio Michilini, are officially recognized as a national treasure, they are covered with drapes most of the time now because of the political and theological controversy they convey. The artist depicted the valiant faith and activism of members of that parish and their struggle for freedom from imperialism and legacies of colonialism.

Some of the images in the murals, like that of a priest with a gun, appear provocative and can startle North American eyes. This artwork invites struggle with theological questions and sincere spiritual seeking. The faith and spiritual practice of Christians in Nicaragua expand faith horizons of JustHope partners. The questions that emerge are not abstractions but living summons to solidarity. In the words of Father Uriel Molina, "Students must not merely learn, but learn to act."[25] Acting requires commitment. It requires putting one's body on the line.

The revolutionary nature of Nicaraguan solidarity appeals to some and repels others. JustHope does not advocate any political party. Instead, the organization seeks to promote understanding, dialogue, and most of all, the ability of North Americans to listen without trying to control Nicaraguan politics. The religious symbols, rhetoric, and language used by the Sandinistas and other groups sparked controversy from the beginning. Father Miguel d'Escoto said that the church could never forgive Marx for caring more about the plight of the poor than they did. JustHope partners discover new questions about what it means to be human and to live in community. What is required for social justice? Through JustHope, partners collaborate to seek sustainable, mutual, ways

23. Hidalgo, *"Ponte A Nuestro Lado!,"* 133.
24. Murphy and Caro, *Uriel Molina*, 70.
25. Interview with Uriel Molina, July 2016.

of living. Learning to work and construct shared wisdom together is part of the praxis. The puzzles of international trade and economic redistribution require knowledge that crosses borders.

Marxism pushed Christianity to change because Marxist thinkers refused to stop analyzing the economic, political, and historical consequences of Christian missions. For example, in the recent history of Nicaragua, the legacy of European colonialism and neocolonial influence of the U.S. resulted in economic and social injustice. Liberation theologians link theological and ethical questions to history. In his book *Revolution, Revival, and Religious Conflict in Sandinista Nicaragua* Calvin L. Smith claimed that the Sandinistas "captured religious slogans and symbols, reworking Christianity to make it revolutionary."[26] In contrast, liberation theologians maintain that the Gospel is revolutionary at its core. Rather than label individual leaders in revolutionary political parties in Nicaragua as heroes or villains, I explore theological concepts and motivations in actors from different groups. These questions remain relevant. In discourses about ethics and international development, Marxist analysis continues to pose compelling challenges to neoliberal models. My students and colleagues engage thinkers like Maria Mies as we wrestle with analysis of exploitation in neoliberal models of development.[27]

This work is not charity, or parochial mission, or poverty tourism. JustHope does not presume to have answers or resources to fix economic problems of Nicaraguan partners. We are committed to the practice of solidarity in development and social justice as defined and led by Nicaraguan community leaders. Recognizing the pervasive systems that transcend borders, such as white supremacy, neocolonialism, and global economic realities, JustHope partners engage transnational collaboration with attention to ethical questions. In her book *Borderlands/La Frontera: The New Mestiza* Gloria Anzaldúa wrote, "We are all living in a society where these borders are transgressed constantly."[28] Too often, international partnerships do more harm than good when crossing national borders.

In his book, *Pedagogy of the Oppressed*, Paulo Freire wrote, "In order for the oppressed to be able to wage the struggle for their liberation, they must perceive the reality of oppression not as a closed world from which

---

26. Smith, *Revolution, Revival, and Religious Conflict*, 145.
27. Mies, *Patriarchy and Accumulation on a World Scale*, 198.
28. Anzaldúa, *Borderlands*, 233.

there is no exit, but as a limiting situation which they can transform."[29] Nicaraguan priests like Father Uriel Molina drew on the critical pedagogy of Freire and others who taught that "original thinking is possible and creativity can be put into practice."[30] The practice of faith in action is connected with the everyday, local experience of seeking a more just world. Liberation theology has been intertwined with Freire's work from the beginning. He writes:

> Liberation is thus a childbirth, and a painful one. The man or woman who emerges is a new person, viable only as the oppressor-oppressed contradiction is superseded by the humanization of all people. Or to put it another way, the solution of this contradiction is born in the labor: which brings into the world this new being: no longer oppressor nor longer oppressed, but human in the process of achieving freedom.[31]

Freire's educational methods intersected with a theological and pastoral liberation method of viewing the work of Jesus through a lens of his socioeconomic and political context in community. This corresponds with the vision of Latin American liberation theologians like Leonardo Boff who taught that the church must be continuously reborn.[32] This model requires work for the transformation of all persons through partnerships in community like feminist liberationist theologian Rosemary Radford Ruether taught. Ruether was a friend and supporter of Maryknolls like Sister Joan Uhlen who worked in Nicaragua and provided financial support as well as theoretical tools for analyzing social systems and identifying the economic and political implications of ecclesial practices and frameworks.[33] JustHope draws on this wisdom for both Nicaraguans and North Americans to be more fully human.

---

29. Freire and Macedo, *Pedagogy of the Oppressed*, 5.
30. Murphy and Caro, *Uriel Molina*, 70.
31. Freire and Macedo, *Pedagogy of the Oppressed*, 5.
32. Boff, *Church*.
33. Ruether, *Christianity and Social Systems*.

— 2 —

Preparations for Border Crossing

I WAS EXCITED ABOUT integrating my work as a theological educator, my work as a social activist, and my passion for JustHope. I wanted this class of graduate students to understand that traveling as a JustHope team would require each of us to stretch our comfort zones in many ways. We would be working, eating, sleeping, and traveling in close quarters that would challenge us with culture shock, new self-awareness, and consciousness-raising about global realities. Students were excited to meet Leslie Penrose. Many knew of her reputation as a gifted pastor and respected community leader. The rare opportunity to learn from her and Nicaraguan leaders attracted students to join the immersion travel course. To embrace this opportunity for relational work, our small group of nine volunteers prepared through intentional reading, discussion, and team-building activities like other JustHope groups. Relationship building takes time, so our class met to begin forging community and preparing for our shared journey one month before our travel date.

Leslie Penrose served as our JustHope liaison for the trip, so she joined the circle for our first meeting before we traveled to Nicaragua. We began with initial, brief introductions. Some participants already knew each other as peers in graduate education at Phillips Theological Seminary in Tulsa, Oklahoma. All were pursuing some form of ministry or social justice leadership. The learning within the immersion experience is profoundly personal; it requires scholarly research and professional development alongside spiritual formation. The goals of the course included self-examination and collaboration with classmates to dismantle personal blocks to genuine partnership. We began to share our stories. One student, George, said he was a second-career student whose wife is a doctor. He was working as a radiology tech and was especially interested in the JustHope medical partnership teams. He was preparing to work as a hospital chaplain. He said that he had been trying to learn a little Spanish, but the assigned reading reminded him that he would be relying on translators. The group laughed in mutual affirmation.

Laura, a student pastor in a suburban church in Tulsa, began by saying, "I need to know whether I should bring a coffee pot. If I have my coffee, I can cope." She shared her anxiety about the trip because she was a "city girl." She was nervous about bugs, dirt, farm smells, and rural life we might encounter. She had traveled a lot, but mostly on business trips with her husband. Laura said she was excited about seeing the old cathedrals from the sixteenth century.

Another student in the class, Rose, was a kindergarten teacher who was working toward her Master of Theological Studies (MTS) degree to work in Christian education. Rose inspired each of us as she spoke about her passion for children and hope to learn with teachers in Nicaragua. She had a friend who had been part of a JustHope team that had volunteered in a school before.

Martin and Paula, a younger, married couple were both in their final year of graduate studies and hoped to start a new inner-city ministry in Chicago. They had heard from other students about how powerful the experience in Nicaragua had been. Both shared candid doubts about the relevance of churches in the U.S. They hoped to find inspiration in social justice movements in Nicaragua.

An older student named Bill had recently retired from a career in business and was serving as a pastor in a farming community. Bill shared that this would be his first trip outside of the United States. He had heard about the JustHope model farm program, and he was keen to see that in person. Elizabeth explained that she had worked as a librarian for a decade and felt called to explore nonprofit management. She was almost finished with the Masters in Social Justice degree and was beginning a job search. She expressed her interest in learning more about how JustHope was organized and administered. Nick was the last student to introduce himself. He warned the group that he was shy and introverted. As a student pastor in a county seat town in Kansas, he had discovered that he sometimes gave people the impression that he was unfriendly. He asked the group to keep that in mind and not take his silence personally.

I introduced myself not only as a professor but also as a supporter of JustHope who had served as a pastor for twenty-five years, an avid gardener, and a grandmother. Leslie introduced herself as a UCC pastor who had also taught at the seminary in the past, founded JustHope, and served as executive director of the nonprofit. She was in the process of retiring from that position but intended to continue in a volunteer role as part of retirement. I reminded the class that we would be sharing potent experiences through this service-learning immersion travel course as a JustHope team, so building relationships with each other and new friends in Nicaragua was an essential part of our class. We would live in close quarters away from many comforts of home. We were traveling to learn more about Nicaragua and JustHope partnerships but also about ourselves and the systems and structures of our communities.

While I could not fully prepare students for the types of experiences that would await them, part of my work as a professor includes reminding students that immersion learning is communal in a way that differs from classroom learning. "Expect to encounter moments of discomfort and challenge," I told the group. "How do you feel about your ability to relinquish control? Each of us will need to be flexible and recognize that letting go and staying open are spiritual and ethical principles." I shared about my previous trips and an experience of being in Nicaragua for a week before my suitcase arrived. As much as we try to prepare, it helps to anticipate surprises. "We will be sleeping in bunk beds in small rooms and sharing tight bathroom facilities. We are going to get to know each other in ways that will likely be uncomfortable at times. In fact, we will have opportunities to get to know ourselves better on this trip," I said. This learning is part of the experience of the practice of solidarity for social justice. Detachment from material and economic luxuries is part of the experience of a JustHope team.

After these initial introductions, we began to review the readings and to address practical questions in preparation for our trip. The history and politics of Nicaragua can seem overwhelming at first. My goal for this initial session was to identify a few key points to help students situate themselves within the experience. JustHope encourages all partner teams to read and learn about the historical context and culture of Nicaragua in preparation for their trips. "Read as much as possible before we travel, but at least make sure you are prepared to watch for examples of these frameworks: Spanish colonialism beginning in the early 1500s, the Contra War in the 1980s, the folk mass and music as illustrative of popular liberation theology, and the national hero, Sandino, whose image pervades the culture," I suggested. These four conceptual frames serve as moorings to begin understanding the complexity of Nicaraguan history and contemporary international relations. Rather than being overwhelmed by all the details of the history, students benefit by mastering a few central dynamics of the history of U.S./Nicaraguan international relations. For example, many students are jolted toward greater awareness when they discover that what people in the U.S. call the Contra War is referred to by Nicaraguans as the War with the U.S. We discussed the reading list and writing assignments with a focus on these four initial concepts.

Then, because the class was also studying the ethos and values of JustHope with the commitment to best practices, Leslie led our discussion about the JustHope values of mutuality, partnership, solidarity, and collaboration. These values would serve as safeguards against perpetuating injustice and inequality, and they would help us to recognize the ways through which older models of mission continued the grip of imperialism and oppression. We compared and contrasted older models of mission based in efforts for conversion or unidirectional aid with the JustHope model. We would return to these topics throughout our time in Nicaragua and in our reflections after travel.

I asked the team to consider the possibility that we might need to unlearn or let go of some assumptions. For example, many of us were formed by the idea that what it means to be a person of faith is to believe certain ideas. Put another way, we were taught that agreeing with cognitive claims about who Jesus was defines whether we are Christian or not. Furthermore, most of us learned to think of salvation as an individual, mostly private matter. In contrast, liberation theology as it developed in Nicaragua calls for direct action that results from seeing with new eyes. Salvation is about transformation of economic and social structures, including political systems. However, liberation theology requires transformation of the individual from false consciousness to new ways of being. I shared about my own process of resistance and slowness in changing my life to integrate new awareness and values. Nothing less than spiritual formation and reformation is necessary.

"Look for examples of the commitment to recognizing the journey toward a new way of being that both feminist liberation theologians and Latin American liberation theologians explore," I said. "I hope you will consider but also critique liberation theology. Some scholars reject liberation theology on the grounds that it relies on a type of standpoint epistemology that divides people. Others note that history and society divide people, and our context determines much of what we experience and believe. We will think together about these questions as we travel. JustHope partners engage opportunities to grapple with deconstructing and dismantling ideas about what faith means, but the engagement with the ideas is far more demanding than reading or thinking about the questions. I continue to discover ways that my ego can be an obstacle to the flourishing of community," I said. "This is also a process of liberation."

To illustrate this point, I passed out lyrics of a beloved Nicaraguan song, "El Cristo de Palacagüina," written in Spanish along with an English translation. As part of their assigned reading, the group had already learned that folk dance and music became emblematic of movements in the revolution and anti-imperialist, Nicaraguan national consciousness movements. One of the most enduring and beloved examples of this reclamation of national identity is expressed in this song from the Misa campesina nicaragüense (Nicaraguan Peasant Mass) of 1975. After allowing a few moments to read in silence, I asked for a volunteer to read the words aloud. Martin volunteered and read the lyrics slowly.

> On the hilltop of the Iguana, a mountain peak in the Segovias, an extraordinary splendor shone out like a dawn in the middle of the night. The cornfields caught fire, the fireflies began to glow, light showered on Moyogalpa, on Telpaneca and on Chichigalpa.
>
> Christ is here and now, born in Palacagüina! of a fellow named José and a village girl named María. She goes about her work with great humility washing and ironing the clothes that please the landlord's lady.
>
> The folks gathered round in clusters to look on him and see him. The Indian Joaquín brought him string cheese in braids, from Nagarote; and as far as I can tell, instead of incense, gold, and myrrh, they gave him caramel-candies, and pastries from Guadalupe.
>
> Christ is here and now, born in Palacagüina! . . . José, the poor day laborer works at it all day long; the joints in his hands are aching from his years at carpentry. María dreams that the child, like his father, go into woodcraft; but already the little

one's thinking: "Tomorrow I'll fight for the freedom of all!"
Christ is here and now, born in Palacagüina![1]

We sat in silence for a few moments as we absorbed the rich images in the lyrics. We explored the lyrics and associations with our own experience. The group was getting acquainted with each other and some key issues that would challenge our thinking during our travel experience.

"Which words or phrases stand out as you hear this?" Leslie asked.

"The aching of José's hands from his carpentry work," said Bill. "It calls to mind a memory of my own father, tired, sweaty and dusty from manual labor."

"María dreaming about what her child will be when he grows up," said Rose. "Babies smell so good; it is interesting to imagine this young Nicaraguan mother and her baby. I can feel the warm connection between them, as if they were one body."

"María pregnant and ironing expensive clothes of the rich landlady," said Laura. "I picture Maria looking like a teenager. I imagine how she felt laundering clothes she couldn't imagine wearing herself. It is painful to imagine this."

"People bringing gifts of their favorite local food like cheese," Paula said.

Elizabeth added, "the glowing fireflies and starry sky."

"What feelings do you have as you read these words?" I asked.

George said, "It is difficult to appreciate the familiarity and local sense of these descriptions because the places named in the song seem as foreign to me as Bethlehem or ancient Palestine. Yet, I realize that Nicaraguans singing this would experience the words as locating the story in their own context. I feel curious about seeing the Nicaraguan countryside."

"Yes, I'm glad you said that. As I study these lyrics, I can tell they evoke familiarity and local connections for Nicaraguans, but they make me sharply aware of my own local roots in different land, food, and culture," Paula said.

"The contrast between the rich landlord and the hard-working María and José make me think more about class differences and economic structures of inequality," said Martin. "I have to admit, I am more like the landlord in the narrative. I recognize in myself some feelings of guilt and unease about my class privilege."

1. Godoy, "Letra el Cristo de Palacagüina." Translated by Juan Pedro Gaffney.

Leslie asked, "What questions or thoughts do you have about this song as an expression of faith?"

Martin said the descriptions of the natural setting: the mountains, the cornfields, and glowing fireflies felt nourishing for his own faith. "Somehow, the physicality of the food, the terrain, and the particular land connects me with my embodiment in ways that I need for my spirituality to flourish."

We listed the gifts people brought to the child: local cheese, Nicaraguan caramels, and pastries. We tried to think of common gifts that would represent our own communities that are everyday items people make with their hands. Laura suggested a loaf of homemade bread. Paula suggested tomatoes from her garden. We wondered together about ways this song might challenge or deepen our imagination about the idea of incarnation.

Paula said, "I like the chorus, 'Christ is here and now.' I'm not sure how to affirm that in my own context, but I like the idea of seeing Christ in Nicaragua. I like the references to places that would be familiar to people there. If people from my own community sang about Christ being here and now in Chicago that would be powerful."

George responded, "I don't get it when people talk like that. I think studying Jesus as an historical figure is meaningful, but when people start all that talk about Jesus being their buddy here and now, it bothers me. What does that even mean?"

Paula replied, "I find it helpful to distinguish between the historical Jesus and the Christ Spirit that I think of as divine love. In other words, Jesus was a real guy who lived long ago and far away, but, he is also the Christ Spirit of the power of love. It is personal to me, but also political. I do see that power in the community organizers I've worked with in Chicago."

Bill said, "I think it would be powerful if we in the United States sang about Christ being born in some small, rural town in Oklahoma like Muskogee or Durant. That sounds like something my folks would appreciate back home. But doesn't this song depict Christ as a freedom fighter and revolutionary?" Bill asked. "It seems to politicize Jesus. I think it sounds more like the birth of Sandino than the birth of Christ."

"Yes, I certainly see the connection between Sandino, the Nicaraguan revolutionary movements, and the Jesus narrative. I am wondering about the type of freedom that the Christ child imagines fighting for," said Elizabeth.

Bill looked red in the face and agitated. Others shifted uncomfortably in their seats. I tried to allow a pause for silence to let the challenges unfold.

After a few moments Leslie said, "These are good questions, and I am glad we are already raising them. During our trip, we will have a reflection time at the end of each day to process thoughts and feelings about our shared experience. This is an essential part of the work of praxis. We will not answer all of these questions, but we will explore them more deeply. Let's keep thinking about our discomfort with these issues as we introduce ourselves more fully."

Leslie asked us to keep the song in mind as we completed an exercise of naming various identity markers that are part of our social location. In other words, we wanted to be conscious of ways that our subject position and context influenced how we interacted with others. How did access to financial resources shape our formative years? How had our race relations affected our family? Were we more comfortable in a city or a rural setting? Leslie shared a little about herself, her family, and her own seminary education. She described the influence liberation theology had on her life and thought. She talked about how the people in Nicaragua have taught her to be more humane in many ways. For example, she contrasted our North American expectations regarding time and schedule with what she called "Nica time." Although people from the U.S. may judge Nicaraguans negatively for lack of punctuality according to the clock, Leslie has learned to appreciate an approach to time that values relationships above all. She said that people in Chacraseca experience time as encounters. When one experience or encounter is over, another happens. If a meeting runs longer than planned because people are talking and sharing, the next event can begin later. There is much more flexibility and less stress about schedule in Nicaragua than in U.S. society. She encouraged us to be open-minded and open-hearted about this type of cultural difference.

As we worked through these and other questions, students drew connections with contextual analysis which they had explored in previous seminary courses. Rose said that she was curious about how being the only Black person in our group would affect her experience. Laura said that she had heard that machismo was prevalent in Latin America, and as a feminist, she wondered if anyone would take her seriously as a pastor. Bill said that we were all children of God, and he was sure things like that would not be a problem on our trip. Paula asked if we would be attending a church service while we were there. She explained why past experiences of growing up Catholic made her anxious in Catholic services now. These vulnerable disclosures made it possible for participants to see one another as complex individuals and deepened our relationships. We were beginning to see one another more fully. Leslie reminded us to be gentle with each other and ourselves as we continued to reflect deeply on how our context and identity affected our experience. We took ample time for introductions that went deeper than the superficial because building and maintaining strong relationships is essential work in the JustHope model.

Then Leslie asked us to spend some moments writing in silence in response to this question: Why am I going on this trip? I sat in silence staring at the blank page of my notebook. I had gone to Nicaragua with groups in the early 1990s. I had led groups with JustHope and participated in many trips like this before. What were my true motivations? My own journey of spiritual practice and reflection continues to deepen and expand. I realized I would need to spend some serious, prayerful discernment with the question later. I knew that I needed to think more deeply about what drove me in addition to the obvious motivations of teaching the class or serving to support friends in Nicaragua. Leslie was asking us to go deep. Why was I choosing to invest my time, energy, and resources on this trip? After moments when only the sound of pens scratching on paper broke the silence, Leslie invited people to share their thoughts about this question.

Laura spoke up immediately, saying, "I have always wanted to go on a mission trip. I've heard other students say it was life changing. It will be wonderful to be able to share our faith and help people in need."

I made a mental note to continue inviting the group to reconsider what we assume about mission trips. I was a little nervous about Laura's persistent references to mission trips and hoped she would think critically about models of missions. That mission trip mentality is a patronizing approach that undermines solidarity.

Bill spoke next, "We are so blessed in this country. Even though there are poor people in my own rural community, we don't even know what real poverty is in the United States. I want to be able to take members of my church on these mission trips in the future."

I thought to myself about the pervasiveness of the old concept of mission trips. I knew that would be a distinction we would discuss during our trip.

Paula said, "I want to learn more about intercultural communication. I wish that I could speak Spanish better. I am working on cultural competency."

As various students responded, Leslie wrote words on newsprint, capturing highlights of their comments. The group generated words and watched them go up on the page: mission, faith, help, learning, new friends, increased awareness, faith in action, service, etc.

After the sharing tapered off, Leslie spoke about contrasting models of mission versus solidarity. Older mission models assume that trying to witness, even if only through actions, is a central purpose of the travel. In contrast, JustHope mutuality may mean that we witness things that change us. It is not uncommon for friends or relatives to presume that we are going to convert people. Conversely, JustHope invites North American travelers to open themselves to a long-term process of being changed by Nicaraguans as much as thinking that we have something to offer. I reminded the class that we would return to contrasting models of mission throughout our week in Nicaragua.

Drawing on their assigned reading, I shared Father Uriel Molina's concept that we, as students of the gospels, were participating in a type of education that might free us from our own materialism, egoism, and elitism.[2] I asked the group to continue to reflect on assigned readings, noting questions about liberation theology and understandings of the types of change that faith requires.

"Keep thinking about the analysis of Rosemary Radford Ruether," I said. She wrote about the tendency of the U.S. to act like a world empire by dominating other nations like Nicaragua. She says that resistance to "empire is seen as crucial to authentic Christian faith, along with the defense of peace, social justice, and ecological integrity."[3]

"Remember that challenge to consider anti-imperial Christianity as articulated in the 2006 World Alliance of Reformed Churches' document 'An Ecumenical Faith Stance against Global Empire for a Liberated Earth Community,'" I said. "We will do a deep dive into liberation theology."

"This kind of theology requires that we study economic and political analysis, too," I continued. "For instance, we will discuss international trade agreements and their consequences for people we meet." I reminded myself to share the work of William Greider who writes,

> What is emerging for now is a power system that more nearly resembles a kind of global feudalism—a system in which the private economic enterprises function like rival dukes and barons, warring for territories across the world and oblivious to

---

2. Murphy and Caro, *Uriel Molina*.
3. Ruether, *Christianity and Social Systems*, 252.

local interests, since none of the local centers are strong enough to govern them.[4]

I agree with his assessment of international trade injustices. Leslie challenged us to continue exploring these concepts through connections with the JustHope mission and values. We agreed to continue examining our own assumptions about the goals for our trip and our own motivations for the upcoming travel.

I had stated that goals for the class included seeking partnership true to the values of solidarity, mutuality, collaboration, and sustainability. Could we avoid the tourist mentality with the cultural elitism and paternalism that characterizes many teams? We were all U.S. citizens, and international travel raises opportunities to be aware of our national identity in new ways. One goal of our trip was to gain deeper awareness of our unexamined assumptions. Our world needs skillful intercultural cooperation, and we must learn to recognize the European and North American tendency to ethnocentrism that undermines understanding and collaboration.[5] Holding each other accountable to JustHope values and increasing our consciousness about systemic injustice would require diligence. Our group would work to be mindful of the imperialist roots of tourism. In the words of M. Jacqui Alexander, "Ultimately, tourism as a metasystem makes it possible for the state to circumscribe boundaries around the nation while servicing imperialism."[6] By examining our privilege as travelers, we could learn more about global systems through a kind of grass roots international exchange.

Practical Travel Questions

Leslie also answered practical questions regarding preparation for the trip. Each of the students in the group had questions about how to pack. Leslie reminded us of the suggested packing list on the JustHope website, and patiently answered each question. We laughed and continued to bond as a team while raising questions about what comfort, safety, health, and cultural conditions we should expect. What would bathroom facilities be like? Would we have internet connection? What would the food be like? Laura was concerned about the type of electrical outlets

4. Greider, *Case against "Free Trade,"* 213.
5. Besley and Peters, *Interculturalism*, 12.
6. Alexander, *Pedagogies of Crossing*, 61.

available and whether her hair curling iron would work. Bill asked about taking his c-pap machine. Martin asked about access to a coffee maker and affirmed Laura's interest in ensuring the group could count on ways to continue their coffee habits.

Despite a desire to help people prepare, it is difficult to anticipate or communicate about the discoveries of transformational encounter and spiritual journey inherent in the experience. Students worried about how they would cope with the heat, the lodging, the physical demands, health risks, safety, and the food. Since few North Americans live without air conditioning, even in our cars, the Nicaraguan humidity and heat can seem daunting. Students had heard from classmates on previous trips that the heat was hard to take.

Leslie stressed that warnings about tropical, mosquito borne illnesses like malaria, dengue, or West Nile virus are no laughing matter. JustHope recommends that travelers wear mosquito repellent with at least forty percent Deet.

Martin said, "There are organic alternatives that I will use. Those chemicals are worse for you than the mosquitos."

Laura replied, "One of our classmates who went on this trip last year got dengue fever. She was in the hospital and then had lingering problems for months. We need to take this seriously."

Rose said, "When I told my neighbor I am preparing to travel to Nicaragua, she asked: 'Isn't that dangerous?' I wasn't sure whether she was talking about dangers of illness or other issues."

Leslie reminded the group that JustHope cannot give medical advice and recommends that each traveler consult their doctor. However, she did share what she does to take care of herself. "I keep myself covered with bug spray all the time. I don't take pills to prevent malaria anymore, because there have been no cases of malaria in the areas where we travel in years. The malaria medicine made me sick, too. I make sure my tetanus shot is current. Although there are crimes like theft, there is little violent crime in Nicaragua. I don't worry about crime, but we do recommend being mindful of your backpack or bag when we are in a crowed public area."

Like all JustHope volunteers, the students had to do some research and make choices regarding health precautions. Because Nicaragua has a high level of food insecurity and poverty, questions about food and access to safe water are not irrational. However, the most troubling discomforts for volunteers are often consequences of the privilege and security we typically enjoy as North Americans in comparison with Nicaraguan partners. During our conversations and communication before the trip, I tried to prepare the students for the culture shock that can be intense. JustHope trips require close, deeply personal interaction, so tending to relationships with each other is crucial. It is common for participants to form strong bonds of friendship during the trips. It is also common for people to face challenges in living so closely together, sharing bathrooms, dishes, and tight quarters. Naming the priority of attending to healthy personal relationships within our group, we discussed our differing needs for space, silence, conversation, and sleep.

"How different is our class from other JustHope teams?" Martin asked Leslie as our meeting wrapped up.

"Most JustHope teams are people who already know each other somewhat from their membership in a congregation, but there are other education institutions that send classes of students, too. The amount of reading and studying varies in every group." Despite globalization and increased access to information through the internet, even moderately well-informed North Americans often know little about smaller, less prosperous nations. For example, before their first trip with JustHope, many volunteers need help locating Nicaragua on a map.

"Nicaraguans tend to be much more aware than U.S. citizens about international relations between our countries," Leslie said. North Americans who were adults during the Reagan presidency may remember news insinuating the communist threat from the Sandinistas and congressional controversy related to military intervention. However, many North Americans lack thorough comprehension of the complexities of the Iran-Contra scandal and the U.S. role in the history of Nicaragua. All JustHope teams prepare to travel to Nicaragua by engaging in meetings focused on education, team building, and reflection. It is not unusual for team members to start with little or no awareness about Nicaraguan history and identity. JustHope offers a bibliography of suggested history books and articles, including some of the books and articles our class read.

Our meeting had been productive. We had discussed the need to practice flexibility, openness to community, and decentering ourselves as spiritual practices. We had begun to explore Nicaraguan culture and geopolitical history. We had covered some practical tips for packing and preparing to travel. As we ended our first meeting, Leslie reminded us that she would meet us at the airport in Managua, but we would need to coordinate our travel plans from Tulsa and other parts of the U.S. Paula and Martin were flying from Chicago. Most of us were departing on the same flight in Tulsa, but our class would see each other next in Houston for our flight to Nicaragua.

Flight to Managua

On May 24th, we prepared for the final flight that would take us to Managua. We were excited to meet the rest of our classmates in Houston. As we approached the gate, I saw Paula in a loose, cotton sundress and Martin wearing a black t-shirt with a red image of Che Guevara on the front. After finding a place to group our carry-on bags and sit together, we took turns walking around as we waited to board the flight.

George and Bill discussed how early they had left home that morning. Rose and Paula chatted and smiled, wondering what they had forgotten to pack. We were already feeling the stress of air travel and anticipation of being away from home and loved ones for over a week. At the same time, our mood was bright with anticipation for the opportunity of making the trip. We laughed with each other about who had managed to pack most efficiently in the smallest bag. As departure time grew nearer, the gate area grew more crowded.

Many of our fellow passengers were speaking Spanish. We eyed people waiting for the flight, and we wondered which travelers were Nicaraguans returning home. But one large group was clearly not Nicaraguan. This energetic, boisterous group spoke English loudly and wore bright yellow, matching t-shirts. I asked one of them where they were from. "We are a mission team from Dallas, Texas," the young man responded. Bill interjected, "Have you been to Nicaragua before?" The two exchanged names and discussed their home churches. Martin joined the conversation saying, "I used to live in Dallas. What are you going to do in Nicaragua?"

"We are going to offer the way of salvation through a Vacation Bible School for kids," the young man answered. Martin smiled quietly and nodded without saying anything in response to that. Several members of our team who were listening also remained quiet but began drifting away in the gate waiting area. At that moment, a leader of the mission group called his group to form a circle for prayer before their flight. Since there were more than twenty people in their group, their presence and energy dominated the space in the gate area.

"Leslie calls groups like that 't-shirt groups,'" I said quietly to Martin and Bill. "This time of year, many church groups come to Nicaragua." Our team looked thoughtful, reflecting on advantages and disadvantages of different mission group styles and approaches. A certain edge between excitement and anxiety pervaded the waiting travelers.

Rose said she had seen a place in the airport where we could exchange money. "Should we go ahead and get some Nicaraguan money now?" she asked. I assured the group that we would get a better exchange rate with fewer fees if we waited to change money until we were in Nicaragua. George said he had exchanged money through his banking service and already had some cordobas, the Nicaraguan currency. He pulled out a wad of bills, and his classmates examined the intriguing designs and symbols on the bills. Rose and Bill both agreed that they felt strange traveling without money they could use. Rose said, "I guess this is an example of the discomfort of feeling out of control. Maybe I want some money in order to feel more in command of the situation."

Laura and Elizabeth both agreed that they felt a little vulnerable without money they could use. The classmates agreed they looked forward to exchanging money, so they would have some cash in their pockets.

Martin said, "Maybe we can make that one of our first priorities when we arrive. I need to change money, too."

"Exchanging money does signify border-crossing and transition from one culture to another, doesn't it?" Elizabeth asked. "One more learning experience about being decentered," she laughed.

"I hope we can reflect more about the pervasiveness of trust in money as power that we, as North Americans, may not be aware we carry," I said. Watching the students' anxious desire to have money at hand made me realize that I had the same urge on previous trips. To be without financial resources adds to a feeling of vulnerability.

"A person could write an excellent reflection paper on the many ways that money and financial resources figure in our collaboration this week," I said.

Soon, boarding announcements blared over the speakers, and we began lining up to board with passports in hand. Before long, we were flying over the Gulf of Mexico. Crossing over national borders and geographical barriers constitutes a stupefying reality of leaping from one culture to another. One of the most marked differences between us and our Nicaraguan partners was our financial means for international travel. Although we sought to dismantle that type of unequal privilege, we needed to remain aware of that access to power we often took for granted. The privilege of crossing international borders calls for examination in relationship to systemic oppression.[7] Although Bill had never been outside of the United States before this trip, most members of our group were accustomed to air travel. Laura was seated next to one of the group wearing a yellow t-shirt and seemed to be engaging in a lively conversation with plenty of laughter. George and Nick both dozed. Other students read or made notes while we flew. The flight from Houston to Managua took less than three hours.

Getting through Customs

During the final hour of our flight, attendants distributed immigration and customs forms for us to complete. We strained our eyes to read the tiny, close print. We had to look up our passport numbers, find our arriving flight number, and share pens to write on the forms. We discussed how to describe or price the items we were bringing with us. Since we had to have these forms completed before we could enter the immigration and customs lines, we made sure to be thorough in filling out the forms. We were prepared with cash to pay the national entrance fee. The amount fluctuated over the years. Leslie had reminded us to be flexible; the immigration and customs process changed frequently.

Soon, we saw the twinkling blanket of lights that was the city of Managua. It was too dark to see the volcanos and mountains, but neon signs and traffic lights colored the landscape below. Before long, our plane was touching down in Managua. I thought back to my first trip in 1994 and noticed changes in procedures. In those days, flight attendants made all announcements in Spanish first, then translated the announcements to English. That had changed. Back then, gringo passengers were a small minority on the plane. It was the custom for passengers to applaud joyfully when the plane landed successfully. Now, as international travel has become much more common, and local customs fade, that applause is rare. I miss the applause on the plane.

Managua has the only commercial airport in the country. The mass of people arriving from our plane crowded through the airport and stood in various lines waiting to pass through immigration and customs. As we moved slowly through the process and wondered about our luggage,

---

7. McCallie, "Toward a Pedagogy of Privilege."

we heard less English spoken and more Spanish around us. Our group nervously flocked toward me, asking about how to negotiate the lines. I felt myself shifting from the driven, fast pace of U.S. international airport culture to the slower, warmer customs of Nicaragua. I smiled to myself, thinking that we were literally passing through zones with different customs. There was no use pushing or rushing now. People crowded in lines that seemed stalled. There was nothing to do but wait patiently. One by one, we stepped up to the immigration administrator. With a thick, glass divider separating us from the official, it was difficult to hear the few questions each of us were asked, first in Spanish and then in faltering English. What was our profession? What was the purpose of our travel? The official took our photos, flipped through our passports, entered information on a computer, and asked each of us for the ten-dollar entrance fee.

Once through immigration and customs, we entered a large room with a baggage carousel and looked for our luggage. We grouped together and waited until everyone found every bag. Then, we had to produce the paper baggage receipt to show that our luggage matched our ticket before moving to the next area where we placed our bags on a large belt for scanning. Laura said, "This is strange that they are only scanning our bags after we have already gone through customs. Wouldn't it make more sense to do this first?" The fatigue from the long day of travel was beginning to wear on all of us. I could sense the impatience with the unfamiliar systems and inability to communicate easily with the Nicaraguan administrators waving us along.

The large group of travelers in yellow t-shirts from Dallas swirled around us in various lines. Their bright faces and exuberant voices dominated the space. We could not avoid overhearing one of their group leaders saying, "I was here before, and this process always takes too long." Yellow shirts seemed to permeate the areas as we passed through the lines and moved together through the scanning machines. However, the more steps we took into the Managuan airport, the more we found ourselves engulfed in Nicaraguans coming home. We heard more Spanish and less English.

Unfortunately, when George recovered his large suitcase as it came through the scanner, an officer pulled him aside and waved him toward a long line for additional inspection. He shrugged at the rest of us and moved toward that line with about fifteen people ahead of him. The line was not moving. The rest of us could do nothing but huddle up and wait for him. He stood in the line. We stood and watched, unable to help him. "Another opportunity to experience being out of control!" Elizabeth said ruefully. We were quickly running out of patience. All the members of the yellow t-shirt group were gone. Our group of gringos stood out conspicuously in the swirling mass of Nicaraguans.

Twenty minutes later, the line was still not moving. We could see a man in a uniform behind a counter at the head of the line talking with a woman who seemed to be the owner of the bag he was inspecting. He was piling every item of clothing on the counter and searching intently through everything. The rest of our group continued to exchange frustrated eye contact with George. George was beyond earshot of the rest of our group, but he held up his hands in a gesture of surrender occasionally to express his frustration.

Laura said, "This is crazy. We are never going to get out of here. What are they looking for?" No one answered her. A few minutes later, Rose sighed audibly, and Martin rolled his eyes. We were all weary from travel. We shifted in discomfort as we stood on the concrete floor waiting. I thought about our opportunity to experience feeling culturally uprooted and dislocated in ways that emphasized our lack of ability to control the system. Clearly, we were not in charge. The people who were in charge did not speak our language or look like us. I thought about what a great learning opportunity this was, but it was difficult to be patient. If we were in the U.S., at least one of us would demand some answers and solutions. In this situation, we were all too aware of our powerlessness and could only wait.

As the minutes ticked by, we could see George growing dejected with sweat glistening on his face. I wondered if I should take the rest of the group out of the airport arrival area, but I knew that we would not be readmitted once we exited. Past the exit door from this area, we could see a thick crowd of people awaiting passengers. We needed to stick together in case George encountered more problems. We were getting a full taste of being at the mercy of uniformed workers whose culture and language were not our own.

Eventually, the line began moving, but almost an hour had passed before we saw George step up to the counter. Knowing that George did not speak Spanish, I considered trying to join him there, but the uniformed security officers blocked us from approaching. We could see the officer ask George questions and pull clothing from his suitcase. After a few minutes that seemed like another hour, the officer piled items back in George's bag, zipped it up, and waved George on. George seemed both apologetic and relieved as he finally got through. "Welcome to Nicaragua," George said sardonically as he rejoined our group.

"What did they ask you?" Laura asked.

"I really don't know for sure. It seemed as if they wanted to know if I was selling shoes because I have six pairs of shoes in my bag. My church sent some as donations. I guess it is true what they say: that no good deed goes unpunished," George laughed.

"I'm glad I didn't bring those bottles of vitamins my church wanted to send," Laura said pensively.

"I'm glad they didn't pull me over," Bill said. "I have diabetic supplies including syringes in my bag."

"Should we exchange some money now?" Martin asked.

"We will have an opportunity to do that tomorrow," I said. "Let's go find Leslie and our ride."

Together, we stepped through the next set of doors and encountered a dramatic passage from the air-conditioned section of the airport into the wall of humidity and heat, as well as the press of Nicaraguans greeting their arriving friends and family members. Later, students recounted their first impression of the crowded public airport lobby. We had clearly entered a different context, where personal space, language, and traditions were unfamiliar. The sound of a crowd speaking Spanish washed over us like a wave. Scanning the crowd for a sight of Leslie or our driver, I quickly picked out her white face in the crowd. Leslie greeted each of us with warm smiles. "Were you worried about how long we took to get through customs?" Rose asked.

"No, it often takes a long time," Leslie explained. She welcomed each student by name and shepherded us through the crowds. She led the way to the van that would transport us all week. We worked to stay together, keeping our eye on Leslie as we waded through the press of the crowds waiting to greet travelers. As we exited the airport, Managua enveloped us with traffic noise, horns honking and motorcycles rumbling, and the smell of diesel engines. Men holding handmade signs that read "taxi" called out hopefully. Leslie quickly found our van driver, Juan Pablo, who greeted us warmly and began loading our luggage on the van.

It wasn't long before we were headed toward a hotel in Managua where we would spend the first night. Martin sat in the front passenger seat and tried out his Spanish in halting conversation with Juan Pablo, who drove with ease through the busy streets. We peered through the open van windows to catch our first glimpses of Managua. A tired, dusty horse clip-clopped past, pulling a weathered cart alongside semis, buses, and cars on the highway in front of the airport. We saw streets crowded with people walking, many holding hands of children beside them, or balancing on bicycles. Horns beeped constantly, and the rumble of large truck engines and buses added to the noise of the traffic.

As we drove through the sprawling city, Leslie pointed out sights and answered questions about everything from the steel and neon tree sculptures to the graffiti, the murals, and the historical memorials to the revolution. We passed contemporary looking businesses that seemed like those we would see back home. We also saw neighborhoods where scraps of aluminum were wired up on limbs to create shelter for housing. We passed groups of people who were enjoying the evening gathered in plastic chairs around small food stands. The night was alive with smells of charcoal and food, with music and car horns, with bright store windows and inky skies dotted with stars. Leslie patiently answered questions.

George tried to calculate the price of gas as we passed several gas stations.

"Gas prices here are less than at home, once you apply the exchange rate from cordobas to dollars," he said. Our driver, Juan Pablo, who can understand English and speak a little English, responded in his quiet way. He explained that in Nicaragua the price on the signs is per liter not gallon. So, gas prices are higher in Nicaragua than in the United States. George was thoughtful as he took in the information.

Paula and Martin expressed surprise when they saw a Pizza Hut and then a McDonalds. Signs of the global economy were evident all around. Clearly, some people here had access to money. Yet, at almost every corner with an Alto sign, we noticed visible signs of poverty, including children braving the traffic to sell wiper blades, tortillas, water, or newspapers. We absorbed the sights, sounds, and smells as we rolled along.

Laura asked, "So, Leslie, how did you get involved here in Nicaragua?"

Leslie shared part of her story:

> I first came in the early 1980s during a heavy conflict time between the Contras and the Sandinistas. I had been working with refugees from Central America in the sanctuary movement, so I came on a study trip with the Center for Global Education. It was really the middle of the Contra War. We went up to the area of Jinotega in the mountains, and we met with a group of farmers. A year earlier, these farmers had been given land by the Sandinistas. In the agrarian reform, the government confiscated

land from the wealthy and doled it out to the poor. So, this group of farmers had been given land to own cooperatively. They were bursting with pride because they had just gathered their first harvest. They grew tomatoes as big as soft balls and carrots as long as your arm. They were showing us all this amazing produce they had grown. Before the revolution, they had lived there for generations and as sharecroppers had worked the land someone else owned. That was when Somoza owned it or one of Somoza's cronies, I can't remember. So, at some point we were standing in this circle. They were guarding us from the Contras. I kept thinking we were in the mountains, where there were Contras. My own U.S. government was paying the Contras to try to kill us, but these farmers were protecting us. Looking around the circle, I said, "Tell me what's different? Why are these vegetables so fabulous? You have been farming this land forever; what's different?" They hemmed and hawed a minute. Then this one little farmer, older than God, looked at me and said, "We have always had hope, always, but now our hope has the strong legs of justice." I wrote in my journal that night that at that moment I heard the Holy Spirit say, "That's your life's work, to give hope the strong legs of justice." So, I've been going back to Nicaragua ever since to learn what that means.[8]

Students listened thoughtfully to Leslie's story, still fascinated by the sights and smells of the city as we rode. It took half an hour to reach El Güegüense Hotelito, the small hotel in Managua where we would stay for the night. Our van stopped on a narrow street with walls and gates facing sidewalks on both sides. Leslie jumped out of the van and knocked on a metal gate to call the manager of the small hotel. A few minutes later, a light clicked on inside, and a woman opened a small panel in the gate to talk. After a brief conversation with Leslie, the woman slid the metal gate open. We unloaded our backpacks and luggage, tired after traveling all day. Leslie assisted us in getting keys and finding rooms. She reminded us to use bottled water to brush our teeth. Too tired to have a reflection circle that night, we agreed to reconnect the next morning.

That evening I was still wrestling with the big question of why I was engaged in this travel to Nicaragua again. I had asked each group member to do some reflective writing and self-examination each evening, remembering the challenges of avoiding charity or savior models of mission travel. That night, I wrote in my journal:

8. Interview with Leslie Penrose, May 2019. Transcribed by Kathleen McCallie.

The work of building the blessed commonwealth requires consciousness-raising or mindfulness as well as commitment to dismantling privilege. The elevated status, advantages, and systemic capabilities based in unequal wealth are barriers that block true relationships required for the good life. The full community of sharing sorrows, hungers, diseases, and blessings with neighbors is the goal of discipleship and the process of discipleship. No advantage can be enjoyed fully unless all share the sweetness. We North Americans are usually oblivious to the privileges we enjoy. We take them for granted and deny the ways we benefit from systems that keep others in poverty.

By traveling to geopolitical contexts distant from my daily life, I become more able to face realities of oppressive economic systems. Eventually, I became more able to recognize and understand the similar and interlocking systemic injustice of my own community back home. My motives for coming to Nicaragua include educating North Americans and simultaneously continuing to root out the seeds of greed in my own heart. In these ways, I participate in solidarity with my sisters and brothers in Nicaragua and elsewhere beyond borders. My responsibility and friendship are not circumscribed by national borders.

Besides, the recent history of Nicaragua over the past century provides an opportunity to contemplate attempts at revolutionary, creative, and communal work where utopian visions converge. The courage and faith of the people continue to shine like a beacon. Theologians, poets, philosophers, artists, musicians, social scientists, humanists, and students of the power of the people have connected in Nicaragua from around the world. Unlike the finite minerals and precious natural resources that colonists plundered from the rich, fertile land in Nicaragua, the treasures of inspiration, wisdom, and hope found in Nicaragua do not diminish when internationals visit. In fact, the complex problems confronting the world today require collaboration across cultures and borders. So, connecting people from the U.S. with communities in Nicaragua is a strategic part of expanding imaginaries and constructing transformational relationships.

3

Holy Ground
Ethnography of a Partnership

> I come to Nicaragua from a country where, by contrast nothing seems sacred, where the simulacra of the sacred, such as public prayer or the flag, are turned into a mockery by the arrogance and violence of government policies toward Nicaragua and throughout the world—continuing a long tradition of imperialist cynicism and religious hypocrisy.
>
> —John Brentlinger[1]

Bill was already drinking coffee when I arrived at the breakfast area of our hotel the next morning. Rose and Elizabeth sat with him in the open-air space where four sets of plastic chairs and tables were covered with bright, floral tablecloths. The smell of coffee and toast floated in the morning air. Bill said, "I heard a rooster in the middle of the night and thought it must be about time to get up. These Nicaraguan roosters are on a different time zone." The humid air and high temperature were already making the space uncomfortably warm.

Paula and Martin walked in looking fresh and rested. "Did your air conditioner work? Our room had a unit, but we could never get it to turn on," said Martin.

---

1. Brentlinger, *Best of What We Are*, 348.

Elizabeth and Rose laughed and shared stories from their experience the night before, trying to figure out the small electric water heating devices on the showers and the light switches. "Those electrical wires up over the showerhead made me nervous," Elizabeth said. "I decided a cold shower was the best bet."

Before long, our whole group had gathered. Leslie talked with the cook who began bringing out plates of rice and beans, eggs, and toast. After we ate breakfast, Leslie walked us through highlights of the colorful murals on the walls of the lobby and patio that offered an introduction to geographical regions of the country, depicting typical food, work, and stories unique to each of the various regions in Nicaragua.

"As you see murals and public art, look for common images. Often you will see Sandino's hat. Another common image is the hormiguita, or ant, a symbol of the small but persistent work of liberation and justice in the world, achieved by ones who can be overlooked as insignificant or powerless."

Then Leslie went over the schedule planned for the day, explaining that we would stop to see a few historic sites before we drove to Chacraseca. We would get a taste of the history of Nicaragua, first by visiting the central town square and a museum that had been Somoza's fortress. Next, we would visit Father Uriel Molina's church, Maria de los Angeles, before we made our way from Managua to the small community of Chacraseca where we would spend the rest of the week. Soon, we were packing up to leave the hotel.

Juan Pablo looked fresh and enthusiastic as he cheerfully replaced the luggage on the roof of the van. We watched as he scaled the van with the agility of Spiderman to stand in the luggage rack on the roof while arranging parcels. He seemed able to lift trunks of supplies and bulky bags that were heavier than he was. We stood on the sidewalk, lifting bags above our heads as he bent down from the van's roof. We stretched up, and he stretched down, barely able to grasp some of the luggage. Paula and Martin reminded everyone to refill water bottles and put on sunscreen as we shouldered our backpacks and began to fill the van. Rose laughed with Juan Pablo as he secured a waterproof tarp over the luggage on the roof of the van.

"I'm amazed at his strength," Rose said. "Did you see how gracefully he stepped up on that luggage rack? Some of those bags must weigh more than eighty pounds."

"He knows what he is doing," Leslie smiled. "He has done this many times."

Already the sun was beginning to cook the asphalt street. George and Bill were the last ones on the van, reluctant to squeeze into the hot, tight space until the last minute. As we rolled away from the curb, we absorbed sights of morning routines in the neighborhood: kids in school uniforms with bookbags, women and men in business suits, a few small shops opening, tucked among the doors of houses that lined the streets, a boy selling newspapers among vehicles stopped at an intersection. The city was already busy with traffic and noisy with grinding engines, squealing brakes, honking horns, and radio music.

Our first stop was the central town square where a memorial statue and pavilion stood across from what had once been the National Palace and was now a museum. We piled out of the van and gathered in the shade of a large tree across the square where the old national cathedral loomed. Leslie and I told stories, reminding students of the history they had read about and the famous photograph of the crowds that gathered on this spot in 1979 when the statue of Somoza was pulled down and destroyed. We visited the tombs of revolutionary heroes marked by the red and black Sandinista flag.

Leslie asked the group to think about the question: "Where does America begin and where does it end?" We pondered that question as we enjoyed the cool breeze from the nearby lake.

I was surprised that there were no children begging in the square. Over the years since my first visit there in 1993, I had many memories of visiting that park and being approached by beggars. This time, there were none, and visible improvements had been made to buildings in the area.

"I'm still trying to sort out this history in my mind," George said. "Were the Sandinistas the bad guys or the good guys? And is that the Nicaraguan flag now?"

"The Sandinistas led the revolution to get rid of the U.S. backed dictator, Somoza," Martin reminded the group. "The U.S. basically dominated Nicaragua most of the years after they gained independence from Spanish colonialism. According to our book by Walker and Wade, Ronald Reagan was obsessed with trying to defeat the Sandinistas. The red and black flag was a symbol of the Sandinista movement. The blue and white flag is the official national flag."

"Keep an eye out for the different flags today and this week. You will see the blue and white colors of flag some places and the red and black emblems other places," Leslie said. "I wish it was as simple as 'good guys and bad guys,'" she said. "The Sandinistas split into different groups, and there is plenty of disagreement still. Most Nicaraguans cherish the figure of Augusto Sandino, who fought for freedom from U.S. imperial control of Nicaragua. The Sandinistas took their name and inspiration from his courage and fight for national autonomy."

We walked as close as we could to the old cathedral, damaged beyond repair in the earthquake in 1972. Leslie reminded our group about the devastation of that earthquake and the problems with corruption when international aid poured into the country after that disaster. Walking on these grounds brought new depth of awareness and sense of reality about these historic events that are still so prevalent in the consciousness of Nicaraguans. Before long, we reloaded the van and scanned the neighborhoods we passed as we drove to our next stop. Leslie pointed out the silhouette of Sandino on a hilltop overlooking the city. The gigantic monument stood like a guardian over rolling hills and sprawling city neighborhoods.

"Oh, I've been noticing that guy with the big hat in lots of artwork and graffiti," Laura said. "So, that is Sandino."

"Yes, you will start seeing him everywhere now," Leslie smiled. "His silhouette used to be the tallest point of the city, but recently, newer construction changed that. Our next stop is Tiscapa, the hilltop where Sandino was killed. We will visit a museum there."

"Will we visit his grave?" Elizabeth asked.

"No one knows where he was buried," Leslie said. "He came down from his hideout in the mountains after leaders collaborating with U.S. Marines invited him for peace talks. They took a famous photo shaking hands with him. The next day, they killed him, but that was only verified later by witnesses. At the time, he just seemed to disappear. There were rumors that he had been killed, but his body was never found. Those who killed him probably hid his body to avoid a shrine at his grave. Nicaraguans have a beautiful folk song about his assassination with lines that ask, 'Where is the grave of the freedom fighter?' and the response is: 'The whole country is his grave.' It also memorializes hundreds of disappeared whose bodies were never found or returned to their families. Sandino is a symbolic figure whom Nicaraguans cherish as a leader toward a free Nicaragua."

"Reading about the activities of the U.S. Marines here was painful," said Paula. The group rode in silence for a few minutes. The implications were clear: as U.S. citizens and taxpayers, our national identity and citizenship meant that we were part of this history of international relations. "I feel embarrassed that I never knew this history before," Paula added.

Bill said, "Yes, but I don't agree with the way they are portraying the U.S. I don't think it was that bad. We wouldn't have done all that."

No one responded. An uneasy silence hung over our group. As our van wound through the hills, we continued to catch glimpses of the Sandino silhouette from various vantage points, although often, cell phone towers, billboards, and new buildings eclipsed the iconic figure. The morning routines of people in the streets continued to offer hints about daily life: children in school uniforms, teens laughing, women walking determinedly to work, elders sitting in the shade, talking.

Our next stop was the sanctuary of a church where murals depicting the revolution were designated as national treasures. Leslie explained that this was Maria de Los Angeles, the parish where Father Uriel Molina had started the first base community in Nicaragua. Base communities are manifestations of authentic resistance and locally controlled, grass-roots circles for justice, creative expressions of faith, and centers of organization for enhancing life. They are small groups who often study Scriptures considering economic and political structures. As part of the liberation theology movements, base communities are centers of alternatives to colonial and imperial forms of church. When we arrived, mass had finished an hour earlier, and no one was in the church except the guide who welcomed us. He apologized that Father Uriel was ill and unable to join us.

We entered the sanctuary and took in the circular room with its heavy velvet curtains draped to conceal the murals. Our guide began pulling cords to unveil each wall. The artwork seemed alive with glowing colors, vivid movement in bold lines, and intense scenes depicting revolution and the horrors of oppression at the hands of Somoza and his national guard.

In one scene, a group of soldiers raised their guns. One wore a clerical collar, indicating that he was a priest. The faces of the men looked young, but their eyes seemed ancient and sorrowful.

"How could a priest pick up a gun and join the revolution?" Bill whispered to me and George as we stood looking at the paintings.

"I try to imagine what it would mean to put my body in solidarity with those who were trying to stop Somoza's brutal repression," I said. "No easy answers."

Our guide pointed out another mural, with a young boy. This was the elementary school boy who had been a messenger, helping those who stood against Somoza and his brutal military guard. The guard had tried and tried to catch him and finally did capture the boy. They crushed his body with a tank in the street about a block from this church. Leslie told us that the boy had attended an elementary school in the neighborhood. The bloodied school uniform he was wearing when he was killed is displayed in a glass case in the school.

Rose said, "What a difficult history for children to grow up with! I can't imagine something like that being in a show case at one of my schools."

We were mostly silent, witnessing the genius of the design and skill of the artist. A sense of awe drew us together. We spoke in whispers even though our group was alone in the sanctuary with only our guide.

"It seems like glorifying violence," Laura said. "I can't imagine having all these images of guns and war on the walls of a church."

Leslie shared stories of her first visit to this parish in the 1980s. Known to be a center of revolutionary and activist organizing, this community was famous as a hub of resistance and Sandinista leadership. Students came from around the world to learn about Father Uriel's base community concept. Leslie recalled the sacred energy of the crowded masses she attended during those years.

"We are fortunate to get to hear your stories about those historic experiences," Martin said. After half an hour of viewing the murals, taking pictures, and asking questions, our group prepared to leave. The guide began pulling the heavy drapes back over the murals.

"Why do you keep the murals covered?" Martin asked.

Our guide explained that the murals were covered because the people who worshipped there each week tired of the politicized discourse surrounding the murals. Although they were proud of the history of their parish, the intensity of the conflict wore on the congregation year after year. I thought about the cost of discipleship understood by liberation theologians. The art stands as a witness that confronts our previous assumptions about what it means to be Christian or even what it means to be fully human. I asked our class to continue exploring ethical questions about violence in pursuit of social justice by the artists and the community.

As pastoral leaders or students preparing for vocational ministry, our group was thoughtful as we pondered the complex history of that parish. We had information overload. In addition to jet lag and culture shock, the complicated issues of international relations and our own identities as U.S. citizens were overwhelming. After this full day of sightseeing to deepen our knowledge of Nicaraguan history, we gladly departed the city. It felt refreshing to leave the sweltering heat and noise of the city behind and enjoy the breezy drive into the countryside.

Road to León

From Managua, we traveled by van through the green countryside for a couple of hours to reach León, the closest city to Chacraseca. Along the way, we saw buses that looked like old school buses overflowing with people. We saw people perched atop buses as well. In addition to cars and trucks of various sizes, the highway traffic included numerous bicycles, motorcycles, and carts pulled by a horse or an ox. We saw people walking along the roadside with large bundles balanced on their heads. The brilliant jewel-colored flowers covering trees, vines, and shrubs dotted the landscape. We were awed by the beauty of the countryside we passed.

However, the landscape was arid in some places. We saw irrigation systems in some fields, but many plots of land looked dusty and dry. We passed acres of brown, dead corn stalks that had withered due to lack of rain. People carrying baskets, bundles, and jugs of water walked along many stretches of the highway. Before long, we got a good view of Momotombo, one of the many active volcanoes in Nicaragua. We stopped at a vista to take photographs of the scenic view. The breeze from a large lake was refreshing. Back on the van ten minutes later, we continued the increasingly hot journey.

We stopped halfway in Nagarote, a small community famous for quesillos, a traditional favorite dish of corn tortilla with creamy melted cheese and onions. Quesillos are served rolled up in plastic bags. Our driver, Juan Pablo demonstrated the art of eating quesillos in the traditional way from a plastic bag and without spilling a drop of the cheese sauce. Leslie explained that this rest stop was a popular tradition on the drive between León and Managua. Our group appreciated the bathrooms and cold drinks we enjoyed with the quesillos. Paula laughed when she tried to follow Juan Pablo's example of eating from the plastic bag and found the cheese sauce dripping down the front of her shirt.

When we were on the road again, Bill said, "I remember when no one had air conditioning in their cars. Riding with the windows open like this is kind of nice if we are moving."

Laura said, "These plastic seat covers make my legs sweat. The breeze helps, but air conditioning wouldn't be bad."

Rose pointed out how every little detail of Juan Pablo's van had been freshly painted. Although the van was far from new, it was maintained with obvious care.

"Look at that property on the hill," Martin remarked, pointing to an estate sprawling on a hillside. "There must be some really rich people in Nicaragua. That looks like a walled palace!"

We passed an intersection with an arrow pointing to a turn marked "León Viejo." I explained that if we had time, we would visit the archeological site there.

"Last year I took a tour there. The ruins are all that you can see, but the fortress was built in 1524 by Cordoba to defend against what the Spanish called the rebellions of the Indigenous people. Remember reading about Las Casas? I won't forget the gruesome descriptions of the history of colonialism in this region," I said. I had seen the remains of the buildings and roads built by enslaved persons. I viewed documentation of the brutal history of colonial domination. The population had been decimated by Spanish colonists; locals were captured and shipped to work mines in Peru and elsewhere.

As we drove, Leslie answered questions about sights along the way. Students wanted to know about the entire JustHope staff. Leslie explained that during summer, often the busiest time for partner groups, additional volunteers and interns came to serve as she was doing. The regular JustHope staff in Nicaragua includes only two North Americans and seven Nicaraguans who handle bookkeeping, translating, and organizing projects. The office is in León, and Leslie said we might have time to stop by there later in the week. Since only a few of us in the group spoke a little Spanish, students were relieved to learn about translators who would be with us each day. We knew that JustHope had two employees who live and work in the United States doing communications, organizational development, and fund-raising.

Eventually, we reached the outskirts of León, and traffic picked up. Although we saw little of León that day, we knew we would return later in the week to experience some of the history and vibrant culture there. We merely skirted around the edge of León to reach Chacraseca as soon as possible. We continued to travel about five minutes beyond the edge of the city and then another ten minutes beyond the point where the paved roads ended. The van left a thick cloud of dust as we sped on the dirt road, bumping and lurching in places where ruts and erosion left the road rough. Bill remarked that he was beginning to comprehend what we had been told earlier about how traveling during the season of torrential rains could be prohibitive since the road could be washed out and impassable.

Chacraseca and the Peace House

We turned a corner and had our first glimpses of life in Chacraseca. A few concrete block buildings on either side of the hot, dusty road stood in the glaring sun. Juan Pablo's van pulled up and stopped in front of an open gate in an iron fence. We had arrived at the Peace House, Casa de Paz, where we would be staying during our week in Chacraseca. It felt wonderful to get out of the van, to stretch, and to know we were done traveling for the day. The Peace House is a cinder block building with one large central room and two dorm rooms where we would sleep. We saw the spacious, shady porch in front of the Peace House, and Leslie explained that the space is used for community meetings. The gardens and trees surrounding the building provide vibrant color and natural beauty where dazzling sun and welcome shadows played in the breeze.

We began to unload our luggage, taking in the surroundings. About a dozen people were sitting on benches on the porch of one nearby building. A man was raking leaves in the yard of the Peace House where bright flowers bloomed around a peace pole. Martin was excited to see the peace pole, and he pointed out that it was exactly like the one in front of our seminary building. "We have one like it in front of my church, too." He said. The four-sided pole had writing in different languages engraved with white placards on each side. "That is a peace pole. See the words for peace in Spanish, English, Arabic, and German?"

Elizabeth shared his enthusiasm. "We have one like this in front of our church, too. I think the languages are different on ours. Very cool!"

We carried luggage inside the simple building, past the large, shady front porch with several rocking chairs. A woman sitting behind a desk at an old computer greeted us shyly. Leslie introduced her as Janeth, the administrator of the Peace House. The central room had about ten rocking chairs, a small desk area in the corner where Janeth sat working, and a small altar or worship center with a table in front of a marvelous cross shaped window of jewel toned stained glass that had been built into the concrete block wall.

Leslie showed us the two dorm rooms with space for six people in each. Wooden bunk beds with simple, thin mattresses were the only furnishings. A simple bathroom with a toilet and a shower was accessible from each room. I would share a room with the four female students. Two of us would have to sleep on a top bunk. We would slide our suitcases under the bunks since there was no other place to put them. Students determined which room would be for the men and which for the women. People began choosing beds and settling their things.

Juan Pablo would stay in a smaller, private room on the other side of the small kitchen. Catherine, a JustHope intern, was living for several months in the only other small room. We looked forward to meeting Catherine, but she was working with another JustHope group that day. The other team, a group of teachers, was staying in the annex building nearby. Leslie would stay in another building next door. But, before unloading her bag, Leslie showed us the kitchen. Students were thankful to discover that they had access to a refrigerator and coffee pot. Martin and Laura were both highly interested in the coffee maker. Laura rejoiced to see that there were plastic ice trays, and she began filling one with the bottled water that we all shared.

"If I can have ice, I can deal with just about anything," she joked.

During our first hours at the Peace House, Leslie instructed in a few simple realities like using only bottled water to brush teeth and not flushing toilet paper down the cantankerous plumbing systems. It takes some adjustment to remember to place used toilet paper in the trash can provided next to the toilet. However, Leslie reminded us that if we forgot and stopped up the toilet, instead of having the use of two toilets at the Peace House, the team would have to get by with just one. Although sharing bathrooms seemed challenging, after a few days, our group slowly began to realize it is rare in Chacraseca to have flushing toilets at all. Usually, several families share an outdoor latrine. Showering without hot water seemed like a hardship at first. But our group soon realized that access to indoor plumbing with facilities to shower and wash hands is another uncommon luxury in Chacraseca. Living without air conditioning also seemed difficult at first, but we appreciated the availability of a few fans and electricity.

Leslie gave us a quick tour of the small buildings clustered around some intersecting dirt roads in front of the Peace House. She explained that thirty years earlier there had been nothing except the church here. In this area that Sister Joan called, "Plaza de Paz," Leslie showed us a medical clinic, a building that houses Stitching Hope, the women's sewing cooperative, a large community hall beside the church, a library that was built by another nonprofit group from the United States, and several annex buildings for housing volunteers. There were also a few other buildings used for offices or storage, a small store that sold cold drinks and snacks, and a large building under construction that would be a youth cultural center. A metal building next door to the Peace House contained a small office and some storage rooms. Leslie would be sleeping there.

"Is this the center of Chacraseca, then?" George asked.

"This is the area most concentrated with buildings. There is not really what we would call a town in Chacraseca. It is more like a county. The area is about fifty-five square miles with about 8,000 people living on farmland. There are thirteen primary schools and two high schools; all were built by solidarity groups like yours," Leslie explained.

Our only plan that evening was to meet with leaders from the community who would welcome us and explain their hope for our time together. As the sun dipped behind the tree line, we met Juan Enrique, Armando, and Nimia, three elected leaders of the base community. Chacraseca makes decisions through an organization called ACOPADES, Asociacion de Comte Pastoral Para el Desarrollo Social, that roughly translates as Association for Social and Economic Development. This group meets weekly on Tuesday mornings at the Peace House. These three represented that group to welcome us to the community and begin building relationships with us. We sat in a circle, took time for thorough introductions, and listened to their welcome and orientation to their community. Clearly, they had welcomed many groups like ours before. Julio, our JustHope translator, facilitated communication while the local leaders led the meeting.

In addition to sharing highlights of our schedule, Juan Enrique asked Armando Cabarello to share about his story as a way of introducing the community. Armando relied on our translator, Julio, to relay his story.

> *I was married fifty-six years ago in 1959. I am eighty-one years old. I have three sons and four daughters who are all married. One son lives here and has children; one son lives away and has two children; only one son is single. Even though we are poor, we raised our children well. They went to school. Two finished University. Gracias a Dios. There are many struggles in life. There are good times and bad times. I have come to understand life this way. Now people don't stay married long. I have*

many friends and neighbors who got married in the 90s, but they are not together anymore. I met my wife when we were children. We were neighbors. I only finished first grade. I lived on this land my whole life. I was born near the church and Casa de Paz.

Since I was a child, because of my parents, I used to visit the church. I have been working for this community for thirty years. I started to organize work in the community in 1972. In 1975, I was very tired working for community and church. I would get up at one or two a.m. My wife supported me with much responsibility and love to do this work. We thanked God we were alive, telling about this life.

In 1988, Sister Juanita came to this community. The community was not strong or united then. I was working with Father Donald Mendoza. Donald Mendoza brought the Sister Juanita to the community.

Now, I continue working as a supporter of ACOPADES because I see there is a need for helping people. Anything I can do for the community I will do. Now, I am a supporter because the doctor said I need to rest. In 1988, the community had energy because of people like you that Sister Juanita brought; 2000 was the year we got electricity.

Sister Juanita built schools. It was always her idea looking for help and money. ACOPADES and Sister Juanita were working together.

ACOPADES was formed because of the spiritual part. At first, Father Donald called it a pastoral committee. Later, it became ACOPADES. The committee has been growing up because the law has changed. It became a non-profit; it has a new name now: ACOPADES.

When Sister Juanita was here, she closed the office on Tuesdays. They said prayers in the morning before the committee meeting. That was before the Peace House was built.

I helped build the Peace House with my hands. Before that there was not anything here. In the 1960s, nothing was here except the church. The first construction in 1988 was a brick factory. Then Casa de Paz was started. In 2014, the rooms next to Casa de Paz were built. I worked making the bricks in the factory. One of the workers taught me how to make bricks. Someone in the community had the idea to make a brick factory and suggested it to the committee. We are always thinking of ideas, but if you don't have the resources, what can you do? The brick factory was needed because other sectors needed latrines. There were many families that needed a house.

Sister Juanita developed the sectors with the committee by working to do a census. We formed a committee of six leaders in each sector.

> Sister Juanita said, "So, now we are going to see what problems they have in each sector." Each needed a school. The first school was the Maryknoll school in Raúl Cabeza sector that Sister Juanita built.[2]

Armando and the other leaders enjoyed sharing their memories. They connected the history of the work in Chacraseca with the work that JustHope does. The collaboration and organizing was not easy. The leaders laughed with Leslie over stories of struggle. Juan Enrique said, "We used to have Sister Joan; we called her Hermana Juanita, but now we have Leslie. JustHope helps continue the work." They showed our group a map of Chacraseca, a long, rectangular area, stretching about ten miles. We were in the southwestern region of Nicaragua, just south and east of the city of León.

Leslie and the leaders gave us an overview of the main projects that JustHope conducts in the community. Each of these projects began at the request of local leaders who had identified needs and sought partners for the projects. Leslie taught us about the social enterprise projects like the hardware store that was owned and run by women, the sewing cooperative, and the micro-credit loan program. We heard about education programs like the teacher-training project, the backpack initiative, the scholarship program, and the cultural center where music, dance, and art lessons would be offered for children and youth. She introduced us to the concepts of the model farm where innovation and education are balanced with ongoing production. She spoke about the health programs within the regular clinics of Chacraseca and the temporary day-clinics set up in out-lying regions when possible. After reaching the saturation point with new information, we were glad to remember that we would be visiting a different project each day, with some opportunity to join in the work and learn more.

Nimia explained how local women who were leaders in the church next door cooked meals for JustHope teams to earn extra income. Because the cooks had to walk miles from their homes to get to the church, we would eat our evening meals here in the Peace House. That way the cooks could prepare the meal early and start walking home in time to arrive before dark. Nimia and the other leaders said they would see us in the days to come. They said good night and left our group to eat supper and share our evening group reflections.

---

2. Interview with Armando Cabarello, May 2016. Translated by Julio Delgado, transcribed by Donna Greene.

Although it was beginning to get dark, Leslie also showed us a labyrinth sculpted from hedges on one side of the building. Leslie told us that Sister Joan always made groups walk the labyrinth as a form of meditative prayer when they first arrived. On the opposite side of the building, Leslie showed us a sign that said, "Forest of Meditation." This section of beautiful, tall trees had been planted at the time the Peace House was built in 2000. Before that, the area was just a dusty field. We could see a small gazebo in the center of the wooded area. Stations of the cross in small grottos made from volcanic rock encircled the perimeter of the woods. Leslie said we could have morning meditations there during the week, but the night was growing dark. The rest of our exploration of the area would have to wait until the next day. We moved indoors.

The common room in the Peace House was furnished with sturdy rocking chairs. Leslie explained that Sister Joan called her ministry "Rocking Chair" ministry because she spent lots of time sitting out on the porch in a rocking chair and visiting with people. The rocking chairs were made locally of rich wood and woven bamboo cane. Several fans made the room more comfortable. We were thankful to eat supper. We found the large plastic bowls of food on the table in the central room of the Peace House. Laura flipped open the lid on her bottle of hand sanitizer, squeezed a dollop in her palm, and asked if anyone else wanted some. We passed the little bottle around, disinfecting our hands. The chicken, carrots, squash, tortillas, rice, and beans tasted great.

"I'm surprised the food is not spicy," Bill said.

Leslie replied, "Most Nicaraguans don't like spicy food. After we finish eating, we will each wash our own plates. That is easier than taking turns to do dishes. Unlike the liquid dish soap many North Americans use, Nicaraguans typically wash dishes using a cake of soap that melts in a small bowl of water used as a container for a scrubbing brush. A person swipes the brush in the soft soap and then scrubs the dish as they rinse it. You will find a little bowl that has a scrubber and a bar of soap made for dishes beside the kitchen sink. Just scrub and rinse your dishes and leave them stacked in the drainer."

"What about the leftover food?" Rose asked.

"We will cover the bowls and put them in the refrigerator," Leslie explained. "Just remember, you can store your own food items in the refrigerator, but someone else might take them. That space is considered community space."

"I'm still thankful to have ice," Laura said.

During our first discussion circle in the Peace House that evening, we admired a colorful painting in the local, primitivist style depicting Sister Joan's dream. The painting is entitled "Chacraseca Is Becoming Chacraverde." The painting includes the Peace House at the center of gardens with a labyrinth on one side and an arboretum with a gazebo and grottos for the stations of the cross on the other side. The painting is bright with luxuriant greens and colorful flowers. Leslie explained that the word "Chacraseca" could be translated "dry husk." "Seca" means dry, and "chakra" is the stalk or shoot of a growing plant. It was Sister Joan who first began to speak of the dream that the dry husk could be transformed into a fertile shoot: Chacraseca could become Chacraverde.

We had seen the dusty streets of the community with its black, volcanic sandy soil lined with verdant tropical trees, shrubs, and flowers which the rain had brought forth. Leslie told us that much of the year all the vegetation seems dusty and parched, longing for renewal and moisture. Decades earlier, the fields had been depleted by overgrazing and unsustainable monocultural agriculture. The area had been deforested and used as a banana plantation. Later, cotton and peanuts grown for commercial demand stripped the soil of nutrients. The area around the church and Peace House contained open fields before the Maryknoll sisters began reforestation projects, planting an arboretum that now towers around the buildings. We studied a bulletin board with fading photographs of the work of these recent decades, documenting the transformation of the location from an empty, treeless field to the buildings and gardens that were now flourishing.

After we put away the leftover food and washed our plastic plates, we gathered in the common room again for our evening reflection time. We had barely been in Nicaragua twenty-four hours, yet our minds were saturated with new questions, information, and sensory overload. I asked the group what images stood out in their minds from their experience so far. I was particularly interested in hearing reflections on our visits to the central town square and museum that morning.

Rose said, "I keep thinking about those families we saw riding motorcycles or bikes with three or four people on one bike. I saw a few people with helmets, but so many little kids without them... Some even had little babies in their arms!"

Bill added, "And then there were all the people walking along the highway with small children. Did you see that woman with that huge basket on her head? I wonder what that weighed?"

Nick said, "I wish I could forget the images of those cages and torture chambers at the Sandino Museum. There is something potent about the fact that we can't go visit the grave of Sandino. It leaves an unfinished, unresolved feeling about it."

"Like a social movement that is still ongoing," Paula said quietly.

"I have thought about the fact that in the U.S. our heroes have mostly been victors like George Washington or Abraham Lincoln. They were on the winning side. In contrast, Nicaraguan heroes are martyrs. Think about how that affects the psyche," Leslie said.

"I keep thinking about that mission team we met in the airport—the ones with the yellow t-shirts," said Martin. "That could have been me five years ago. I wonder what their group is doing today."

The group continued to ponder and reflect over their experience so far. After checking in about needs or concerns each group member had, we reviewed our plans for the next day. We would spend our mornings doing some volunteer work and our afternoons visiting various JustHope programs. Monday, we would help build a latrine as part of a community project JustHope offered. In the afternoon, we would learn about the micro-credit lending circles.

After we finished discussing logistics for the next day, I said, "Another song that Carlos Mejía Godoy performed as part of the Nicaraguan folk mass is about houses made of cardboard, "Casas de Cartón." The lyrics were written by Marco Antonio Solis. All day I kept thinking of a few lines from that song: "Here comes the worker almost dragging each step, carrying suffering's weight. Today is the same as yesterday, his world doesn't have a tomorrow . . . Millionaires feed like tapeworms; and, because of that, how sadly live the children in the houses made of cardboard."[3] It is a great song. I found the lyrics after I heard Carlos Mejía Godoy sing it in concert." Several students made note of the song, appreciative of the powerful poetry.

Nick said, "I just pulled up the lyrics on my phone. Those are some powerful words."

I asked the group to continue reflecting on questions and feelings they had during the day. The hum of the fan and the creak of rocking chairs was the only sound for several minutes.

Then Martin said. "My mind is flooded with images of the shacks we drove past that looked as if they were made of scraps of trash. I feel

---

3. Solis, "Cardboard Houses." Translated by Kathleen D. McCallie.

overwhelmed by frustration at the chasms between inadequate shelter versus obscene levels of luxury in the world. I have no doubt there is a spiritual core to this heartache I feel, but I don't know what to do with it."

"And I can see those people along the roadside who were carrying huge bundles of firewood on their backs, or big plastic tubs on their heads," Rose said. "Like 'carrying suffering's weight' as that song said."

"And the poor housing looked worse in the crowded city," Paula said. "I thought Juan Pablo would never get through Managua this morning. It was so hot and cluttered everywhere on those small little streets. It must be much nicer to live in the countryside like this rather than live in the city," she added.

"I keep remembering little kids playing in the dirt with bare feet and not many clothes," said George. "If I tried to describe it to my wife, she wouldn't believe me."

"Millionaires feed like tapeworms," I said. "What a powerful line! Hungry people who also suffer parasites give the lyrics new potency."

"I could get overwhelmed by sadness real fast," Laura said.

Leslie smiled quietly. "Many people only see the poverty and not the strength and beauty of the people. I recently read that we should always use the term 'people made poor' instead of referring to people as 'the poor.' We need reminders that poverty is a result of economic structures and history rather than a natural state into which people are born. I don't want to think of these people as 'the poor,' but I want to remember they have been *made* poor. Let's continue reflection on what is at stake in being open to all we can learn here." We sat in heavy silence a few moments.

I thought about the process I hoped the students could go through as part of this class: waking up to economic and national privilege, allowing the dissonance between our worldview and the world of Nicaraguan campesinos to shake up our spirituality and faith, committing to an activism to transform political systems and redistribute resources.

"Leslie, please say a little more about the concept of the struggle and resistance in your work," I asked.

Leslie said, "In Nicaragua, people often talk about the struggle as a sacred act. It is a spiritual concept related to the revolution within the self, the community, and the world. The dream of working for justice is not yet achieved; the struggle continues. Resisting injustice is the struggle. People who join the work find community, hope, and joy in the struggle."

"That makes me think of Alice Walker's book, *Possessing the Secret of Joy*, with resistance as the center of the secret," I said. "Womanist and

Latin American liberation theologians both emphasize resistance in the struggle for justice as a crucial element of becoming human. It is interesting to notice that people often think spirituality should be comforting. In my experience the spiritual journey is often disturbing and disruptive, too."

Others nodded. It had been a long day, and we were all weary. Our conversation tapered off. Then, we closed our reflections for the evening and said good night.

Liberationist Theory

Feminist Liberation Theologians in the 1980s wrote about the process of being freed from unjust structures and freed for true community. The struggle to change economic, political, and material systems goes hand in hand with internal liberation from crippling narratives and ideology. The movements for justice lead to intersectionality and relationships that defy borders. Justice and freedom are manifest through relationships. Beverly Wildung Harrison writes:

> We do not, from a liberation perspective, possess blueprints for a just world. It is only virtue of our engaging in the struggle for justice—a struggle we must suppose will endure for as long as time and history continue—that we gain intimations of what rightly ordered community and God's transcendence may mean.[4]

The UN Human Development Index measures economic and social factors to compare what it takes to live in various countries. Nicaragua ranks low in comparison to other nations. Walker and Wade observed that Nicaragua "dropped from 60th at the time of Chamorro's inauguration to 116th ten years later."[5] The wealth disparity between the United States and Nicaragua is largely a result of political actions and policies. Although the motives of some revolutionaries were mixed, the Nicaraguans who fought to oust Somoza understood themselves to be fighting against "the beast" or the United States. Tomás Borge, a Sandinista leader, said, "Our revolution was not made to maintain the exploitation of humans by humans, to maintain the privileges of millionaires, but to restore the rights of the humble and the poor."[6] When the political movement fractured into different political parties, each group continued to claim

---

4. Harrison, *Justice in the Making*, 21.
5. Wade and Walker, *Nicaragua*, ix.
6. Borge, *Christianity and Revolution*, 49.

solidarity with the poor. Sandinistas lost the election in 1990 and dashed the hopes of many who had equated the movement with the FSLN party. But the popular understanding of the fight to continue the revolution was united in commitment to justice for the poor.

Fernando Cardenal reported a conversation in 1990 with an eleven-year-old girl. He asked her, "Who are we working for in the revolution?" She replied, "For the poor."[7] He said that although they had lost the election, Nicaraguans would continue working for the poor. Yet, he acknowledged that corruption and impure motives had plagued the revolution, too. Cardenal wrote, "The problem, and the enormous tragedy, was not losing the election. The tragedy was losing our moral standing because of corruption."[8] The robust self-examination and theological reflection in the social movement that was the Sandinista revolution continues. International partners and aid workers have been drawn to Nicaragua because of the richness of the idealism and vision of true egalitarian collaboration for a more just and humane society. Nicaraguans offer a mirror to illustrate the hypocrisy, injustice, and greed of the United States. By drawing on the prophetic tradition of Scripture as a model for critiquing political and economic systems, Nicaraguans identified the actions of the United States as the beast. Although it is painful and challenging for U.S. citizens to comprehend this perspective, it is a gift Nicaraguans offer for healing and correction. David Haslam captures one explanation of why our partners in Latin America often view the United States as "the beast." He writes, "The simplest phrase to describe what the Nicaraguan Christians see as the Beast is 'U.S. imperialism,' that is the arrogant, greedy, dominating use of power, and the search for even greater power, by the administration of the United States, backed by the military, industrial and financial interests which are at the heart of the modern U.S. empire."[9] I have observed students and volunteers with JustHope move from defensiveness about policy to dawning comprehension of the injustices that we fund as taxpayers. Our spirituality and faith cannot be sequestered from this insight.

JustHope partners from the United States deepen their awareness and information about international relations and U.S. foreign policy. Many had never heard of the U.S. "blueprint for war" that called for "escalating propaganda activities directed at Nicaragua and the rest of

7. Cardenal, *Faith and Joy*, 228.
8. Cardenal, *Faith and Joy*, 231.
9. Haslam, *Faith in the Struggle*, 115.

the region."[10] Since 1926 when the U.S. sent five thousand marines to protect financial investments of U.S. citizens, most Americans have been blind to this action. Sandino and his fighters were described as bandits or outlaws. In U.S. popular media, Sandinistas sounded like dangerous enemies. However, the Sandinista revolution was fought in the name of equality and liberty. Howard Zinn writes:

> The Sandinistas, a coalition of Marxists, left-wing priests, and assorted nationalists, set about to give more land to the peasants and to spread education and health care among the very poor and long-oppressed people of Nicaragua. Almost immediately, the Reagan administration began to wage a secret war against them.[11]

The methods used against the Sandinistas were not consistent with principles of just war. Zinn and other historians documented the testimony of Colonel Edgar Chamorro, the Contra's public relations person. In a statement to the World Court, Chamorro said,

> We were told that the only way to defeat the Sandinistas was to use the tactics the Agency (the CIA) attributed to Communist insurgencies elsewhere: kill, kidnap, rob and torture . . . Many civilians were killed in cold blood. Many others were tortured, mutilated, raped, robbed, or otherwise abused . . . When I agreed to join in 1981, I had hoped that it would be an organization of Nicaraguans, controlled by Nicaraguans . . . [It] turned out to be an instrument of the U.S. government, and specifically of the CIA.[12]

This type of well documented information supports the argument of Noam Chomsky, who has said that "the primary concern of U.S. foreign policy is to guarantee the freedom to rob and to exploit."[13] Of course, most U.S. citizens are unaware of this history and the continuing economic structures that dominate and exploit nations like Nicaragua.

The consciousness-raising that JustHope offers does not happen quickly or easily, since many travelers from the U.S. may have vested interests in remaining uninformed. The process of coming to realize the history of unjust international relations can be quite painful for JustHope partners from the U.S. New insights and information can seem

---

10. Kornbluh, *Price of Intervention*, 212.
11. Zinn, *Declarations of Independence*, 223.
12. Zinn, *Declarations of Independence*, 224.
13. Chomsky, *On Power and Ideology*, 7.

unpalatable. However, those who feel convicted by the Christian ethic of unconditional love, regardless of the consequences, continue discerning how to integrate faith with public life and thus with political action. Feminist ethicist Beverly Wildung Harrison claims that "mature spirituality" requires both "doing the practice of the love of God" in relationship with others and also discourse that includes "good socio-moral analysis."[14] No one can secure a border between politics and faith. JustHope partnerships press participants to reflect on how to faithfully mix them.[15]

I tell my students about the ministry of Father Miguel d'Escoto who has been an important teacher and guide in my own spiritual formation. When I first met him in Managua in 1994, I experienced him as a warm, loving, wise priest and community organizer. He was jovial and utterly humble. I learned that bodyguards protected him constantly then, and he was still threatened because of his leadership in the revolution and the Sandinista resistance to the U.S. Slowly, I came to realize that he was a famous statesman and international diplomat who had served as Foreign Affairs Minister and even as president of the General Assembly of the United Nations. I learned that the Vatican had revoked his priesthood because of his political activism. I learned that he had led the Nicaraguan case against the U.S. in the World Court of Justice in 1986, to protest the mining of Nicaragua's harbor. In that case, the U.S. was condemned by the World Court in a decision that demonstrated criticism of the U.S. war against Nicaragua. Over the years, I was blessed to meet with Father Miguel numerous times, as he welcomed groups of volunteers and taught about liberation theology and spirituality as well as history.

Father Miguel said:

> The American people are systematically lied to, systematically deceived concerning not only the purposes of U.S. foreign policy, not only the objectives but also the content—what the U.S. leaders really do. The American people have been betrayed, betrayed by their churches in the worst way. The American churches have been bought.[16]

His point about the churches in North America is evidenced in the fact that I learned postcolonial theory in Nicaragua. Sadly, deception is not limited to politicians in the U.S., but through transnational friendships,

---

14. Harrison, *Justice in the Making*, 151.
15. Baker, *When Faith Storms the Public Square*, 25.
16. McCallie, "Liberation and Liberal Freedom," 346.

I learned to think critically and trust new sources of information. It was only from Father Miguel that I began to learn about Tolstoy, Dorothy Day, and the critique of neoliberalism as part of the ways of Jesus. Father Miguel said:

> Dorothy was always in jail. And in spite of all the hypocrisy today of the Catholic church, they want to cardinalize her. They should be stopped. We don't want them to touch her, not to dirty her. She is a saint by acclamation of the people. Of course, in my book Marx is a saint. He was the only one, the only conscience of humanity that saw what man was doing to man in the industrial revolution . . . And he was the first one to explain to us the workings of capital. And so there you have it. I was saying Dorothy is a saint, Marx is a saint, Gandhi a great saint, Martin Luther King, those are our saints. We don't need the church to canonize them.[17]

JustHope partners are invited to struggle with their spiritual path and act in resistance to the dominant messages of civil religion in the U.S. In contrast to the focus on personal piety and palatable narratives most Christians in the U.S. know, solidarity with Christians in Latin America can seem subversive. In her 2014 book, *Solidarity Ethics*, Rebecca Todd Peters offered keen articulation of the problem. She wrote:

> Today, Christians in the first world are being called to account by our brothers and sisters from the global South for our participation in the systems and structures of empire and globalization that are impoverishing and exploiting their lives, their families, and their communities. As people of faith, as brothers and sisters in Christ, we are called to listen to their voices, their stories, and their experiences—and to examine our own lives in the process.[18]

Peters admitted that this work is hard because as North Americans we benefit from the wealth amassed by our nation. We are often blind to the public goods like transportation, education, and other public resources that place us on a different level from our birth. We have capabilities by virtue of living in a wealthy country that others cannot access.

I asked my students to engage deeply with this statement Peters wrote: "Trying to figure out what solidarity with the two-thirds world looks like is a difficult topic for people who live in the first world. One

17. McCallie, "Liberation and Liberal Freedom," 347.
18. Peters, *Solidarity Ethics*, 119.

reason for this is that they undoubtedly benefit from the current model of economic globalization that dominates our world."[19] Students and I squirm with unease in this process of becoming more keenly aware of what is at stake for us personally in unmasking the inequities and the human systems that create and maintain unjust wealth and poverty. Our Nicaraguan partners confront us with a haunting question: how deeply will we allow ourselves to be transformed by our faith? John Brentlinger was a North American historian who articulated a similar spirituality enlivened by liberation theology. He wrote about his own transformational encounters in Nicaragua. He and Leslie Penrose were great friends and shared their appreciation for the liberative praxis of activism in Nicaragua. Brentlinger described the spiritual calling he developed in Nicaragua well, saying, "We need to reconstitute and nurture our human capacity to feel deeply bonded together as part of one historical struggle, on the same earth, within the same creative, evolutionary process."[20] That spiritual transformation is the process that Elba calls becoming "humanized."

19. Peters, *Solidarity Ethics*, 93.
20. Brentlinger, *Best of What We Are*, 349.

— 4 —

Solidarity in Dignified Work

> Prayer is more than words, more even than listening to the "still, small voice of God." It is also about seeing—seeing the God who is with us and in our neighbor and the love of God that surrounds, embraces, and fills us.
>
> —MARYKNOLL BOOK OF PRAYER[1]

LIGHT DAWNED MONDAY AROUND 5:00 a.m. in Chacraseca. Some of our team slept a little later, but a few of us were up before our alarm clocks rang, ready to embrace our first full day in the countryside. Martin had brought a special roast of coffee beans and a grinder. He had graciously offered to share the fruit of his elaborate coffee-making process with early risers. The delicious smell got me out of bed by 5:30, to enjoy the blessed quiet of the morning and the plentiful birds' music. I found Bill and Martin in rocking chairs on the porch, savoring coffee and enjoying the lush, tropical surroundings and peaceful stillness. Just as I was returning with another chair and a mug of coffee, several sharp, loud cracks split the air. The sound like fireworks exploding nearby jolted us all. Our eyes met while we wondered if others were sharing the same thought. Did that sound more like gun shots or fireworks? Through the screen window of

---

1. Leach and Perry, *Maryknoll Book of Prayer*, 56.

the nearby bedroom, we heard George yell, "What the hell was that?" Moments later, Laura, still in her pajamas, hurried out to the patio asking, "What was that? It sounded like gun shots!" The startling reaction illustrated the vulnerability of being far from home in an unfamiliar setting and culture. Sounds like gunshots in the Nicaraguan countryside brought all kinds of associations to mind.

At the same moment, Leslie walked up looking relaxed, refreshed, fully dressed, and ready for the day. "It was fireworks," she explained. "There is a small fireworks factory right over there. They test fireworks most mornings and sometimes at various times of the day or night." We all relaxed and felt amused at ourselves.

Laura looked doubtful, but she headed back toward the women's bedroom area. Another volley of fireworks went off, and we all jumped again. Despite that excitement, the early morning was mostly serene. Martin, Bill, Leslie, and I visited as we sipped our coffee. Mostly we sat together in prayerful silence, soaking up the beauty surrounding us. The Peace House porch invites meditation, reflection, and spiritual practice. We had ample time for journaling and morning routines. Over the next hour, others who had showered and dressed joined us, while I returned to finish dressing for the day.

We took turns in the shared bathrooms. The cold shower was bracing that early in the morning, and it was frustrating to get clean and to then have to douse immediately with insect repellent. We had already encountered a few mosquitos, even inside the Peace House. By the time I was trying to towel off after my shower and get dressed, I was already sweating again. In the tight space of the shared room, we skirted around each other to get ready to go. I laughed with my roommates about how the sunscreen that I slathered on my face rolled off my skin with perspiration.

We gathered on the porch of the Peace House at 6:45 a.m. for a morning devotional time that Leslie led. We stood in a circle around a small wooden table which held a pan of water. Leslie invited us to take a few moments to connect with the ground under our feet. She asked us to think of the hundreds and thousands of people who had walked on this land. She reminded us that Chacraseca has no surface water; until recently, wells were all dug by hand. People who lived here ages ago, the Spaniards who came and conquered, the plantation owners, workers, leaders, and families who lived here in recent centuries, and their descendants who lived here in recent decades all depended on water. We thought of volunteers from various countries who had come for solidarity during the 1980s and 1990s. We acknowledged the sacredness of this land; we acknowledged the sacredness of all land and water.

What is solidarity? Leslie quoted a friend who taught her that solidarity is when you start to dream another's dream with them instead of dreaming your dream for them. Leslie asked us to go into the day asking ourselves: how do we want to be with people? She read a contemporary reading that was a quotation from Eduardo Galeano: "I don't believe in charity. I believe in solidarity. Charity is vertical, so it's humiliating. It goes from the top to the bottom. Solidarity is horizontal. It respects the other and learns from the other. I have a lot to learn from other people." Our theme for the day was the JustHope value: solidarity. She prayed that our group would have eyes to see what God wanted us to see that day. What illustrations of solidarity would we witness? Soon it was time to head across the dirt road to a building next to the church.

We were intrigued with the gleaming white church building shining in the morning sun. We were a group of church nerds, and we wanted to go explore that church building. Leslie had assured us that later in the week we would get an opportunity to see the sanctuary. However, that morning at 7:00 a.m., we entered the older, dusty community building next to the church instead. Several local women greeted us as we passed through the kitchen; Leslie introduced our cooks, Nimia, whom we met the previous afternoon, and Estella. They both hugged each one of us and said, "Buenos dias! Cómo amanecio?" Leslie explained that this lovely phrase is the most common morning greeting in the community. Literally, it would be translated, "How did you dawn?" So, it is somewhat like asking, "How did you sleep?"

Estella was bent over with age and looked quite elderly. Leslie said that for almost twenty years, Estella had been telling people she was 80 years old. Nimia was younger, with only a few touches of grey in her dark hair. She introduced her young grandchildren playing in a nearby corner of the kitchen. After exchanging warm greetings, they turned back to the wood fire that was roaring under the hot griddle where they cooked tortillas, rice, and beans. The large community hall seemed dark, smoky, and sweltering, despite the wilted fan spinning lazily overhead that Nimia flipped on as we entered. We gathered around long, rectangular tables covered with plastic table clothes; we sat in plastic chairs. We passed around the stack of plastic plates and poured juice into plastic cups.

Julio, our JustHope translator, came in carrying his motorcycle helmet and joined us for breakfast. Juan Pablo and two more JustHope translators came with Julio. Leslie introduced Francis and Roberto, who would be working as translators with us that day too. We passed plates and food as they sat with us to share the meal. As we remarked on the good food, Bill said, "At least there is plenty of local food growing. Do groups always eat this well?" Leslie explained that most people in the community did not have access to the variety, quality, or amount of the food that we were eating. She explained that through JustHope, our team had provided money to buy the food and pay the women who prepared it. That awareness soaked in as we chewed thoughtfully.

Julio explained that almost every Nicaraguan breakfast included the favorite dish in Nicaragua, gallo pinto. Gallo pinto is a combination of brown beans and rice that we were all eating. Julio and Juan Pablo agreed that gallo pinto was their favorite food. In addition to gallo pinto, we ate corn tortillas, bananas, and eggs scrambled with peppers and onion. After everyone was served, Leslie invited the older cook, Estella, to come share a little of her story. Julio translated:

I have been working for the church the past forty-two years. I taught the younger ones who are cooking now. I am always working with the priest preparing meals for events. Sometimes the priest looks for me to come help him out. I don't get any payment for this. This is my way of helping the church. I also work for ACOPADES; I prepare the meals on Tuesday. I came here because of Sister Joan. I remember that in all the meetings and religious celebrations, she needed somebody. I said, "Here I am, I am present."

When the Peace House started, I was the number one cook every single day for nuns and groups. I remember when we started cutting the weeds to build the Peace House. Later, more and more people came to work. Sister Juanita, said, "I need you to cook every day all the meals." We had one or two days of a rotation coming from every sector. My job was to make juices and cook.

I was there from the very beginning to the end of the construction. It took about six months. It was a tough thing to do, a hard work. There was nothing here. Just yuca fields, corn, only the church. I lived here eighty-two years in the same place. I have seen many changes. There was no house for the priest. They would come and go. The first one who stayed was Father Julian. That was after Father Donald.

North American groups started to come when Sister Juanita was here. She opened up the way for them to come. My first memory of

Sister Juanita was that I started to see groups when she first got here. She asked for help. I remember her idea to bring electricity here. She said that we were going to knock on the doors. We were going to ask for help from our brothers and sisters. When she had meetings with us, I said, "Let me know what you need. I will help anyway I can."

I had two sisters and two other half-brothers. When I was a child, there was no joy. There was nothing. The youth now are lucky. Now, for weddings, there are big parties. Now girls have sweet fifteen celebrations. It was more difficult when I was a child, kids are more advanced now. We had to gather wood in the fields. Now kids go and play baseball. Now, they go to school. Before, there were no schools. Everything was just working, eating, go to bed, next day same things. So many changes. I was about sixteen years old when I had my first pair of shoes.

None of my sisters or brothers went to school. We did know that some of our neighbors got to go to school in León because they had money. My first work was helping my mother by grinding corn with stones. There were no machines at that time. If they did exist, they were very expensive. I also helped carrying water from the well far away. We would carry buckets on our heads. My mother's life was very sad. She picked beans, corn, cotton, in the field for other farmers. When she got paid, we had food on the table. My sisters and I worked with her in the field. We left at two a.m. because beans need to be cut before the sun gets hot. The beans have to be kind of wet. At seven or eight o'clock, we went back home. At 2:00 a.m., it was time to go to the fields. All we had to eat was ground corn to mix with water. It was a tough life. When there was nothing to do in the fields, we went to gather wood. We had to buy buckets of water.

I was twenty-two when I left my mother to get married. We didn't get married in the official way. I met him telling me lies, of course. He said, "Once you are with me, you are not going to work. You work hard with your mom." I said, "I don't want to leave her alone." He said, "You are going to visit your mom." I was working in the fields when I had my first child. It was during the time of picking cotton. You had to fill a 100 pound sack. They paid three cords per sack. I remember my goal was to make eighteen cords per week. I had to run take care of baby and go back to field. At 3:00 a.m., I had to grind corn and make tortillas for lunch.

I had eleven kids, six boys and five girls. One died when she was five; one died when she was eleven. Now, one lives at home, because he has a disability, a problem with his spine.

> *What do you think about my destiny? My husband died. Now I am just by myself and my two boys. I work just to support my boy with a disability. He is my boy. I am not just going to let him die. I work for the church with so much love. Especially for Sister Juanita. I cried when she left. The same with Sister Elizabeth. When they left, they said, "You will be in my prayers all the time so God will give you the strength to continue cooking and helping the community.*[2]

Estella paused and reached out to squeeze Julio's hand. He had been translating for her as she told her story. She pinched his cheek as if he were a little boy and said, "I worked with Julito many years."

Julio hugged her affectionately saying, "She calls me 'Julito.' We have been working together here for seventeen years." The tenderness between these two was clear. We thanked Estella and asked if we could talk more in the next few days. Later in the week, several members of our group heard more of her story. Rose, Paula, and I went with her to the cemetery to visit the grave of her husband. But that morning we had to keep moving, since we wanted to get out in the community early. After breakfast we collected work gloves, hats, sunscreen, and bug spray. We refilled our water bottles and headed for the van. We were all sweating as we piled in the hot van again. As we opened windows, I counted the group.

"Who are we missing?" I asked.

Everyone looked around. "Bill isn't here," Rose said.

"He is on Nica time, I guess." Martin laughed. No one laughed. It was too hot to wait cheerfully. Seconds ticked by, and I wondered how much I should step up to take charge. I knew this was an example of living in community rather than acting as individuals.

We were almost ready to send someone in to find Bill when he came hustling out of the Peace House. We were ready to go. Juan Pablo fired up the rumbling van engine and backed on to the dusty road.

Once we got rolling, we savored every breeze, despite the dust, as we drove along the dirt roads. At times, the dust was so thick that I covered my mouth and nose with a bandana. The day had only begun to heat up. We soaked up glimpses of typical morning scenes in Chacraseca. We passed women flinging water from plastic bowls to calm the obsequious dust as they swept and raked the dirt yards and paths around their homes. We passed children in their immaculate white shirts and navy

---

2. Interview with Estella, May 2016. Translated by Julio Delgado, transcribed by Kathleen D. McCallie.

school uniforms walking along the dirt roads toward school. Bill took a photo of a man with two old, aluminum milk cans on a cart that he pulled with his bicycle. A small herd of cattle forced Juan Pablo to slow down until the boy walking behind them drove them into a field. Morning routines blossomed as the sun climbed over the tops of the trees. As we rode, Leslie explained about the latrine project.

Leslie said, "Like the three leaders who first welcomed us to the community on behalf of ACOPADES, all representatives from each sector are elected. In a few minutes, you will meet Scarlet. We will pick her up at the corner by her house. We are going to her sector. She is another leader of the base community who is part of the process to cooperatively make decisions about development goals for Chacraseca."

Fifteen minutes later we stopped and picked up Scarlet, who greeted us and thanked us for coming. As we drove, she answered questions from the group about how ACOPADES invites partner groups like JustHope to work on projects that ACOPADES had prioritized. Housing and latrines have been among the top priorities for years. Scarlet and Leslie explained that although local workers could do the labor and construction, families need financial resources for materials to get the building completed. It costs approximately two hundred dollars to build a latrine. Money for the supplies was provided through JustHope funds by our team.

George asked Scarlet, "It costs lots of money for all of us to fly down here. Wouldn't you rather just have our money to complete more projects?"

Scarlet looked serious and thoughtful as she responded to his question. "We do need funds, but more importantly we need your solidarity. We always agree that it is more important for you to come see, to work side-by-side with us. We want you and other partners to come and share time with our community. We appreciate your collaboration with our families and leaders in different sectors."

After another twenty minutes of riding in the van, we pulled into a dusty driveway where a group of four small, rustic houses were clustered under a few shade trees. Scarlet and Leslie greeted a man who was already working, and Scarlet introduced him as Jorge, our supervisor for the work. Jorge listened to us as we shared our names, and we guessed he was sizing up our abilities to accomplish any of the needed work. Would we be more trouble than our help was worth? The new latrine would be in an area between several houses. Julio translated as one neighbor explained that six families had been sharing the same latrine, so this new latrine would contribute to health and comfort.

Leslie spoke in Spanish with Jorge discussing the fact that the hole in the ground had been started but was only about eight feet deep. The agreement with JustHope was that the holes would be completed and the concrete floor in place when groups arrived. In this case, the man who had been paid to complete the digging process had been taken ill recently, so the project was behind schedule. Leslie made sure a local digger was coming soon. In the meantime, we could volunteer to help dig.

The hole in the ground was approximately four feet square with remarkably straight, smooth walls. Jorge explained that this hole would need to be approximately thirty-five feet deep. It would be completed by a man lowered by rope with a shovel and bucket. Our group exchanged looks of astonishment trying to imagine that work.

"Thirty-five feet deep!" Bill exclaimed. "I would be terrified to be down there, especially relying on this old rope to pull me back up."

Elizabeth raised her eyebrows. "I hope they pay the guy who does that job well. I feel queasy just standing here imagining getting in the hole now. It has to be more than three times as deep as it is now."

However, Martin and George were both ready to try to dig a little. Jorge lowered a thin, metal ladder that was still a couple of feet short of reaching the top of the hole. Martin climbed down first and called up that at least he was out of the glare of the sun now. Jorge lowered a large, plastic bucket and shovel down. Martin began digging and filling the bucket with loose earth. We pulled the heavy buckets up and emptied them nearby. A little dust floated up from the hole, and we could see that Martin was starting to perspire. The rest of us took turns hauling up buckets of dirt and standing in the shade of a nearby tree to escape the blasting sun. After about twenty minutes, Jorge said it was time to switch jobs. He called to Martin, who was about a foot lower than when he started. Martin seemed perfectly willing to climb up the ladder. It was George's turn to dig.

Once he had climbed down in the shadowy hole, George filled buckets until the ground was too hard. Jorge passed down a pickax and explained that chopping the earth first would make more shoveling possible. It was slow work. George filled buckets that we lifted, emptied, and lowered again. After another fifteen or twenty minutes, Juan Pablo, always ready to help, offered to take a turn. He showed us all up with his jovial humor and physical stamina. Then Rose said that she wanted to try digging. The hole was getting deeper than before, but Rose climbed down the ladder and took her turn. She yelled up to those of us watching, "At least it feels a little cooler here out of the sun!" She slowly chipped away, filling buckets that we hoisted up with the rope. She made more progress. Bill, Paula, and I each took a turn, mostly just for the experience. As I lowered my middle-aged body down the slim ladder, stepping below the bright sunlight down into that deep hole, I tried to imagine the local digger who would complete the work many yards deeper. Although I was only in the hole digging for about ten minutes, I had time to think about how this small, deep, four-sided hole was something like a grave. I felt the connection of the earth with my own body, aware of the interconnected web of all creation.

When I climbed back up the ladder after making a symbolic contribution to the work, the sun seemed even more harsh and brutal. Laura looked at my dirty face and arms and shook her head. She said, "No way." We all smiled with understanding. For the next hour or two, we stood around taking turns lifting buckets of earth hauled up from the hole that did not look much deeper.

"I don't think we are making much progress," Martin said.

I laughed and responded, "No worries. I'm sure Jorge will get more done here after we leave. I just wanted to see what it was like. Leslie, maybe we should go on to the other latrine site."

Leslie and Jorge discussed the plans with the neighbors there, explaining that another digger should be arriving soon. When Jorge agreed that other workers would finish digging and constructing the walls and roof, I felt relieved. I was worn out already. George and Rose looked reluctant to leave the task unfinished, but most of us were ready for a break. We were all glad to hear that Jorge would make sure the project was finished after we left. We said our goodbyes to the family and workers, hoping to stop by in a few days to see the progress. Then Jorge led the way to the next latrine work site on his motorcycle, with Juan Pablo driving us in the van.

When we arrived at the second site, we could see the next steps in the process of building a latrine underway. The square hole in the ground had already been covered with a pre-formed, single-unit square, concrete floor that had a toilet sized hole in the center. A couple of workers were busily setting red brick blocks in concrete to construct walls around this molded floor. They had already cemented a concrete stool in place over the hole. As we met these workers, we learned that one was a man who lived in a nearby home, and another was being paid by Jorge. They patiently put us to work, demonstrating how to layer wet cement and add another row of bricks, how to keep the bricks watered, how to use the ingenious wooden form to fill in concrete between the gaps in the bricks, using small sticks to tamp down air holes. With a few of us working at each task, we made steady progress and enjoyed watching the walls rise up, drying quickly in the heat.

We marveled together about accomplishing the work of leveling dirt, mixing concrete, and carrying bricks without equipment like wheelbarrows. When we ran out of wet concrete, we learned about making volcanos, as Jorge called them. He showed us how to sweep a clean area on the hard ground, pour a bag of sand and half a bag of concrete mix, and then blend it thoroughly before we added water. His ability to deftly turn the small pile from the bottom up by using quick, small flips of his shovel was a thing of beauty to behold. He walked around the pile, turning it over completely twice to blend the mixture, and then made a small bowl in the top of the hill for the water. Using a five-gallon bucket of water we had dipped from a large barrel nearby. Jorge showed us how to pour the water slowly in small amounts while a couple of us scooped from the bottom of the pile to mix the concrete. When Jorge went back to supervise others laying another row of blocks, we found out quickly that we were poor substitutes for his mastery of making volcanos. We persisted, nevertheless.

The physical work and fervid temperature demanded that we took turns working and resting. Scarlet had been talking with a few neighbors and family members on the shaded porch of the nearby house. Some of our group had joined the conversation. Paula and Rose struck up a friendship with some kids who came to watch from the shade of some trees as the morning wore on. Rose attempted a little Spanish, asking the kids why they were not in school that day. The kids smiled, and their mother explained that she let them stay home to share in the big event of the delegation's visit and latrine building. Paula and Rose realized that, as international visitors, their presence was an unusual occurrence for the community. Scarlet continued to visit with us and the community members. The air was charged with excitement despite the sun and heat.

Our group kept working. We rotated between the shade, the rising walls of the latrine, and the tasks of carrying bricks, water, and concrete. George, Bill, Martin, and Nick leaned into the strong male manual labor motif. Paula, Rose, Elizabeth, and Leslie stepped up and pitched in as well. Before too long, Paula and Rose moved to the shade and struck up a game with some of the children who had been watching. Soon they were running around giggling and having a great time. At one point Bill stood frowning at them with his hands on his hips.

Leslie noticed and said, "Remember solidarity with the people of the community is our main goal, so playing with the kids and taking breaks to talk with the neighbors is even more important than simply getting the construction work done." I thought about the ways that, as North Americans, we often prioritize achievement and work rather than relationships. JustHope partners can come to see how countercultural it is to rest, slow down, and enjoy relationships. "The people here can do the work themselves if they have the materials," Leslie said. "Your presence and willingness to get acquainted is as valuable as the financial resources you share."

Finally, the latrine was finished, except for the door that Jorge was fashioning from a sheet of metal. It was time for us to go back to the Peace House for lunch. Before we left, we exchanged thanks and affirmation with the family and neighbors who had been working with us. Scarlet represented her sector, including this family, and reminded us that in all sectors, ACOPADES worked collaboratively on projects like this. The families who would share the latrine wished us well. They laughed with us as we took turns having our pictures made while seated on the latrine stool. Then, we gladly got on the van and thanked Juan Pablo for driving us back to the Peace House. We were all too tired to talk much during the ride back.

We were all filthy and soaked with sweat. The breeze from the open windows of the van felt wonderful. Laura and Paula said they couldn't possibly eat until they took showers. We agreed to take fifteen minutes before we went to lunch. We had appointments in the afternoon and needed to stay on schedule. As I braced myself to duck under the cold shower, I imagined jumping in a swimming pool. Once my head was under the cool water, it felt marvelous. I didn't miss hot water at all. Soon, we were walking across the road for lunch.

We found our cooks still working in the sweltering heat of the community building. Although the sultry heat and humidity left us feeling wilted and disinterested in eating, the cold fruit drinks revived us. As we began to pass and fill our plates, Paula asked, "Are we going to pray before we eat?" I asked Paula if she would pray for our meal. As she prayed, blessing the food and the time together, I suspected that I was not the only one pondering what it meant to pray as we piled our plates with chicken, carrots, squash, rice, beans, and tortillas. We knew that the neighbors we left, who had sweated with us around the latrine sites, were probably not enjoying a good meal like ours. There was not much talking as we ate our lunch. We all wanted a nap, but we knew our short time in Nicaragua required that we press on to visit JustHope programs in action.

By 1:00 p.m. we were on our way to visit JustHope programs and leaders in the community. Laura, who had been especially interested in microcredit lending, was enthusiastic about visiting the lending circles in Chacraseca. As we drove to our first visit, Laura told us about how she had been inspired by reading about the work of Muhammad Yunus in Bangladesh, as he started the first microcredit banks.[3] Small loans, each under one hundred dollars, were made to women who formed support and accountability groups. The social support of the group collective was the power that ensured repayment of the loans. By addressing the economic pattern of dependency on middlemen, women increased profits in ways that allowed them to develop assets and advance. In the early 1990s, microcredit projects were expanded in Nicaragua based on that model. Groups from Tulsa, Oklahoma, led by Betty Morrow, set up a number of microcredit banks in Nicaragua with the help of Leslie Penrose and others.

Although Laura looked forward to witnessing the microcredit lending program in person, she said she was nervous about her own courage and grace when it came to visiting Nicaraguan pig farms.

"In the United States, I have driven through rural areas where corporate pork producers dominated the local economy," Laura said. "The smells were so bad that I wanted to run away and never go back. I am unsure how well I will cope with these visits to the farms here. If I can't stand it, I may have to come back to the van and wait for you."

Rose replied, "I bet your enthusiasm for the microcredit program will provide enough determination to push through your aversion. Besides, the smells aren't as bad on small, family farms."

First, our team would pick up Elba, a JustHope staff member in charge of the microcredit program. Elba was waiting at the corner on her motorcycle, ready to lead us to the first home visit. When we pulled into a driveway and parked beside a small farmhouse, we all marveled to see Elba hop off her motorcycle, pull off her helmet and look polished and immaculate, like any professional woman, complete with earrings and

---

3. Yunus, *Banker to the Poor*.

lipstick. In the surroundings of the black, dirt yard near the dusty road, the contrast was striking. A middle-aged woman coming from the house greeted Elba warmly and smiled at the group of visitors. We met Josefina, our host, as she finished arranging plastic lawn chairs in a circle in the shade of a tree. An old pickup truck pulled in the drive, bringing two more women and another stack of plastic chairs. This would be a meeting of United Women, a microcredit lending circle. Others arrived, and soon our group sat in the shaded circle with nine women to learn about their experience with microcredit. Laura was relieved to discover that the sun beating down and the occasional breezes left the yard smelling fresh with no overpowering animal odors.

As a full-time employee of JustHope, Elba Luz Delgado is the only person paid to administer the loans. However, Diana, the JustHope bookkeeper, handles the banking and recordkeeping with Elba. Elba started the first JustHope microcredit circle in Chacraseca in 2009. For many years, the loans were made at an interest rate of one percent. The average loan was approximately $200. In 2015, the interest rate was raised to two percent. Half of that profit goes toward Elba's salary to make the program sustainable. JustHope still subsidizes the project by paying the rest of Elba's salary for other work she does and paying Diana for accounting and bookkeeping. Laura asked how many women have loans now with United Women in Chacraseca. Elba explained that the banks now have $50,000, and 204 women currently have loans.

Elba asked each woman in the circle to introduce herself and talk about her loan. Josefina explained that she got her first microcredit loan three years earlier. She borrowed two hundred dollars and used the money to buy a pregnant sow. Students in the circle asked questions about the expenses involved in raising pigs. Josefina answered questions about the cost of feed and medicines, the amount of work and care involved, and the time it took to raise the piglets until she was ready to sell them. Her profit was more than double the amount of the original loan, so she was able to supplement her income while repaying the loan in full. The next year, she got another loan and continued to expand her pig farm business. We learned that Josefina's husband picked crops when work was available, but in recent years the drought resulted in poor harvests and unreliable work. In addition to Josefina and her husband, their adult daughter and three grandchildren lived with them. Laura asked what Josefina did with the income from the loan. Josefina explained that she spends half of the money to buy food for her family and saves the rest.

"Before I got this loan, I had never even touched a dollar bill," Josefina said. Her husband had always handled all of the money. "When a man has money, he only gives the amount he wants," she said.

Rosa Maria explained that she had gotten a loan to grow one manzana, or approximately one and a half acres, of corn. She paid a neighbor with a tractor to disc her land and plant the corn. Even after paying for this work, she made a profit when she harvested and sold forty sacks of corn.

Luce explained how she was able to buy a horse and cart to sell yuca and pigs. Yuca is a popular crop because it is a local food source and grows well in the area. She supports her grandchildren going to school.

The women spoke with pride about their business ventures. They explained that a loan from a bank would charge a farmer between 18 percent and 24 percent interest per month, but banks would not loan to women. Farmers who owned land or a house might get a bank loan for an agricultural project, but they had to pay that high interest every month. In contrast, Mariela said that her first loan, also for pigs, was for the amount of $225. She paid only 1 percent interest a month, so the total repayment was $250. Even now that the interest rate was 2 percent, she was thankful to have another loan. Her new plan was to build bigger pig pens and expand her business.

Another woman spoke about using her loan to start a vegetable farm. Now she sells vegetables in a market in León. "What did you do to earn money before?" George asked her. She replied that she had only worked as a maid in León, where she made about sixty dollars a month. She didn't like that work because she could only see her children in Chacraseca one day a week. Her mother cared for her children the rest of the time. She was glad she had found a way to make more money while living in Chacraseca.

"What happens if you don't repay your loan?" Bill asked. The women laughed a little, nervously. Josefina said that they meet every month to discuss how their businesses are doing.

"If a woman doesn't show up, we go get her," she said. All the women laughed heartily. "Thanks to God, we have all been able to repay our loans, but we agree to cover the loans for each other if there is a woman who has a hard time. In our sector, there are one hundred women who are on a list requesting these loans. We want to keep this dream alive and share it with more women."

"How do you decide who can have a loan?" Paula asked.

Elba said, "Josephina is the leader of this circle. She and Maura both were part of the original circle the first year, so they have experience. They talked with their neighbors, and women wrote up plans with proposals for the type of project they would like to start with a loan. Then Josephina, Maura, and I chose the first circle of ten women. Since then, other women have been added; the program has grown to ten different circles like this one. The groups decide together with Elba's help which proposals will be accepted for each new year.

Maura spoke up toward the end of our meeting and said, "I like having my own way to earn money and help my family, but the best part is having friends. Before I joined this program, I only left my house to go to church or the store." Other women smiled and nodded in agreement.

"Men said that women could not administrate money but only know how to wash and iron," said one older woman.

"Yes, my husband owns the land. When he has money, he goes to the bar or spends it on cockfighting," said another woman. "My parents didn't have enough money to send all of us to school, so my brothers got to go to school, not me. I am working to make sure my daughters go to school, too."

"We are joyful when we get together," Maura said, her face beaming, and others smiled and nodded in agreement.

Then Josefina proudly invited us to go see her pigs, and we walked around behind the house where we saw the simple pens and shelters where two adult hogs were napping in the mud. Laura did wrinkle up her nose a little as we stepped up close to the pig pen, but she was impressed by watching Josephina lift enormous buckets of water over the fence for her pigs. Laura asked Josefina to share one story of how her life changed after she got her first loan. Josefina laughed and said, "Before I got my loan, my husband never let me handle money. When he didn't have work, he laid around and ordered me to do all the work. After I earned money myself, one day I told him to get out there and feed the pigs. And he did it." She laughed. She admitted that because all the women are responsible for each other's loans, they sometimes worry about the loans. However, they are becoming more confident over time, she told us. Josefina made sure to praise Elba and offer thanks for the opportunity to be part of the program. There could be no doubt that all the women adored and respected Elba.

Our next stops were similar visits with two other women in the microcredit circle. One had received three hundred dollars to buy a dairy cow. Another had obtained a loan to start a tortilla business, selling tortillas along the road in front of her house. The tortilla maker, Julia, answered a few questions about her business plan.

Elizabeth asked, "What is the best part about United Women and the loans?"

Julia did not hesitate and responded enthusiastically, "The loan and the business are nice, but the best part is when we gather for our meetings. I never had a woman friend before."

Each of the women in the program was enthusiastic about the opportunity to earn money through her own business. Between our stops at various houses that morning, Laura continued to share what she had learned about the success of microcredit lending in various parts of the world. Elba answered questions about JustHope's microcredit program. One student asked why all the recipients were women. Elba explained that they found men were less likely to repay the loans. Also, men were more likely to be able to secure credit in other ways. With a repayment rate near one hundred percent in JustHope's program, our group began to see the power of this social enterprise program. We could see why Muhammad Yunus won the Nobel Prize for this revolutionary model that builds economic strength on the power of social relationships. The bonds between the women in the group are the collateral that powers the enterprise.

Next, we stopped at a building on the corner of two intersecting dirt roads. Elba introduced us to Juana, the manager of the women-owned hardware store in Chacraseca. Juana shared the story of being part of the first microcredit circle established by JustHope several years earlier. As the women in her circle gained confidence in themselves, they developed a new dream. They came to the staff of JustHope and said they thought their community needed a hardware store.

They wanted to open the store and run it themselves. Since there was no hardware store at that time, everyone had to go to León to buy even simple things like nails or glue. Most families had no car or truck. Although some had horses or bicycles, many simply walked the ten or more miles to León. In fact, Juana told us how she herself walked to León when she went into labor before giving birth to her first child. As we listened, Rose, Paula, Laura, and I exchanged wide-eyed glances trying to comprehend what it would be like to live outside the city without access to a nearby hospital or transportation to get to one. Juana continued with her story of the women who dreamed of opening a small store that could sell commonly used items as a way of helping the community of Chacraseca and providing work as well.

With the help of JustHope's social enterprise program, the hardware store became a reality. We asked what men in the community thought about a hardware store owned and operated by a group of women. Juana smiled and admitted that at first there was skepticism and resistance from some of the men in the neighborhood. But, after the store opened, the convenience of being able to buy supplies without traveling to León made the store popular even with men who had had doubts. Juana explained how the profits all go back into the store, and that has allowed it to grow over time. After the first year, they dreamed of expanding the building.

"We wanted to prove to the men that we can administer this type of project," Juana said. "It gives us a place, a space to be free."

In 2015, the women who ran the store had a new idea for expanding their business. During times when migrant workers were present to plant or harvest crops, many men stopped by the hardware store looking to buy something for lunch. The idea of a small café serving hot food and cold drinks could offer additional employment and meet another need. The café would require another new structure with a place to cook and a patio for seating. The social enterprise program through JustHope provided the initial investment of funds needed for this expansion.

We saw the small cafe with several outdoor tables and benches where people could eat. The café met needs and created another job opportunity for a woman who sells cold drinks and food there. Juana explained that one woman can run the café for a few months, and then another woman has a turn.

Inside the store, Juana showed us the racks of used clothing for sale, school supplies like crayons and paper on the counter, and building materials like bags of concrete, posts, a few tools, and boxes of nails. She explained that the hardware store is not a privately owned business that benefits the women who started it as if they were private owners. It is a cooperatively owned enterprise operated through a collective decision-making process. Although the women are learning and exploring how to run the store in sustainable, manageable ways, they have already successfully built and grown a place that creates jobs and provides important services for their community.

Before we left the hardware store, Laura asked Juana what the women's next dream is for the hardware store. Juana quickly replied that they dream of securing a truck to make deliveries and allow them to buy more efficiently. If they could travel to Managua to buy items, then they could offer better prices and increase income for the store. Since hardware stores in León offer delivery of heavy items like bricks or bags of concrete, the women had a hard time competing on larger sales since they could not deliver anything. Also, Juana added, if they had a truck, the community could use it as an ambulance for medical emergencies, like when a woman goes into labor. The bold imagination and hard work of these innovative women made a lasting impression on each of us. We looked at Juana and tried to imagine her in labor with her first child, walking all the way to the hospital in León by herself. As we said goodbye and prepared to leave, we were glad to buy cold, canned pop at the cafetín.

The final social enterprise project we visited in Chacraseca was a women's sewing cooperative called Stitching Hope. There, we experienced the leadership skills of Francis, another JustHope translator who serves as a liaison with the women of Stitching Hope. The sewing cooperative is housed in a building a few doors down from the Peace House. Francis explained the JustHope development model of projects that progress through three phases: the start-up, step-up, and stand-up phases. Each JustHope project begins when local leaders express a desire and dream to initiate a new program. When resources, abilities, and opportunities match the requests, JustHope explores possibilities to help a project start. But every project must have the potential to become self-sustaining eventually. To avoid dependency or charity dynamics, projects are required to move toward self-sufficiency by stepping up and then standing up on their own at some point.

The Stitching Hope project illustrates this process. We learned how the project began with the generous support of a leader and a congregation in the United States. Brenda Grawer lives in Ohio, and years ago she came with a team that bonded with Nicaragua women through sharing sewing skills. The idea for the sewing cooperative developed from those partners dreaming together. Brenda returned many times over the years to collaborate with the sixteen women of Stitching Hope in Chacraseca. Members of Brenda's church in Ohio provided funding and sweat equity for the small building, complete with table and sewing machines. The women in Chacraseca now own and operate the business, dying and painting fabric, designing and sewing clothing, and crafting fiber art and items for fair trade exchange. Although Brenda and her congregation provided initial leadership, training, and start-up funds, local women from Chacraseca were part of the start-up effort as well. They shared dreams and labor alongside their partners from the United States. Over time, they invested wisdom and experience as they made decisions collectively regarding how much workers should be paid, what items would be produced, and how the business should grow over time. The project began in 2012, and by 2016 their enterprise was almost self-sustaining. JustHope volunteers help find opportunities in the United States through fair trade markets to sell the products.

During our visit to Stitching Hope, we heard stories of the way the project enhanced the lives of the members who work there. The women articulated numerous benefits of sharing in the work of the cooperative. In contrast to the workers at the sweat shop in the area who typically earn two or three dollars per day, the women at Stitching Hope earn six and a half dollars a day. Furthermore, these women enjoy flexibility when the needs of a sick child or family emergency necessitates taking time off from work. Unlike the free trade zone factory where sweat shop workers labor six days each week with no sick leave, workers at Stitching Hope enjoy more humane conditions. We saw the beauty of the fabrics they dyed with patterns using leaves and flowers they collected. We heard about their efforts to sell in the street fair in León.

After this long, busy day, our group was ready for rest and relaxation. Back at the Peace House, we had about thirty minutes until time for supper. Each of us was unwinding from the day and trying to cool off. I was glad to get in the cold shower.

As I came back to the common room, feeling cleaner and more energized, I heard Laura say, "Hey you guys, who put all these water bottles in the freezer? The ice isn't even freezing because these big water bottles are keeping it too warm."

Martin and Rose went to join her in the kitchen.

"Sorry," Rose said. "I saw others doing this yesterday, and it seemed like a great idea."

Martin said, "Yes, I put mine in last night, and it was frozen solid this morning."

"Well, we need to figure out a way to take turns or something," Laura said. She was clearly irritated. "I don't have ice, and my water isn't cold at all. The freezer cannot keep up with the newly filled bottles of water. I guess solidarity has advantages and disadvantages." The tension of living in close quarters was evident in various ways like this all week. We were accustomed to the luxury of controlling our own space.

Evening Reflection Time

After supper, we gathered as a group again for reflection time. Leslie led our discussion, beginning by asking us to share images: What did we see? What sounds, smells, or experiences stayed with us from the day?

Martin said, "I can still see the square of blue light that was the only sky visible from the vantage point of the bottom of that hole when we were digging for the latrine."

"I saw the kids at that second home where we worked running around the barbed wire fence and construction materials in their flip flops with so little protection," Laura said. "It is a miracle no one was seriously hurt. Did you meet that little boy named Luís? He was adorable. I think he was about seven or eight. He and some of the kids even helped haul those heavy bricks and buckets of water."

"One image that sticks with me is the washed-out dirt road that Juan Pablo managed to drive on," Bill said. "How would people get through during heavy rain?"

Rose said, "I love the photo of me sitting on that concrete latrine stool after the latrine was almost finished. That is an image I may have to frame." We all laughed in agreement.

Just then, we heard a deafening clap of thunder as, simultaneously, heavy rain clattered on the metal roof. The noise escalated as rain hammered. Leslie was just reminding us that the farmers would welcome this rain for their crops when another clap of thunder sounded as if it had struck just outside.

"It sounds louder than what we are used to because of the metal roof without insulation," Bill said. "And all the open windows. Now those roads will be flooded!"

In another moment all the electricity went off, leaving us in total darkness. The wind and pouring rain roared on. George and Laura both turned on flashlights from their cell phones. Leslie got up and lit a few candles. I asked the group to continue to stay in the circle of rocking chairs, hoping the power would come back on soon.

"We need to continue processing experiences and insights from the day together," I said. The drumming rain continued, but our group began to relax again, nonetheless.

The scent of the candles and the flickering shadows they cast in the dark room gave an elemental sense of sanctuary from the tropical storm raging outside.

Leslie reminded us that we had begun the day with reflections about solidarity. "What did solidarity look like in Chacraseca?" She asked.

Paula said, "When I was working as a youth minister, I went on a mission trip to Haiti with a group of teenagers. We worked on building a house, and some of the work we did was similar today: carrying buckets of water, bricks, bags of cement, mixing concrete. What was so different today is that the family and neighbors were there working with us. The time I spent playing with the kids was awesome. I felt a little guilty, as if I wasn't doing my share of work, but then I thought about solidarity. Talking with the neighbors seemed really worthwhile."

Leslie said, "I always remind groups that the relationships we build with people in the community is the most important thing we do."

"I loved visiting the micro-credit loan women," Laura said. "I am fascinated by their willingness to be responsible for each other's loans. That is where I saw solidarity today. I wonder how those pigs are doing with this torrential rain?" We sat a few moments without anyone speaking while we listened to the pouring rain.

Nick asked, "What is yuca? People here keep talking about it, but I don't recognize it as a crop grown where I live."

"It is called cassava some places," Leslie explained. "The roots are like starchy potatoes. It is drought tolerant, and it doesn't need much fertilizer. Everyone here eats it, but it is also used for animal food."

Moments passed in reflective silence as we listened to the patter of rain on the roof.

Elizabeth spoke up next. "I've been thinking about a friend I have back home who was exasperated about my decision to take this trip," Elizabeth said. "She thinks we should take care of the poor in our own communities instead of traveling like this. She has a point. Today I have been reflecting on the question of whether international borders matter in our responsibility toward others. Do our obligations to our home communities differ from ethical duty to reduce income inequality here or in other settings? When I think about the teachings of Jesus, I don't see how national boundaries could limit our call to respond. I keep puzzling over that," Elizabeth said.

"Great questions," I said. "Let's keep thinking about that. There was a learning moment for me today when I realized I had said something culturally insensitive," I continued. "We were talking with the micro-credit women's group, and one mentioned her husband. I asked how old she was when they got married. She looked uncomfortable and then said, 'Well, we never formally married.' I suddenly remembered that many people here don't actually marry in church. I felt terrible. I want to remember to be more careful about that in the future."

"The hardware store is inspiring," Martin said. "It seems like they are depending on people like us to bring materials to sell, though. I keep thinking about the contrast between charity versus solidarity."

"Are they able to make much money on the store?" Bill asked.

Leslie replied, "The people here have a very different approach to finances than we do. They view the store as a service to the community. Instead of thinking about how they could charge more for items for the convenience of buying close to home, they try to figure out how little they can charge in order to help their neighbors. Since we are formed in the capitalist mindset, we would not do it that way."

"Since the store has not been open very long, maybe it will become more sustainable over time," Paula said. "But it is problematic to think that we are encouraging them to be more like capitalists if that isn't their culture."

"But it won't continue if it relies on donations and support from North American partners," Martin said. "If they don't raise their prices and make a profit to expand and get a truck, it won't be sustainable. Socialist economics sound great in theory, but right now they are too dependent on JustHope."

Leslie said, "Yes, the hardware store and Stitching Hope both depend too much on teams right now. We are working toward making these efforts sustainable. I continue to ask the leaders here what would happen if JustHope groups stopped coming. In a way, it is an act of solidarity to dismantle the dependency and strengthen their independence from North America volunteers. At the same time, the act of bringing material and financial resources is also an act of solidarity. In fact, I witness solidarity in your willingness to be present, make friends, and allow Nicaraguans to teach you by sharing their stories."

Martin said, "I need to learn more about the effects of international trade agreements like NAFTA and CAFTA on the economy here. I understand there is a new trade bill being proposed called the Trade Act that would correct some of the problems with NAFTA."

"Witness of Peace has a helpful analysis of types of trade policies that would help countries like Nicaragua," I said. "I trust their research and information. I also appreciate the writing of William Greider on the topic of trade agreements."

"Listening to the women talk about their loans was the highlight of my day," I continued. "I was impressed with their sense of shared success and vulnerability as a group. Back home, I get so sick and tired of competition. Today, I saw ways that concepts of success or progress that depend on winners and losers perpetuate inequalities in access to material resources. I see a spiritual poverty in our economic striving in the United States."

George said, "I kept asking myself what wealth means in my life. Being here is giving me new insight about how the obsession with material possessions in our culture is a construction that may not enhance our lives at all. I realized today that I spend lots of my time thinking about something I want to buy, like a new car."

"Interesting," said Leslie smiling. "Since capitalism requires markets that keep growing and expanding it may not be as sustainable as we have been led to believe."

"The environmental impacts of consumerism make it unsustainable, too," I added. "We need to think collaboratively about how to address poverty. I notice my own impulses to think of solutions that amount to throwing money at problems. It is difficult for me to escape my mentality of fixing problems. When I think about solutions to poverty, my impulse is to get enough money for everyone," I said.

"Yes," Leslie responded, "when we ask ourselves what is needed so that no one will be poor anymore, I notice people here have a different imagination about that. I have heard people in Chac say no one would be poor if everyone had land or if everybody had a job they could depend on."

Nick said, "Today I remembered something that I intended to ask about. As we were driving from Managua to León, I saw several billboards with pictures of Daniel Ortega and the slogan, 'Cristiana, Socialisma, Solidarita.' I wrote it down in my notebook. It looked like a campaign poster."

"Christian Socialism has a different valence here than it does in the U.S.," Leslie said. "You have read about the history of the Nicaraguan revolution and the efforts to avoid privatizing all industry and service sectors. There is tremendous pressure from the IMF, the International Monetary Fund, and World Bank to privatize everything. The social enterprise programs here continue the exploration of alternative economic development," she said.

"It is important to remember that economic socialism can be democratic," I said. "Sometimes I hear people in the U.S. link socialism with Stalinism or repressive totalitarian regimes where censorship is repressive.

But some societies have promoted freedom of speech and religion while engaging in redistributive, socialist economics. Today we saw examples of people who try to make decisions democratically about the enterprise they own cooperatively. There are so many problems with unfettered capitalism that I welcome efforts to find other ways to handle economic issues. I remember when I first started coming to Nicaragua in the early 1990s, we saw posters and graffiti about the efforts to privatize the phone systems. Now, they are working to privatize the water systems," I said.

Leslie reflected, "Our time at Stitching Hope today reminded me of a group of women led by Rev. Lara Blackwood Pickrel, who is a student in the Doctor of Ministry program at Phillips. They came on a JustHope partner trip and participated in a process focused on accompaniment as a new model to replace missions. I liked the emphasis on relationship building and education about systemic problems. They insisted that accompaniment is "Spirit work."[4]

"Yes, she is writing up the report on her project now," I added. "I look forward to reading her conclusions. I appreciate the way her reflections illustrate the spiritual formation and challenges of participating in JustHope partnerships. I think her first trip to Nicaragua was on a seminary class trip led by Mindy McGarrah Sharp."

"Yes," Leslie said. "That was a group of women who engaged in dialogue with women here. They read together and discussed Margaret Randall's book, *Sandino's Daughters*. I remember that some of the women here did not know how many women had been leaders in the revolution. Some of the women in Chacraseca carried around their copies of the book for days everywhere they went. It was thrilling to see. Mindy served on the board of JustHope, and she and her husband Tommy wrote a curriculum for partner groups."

"I was intrigued by the cooperative ownership of Stitching Hope and the hardware store," Bill said. "I wonder if a few of the members really make the decisions? That is often the way it works at my church. Everyone has a vote, but some people seem to let others run most things."

"I was impressed with the flexible, compassionate work arrangements they maintain," Laura said. "It seemed to me that their pride and dignity in their work reflected the kind of collaborative creativity that resulted from balanced investment in the decision-making,"

---

4. Pickrel, "Not Yet Sisters," 71.

"Let's keep asking about that," Leslie suggested. "What are the theological or spiritual issues that connected with your experience today?"

"I noticed that when we visited different groups and saw JustHope projects, the people seemed to express thanks to us, as if we are JustHope. They are thankful to JustHope, but I haven't given a lot of money to JustHope. I haven't put in volunteer hours or worked to build JustHope," Nick responded.

"That is fascinating, isn't it?" I remarked. "We are being received as the face of JustHope. It is a taste of participating as a collective body or community rather than as autonomous individuals. What I notice is a quality of the expression of gratitude that has a performative quality sometimes. It feels awkward, like they are trying to ensure that funding continues."

"Since the work of JustHope depends on donors, there is a reality about the unequal power dynamics resulting for wealth distribution," Leslie said. "Those of us from the U.S. may be looking for relational depth, community, or spiritual growth. People here come to the partnership needing money. If we don't name that honestly up front, we are fooling ourselves. What does that mean to us in terms of our own questions?"

"I am struggling with the disconnect between my own comfortable lifestyle in comparison to the way people are living in sheds and plastic shelters," Laura said. "I keep wondering how I can say the words, 'We are all one in Christ,' after seeing the way those young mothers are trying to survive with their kids. Can you imagine what it is like in a plastic house during this storm?" We sat in silence a few minutes thinking about that. The sounds of the rain drumming on the roof continued in the background.

"I think I am angry with God because these people are suffering so much," Paula said. "How can they be so cheerful and thankful to God in their context? What does God even mean to them?"

"Well, what does God mean to you?" I asked. The group sat listening to the rain. After a few minutes of allowing the silence to agitate us all, I said, "Coming here forces me to face the reality that I don't have a clear understanding of what God means to me. At home I often slip back into the cultural concept of God as a big person with superpowers like knowing everything or being all powerful. But here I see the people born into this cycle of poverty generation after generation, and the devastating consequences of poverty that restrict human capacity. Sometimes I think that God is more like a force, like in Star Wars, rather than a personal being."

"Maybe God is the collective power of relational will and work," Leslie said, "Maybe God is not like a consciousness or personal being."

Martin said, "That would certainly change the way we understood prayer, if we believed that."

We sat in darkness with light and shadows cast by the candles still burning in the center of the room. The rain hammered on the roof.

Leslie said, "This conversation reminds me of a song that is a favorite around here entitled, "No Basta Rezar / Praying Isn't Enough." She raised her voice against the noise of the rain on the metal roof and sang a line from the chorus, "No, no, no, praying is not enough. / Many things are needed to achieve peace."[5]

"Do you believe that?" Bill asked. "I don't think we should be teaching that prayer is not powerful. Do you really believe that prayer is not the best thing we can do to work for peace?"

No one responded to this question for a few moments. The rain clattered on the roof. The darkness and candlelight added to the intensity of the conversation.

Martin replied, "Maybe true prayer is not just saying words but acting for justice and compassion as well. I don't think praying is enough if it only means uttering words."

Then Paula said, "Jesus seemed to act as if feeding the hungry or liberating captives was necessary for the way of faith he taught. I think Jesus would agree that praying is not enough."

"I like Martin's question about how we understand prayer," I asked. "Do we think that when we pray, we are taking an action that could change history because we might persuade God to work for our objective? Some people pray in a way that implies that they need to soften God's heart or remind God to be compassionate. Some prayers imply that God needs to be lobbied for the cause of people or justice."

Since the power was off and the fans stopped, the room was getting uncomfortably warm with the thick humidity. The darkness held us together in the circle.

"So then, what is prayer?" Laura asked.

"I think of prayer as an effort to align myself with God's will. Prayer doesn't change God's mind, prayer changes me to be a better vessel for doing God's will," Leslie said.

---

5. Primera, "No Basta Rezar." Translated by Kathleen D. McCallie.

"Or maybe God isn't a conscious being with a will at all," Martin said. "Maybe prayer is an attempt to shift the collective consciousness of all life. The concern in this song is not about whether prayer is a good thing. The point is that other action is also required."

"Well, I don't think anything is required for salvation besides faith expressed in prayer. I do believe that prayer is enough," Bill said.

"Prayer is not just saying magical words, like an incantation or something," Nick snapped.

Elizabeth said, "I don't think prayer is enough."

Leslie's voice was steady and calm in response to the growing shrillness of the other voices. She asked, "Enough for what? Liberation theology suggests that our concern should not be our own individual salvation. In fact, salvation is understood differently than many modern theologies conceptualize it. The goal of the Christian life is not salvation in the sense of going to heaven instead of hell after you die. Salvation is transformation of the structures and systems of society for the well-being of all. That is what solidarity requires."

The darkness was interrupted by an occasional flash of lightening outside or the glow of cell phones as people glanced at them from time to time.

"I am worried about my phone battery," Martin said.

"We will continue to explore these questions all week, but let's end our conversation by returning to the concept of solidarity, and what JustHope means by solidarity," I said. "We have plenty of hard questions to consider. I don't know about you all, but I am tired from the long day. I bet I can sleep even if the power is off."

"When will the power come back on?" Laura asked, with anxiety in her voice.

"Power outages are a regular part of life in Nicaragua," Leslie explained. "Sometimes during a storm like this, a leader shuts down the grid here in Chacraseca in order to prevent worse damage to the system," she continued. "We might as well go to bed and hope it comes back on during the night. You are getting a taste of challenges of life in Chacraseca. This is what solidarity looks like tonight. Is there anything else we need to discuss before tomorrow?"

"I am a little worried about the toilet in our bathroom," Nick said. "It is not flushing very well. I have found it is hard to remember not to flush the toilet paper." Others agreed.

"Keep an eye on it," Leslie said. "The plumbing in Nicaragua cannot handle even a little paper. Be extra careful not to flush paper."

For a few minutes, we all sat in the darkness, listening to the patter of the rain on the roof. I guessed that we were all thinking about how often we take electricity for granted in our respective homes in the U.S. Through the windows, we occasionally saw silvery reflections on the wet trees and plants when a flash of lightening lit the sky for a second.

"It is too hot to sleep without the fans," Laura complained.

Silence followed.

"This reminds me of something Father Miguel often said to groups from the U.S.," I said. "He said, 'You people are crazy! You leave your comfortable air conditioning, hot water, and good food. You come here with the bugs, diseases, and mosquitos. You are insane! What are you thinking?' And then he would smile and say, 'This is what the world needs, more divine insanity like this.'"

The rain continued to pound on the metal roof. We reviewed plans for the next day, and then we said good night. We prepared for bed with limited light from our cell phones, knowing that the charges of our phones would not last forever. The loud rain would probably keep us all awake, but thoughts of the issues from the day also occupied our thoughts. I lay in the darkness, continuing to ponder our understandings of prayer, community, social goods, property ownership, individuality, and solidarity. Thankful for earplugs that muffled the noise of the rain on the roof, I began to relax. I suspect that I was not the only one who prayed before I slept with vivid images flowing through my mind of our encounters that day in Chacraseca. In the middle of the night, the lights woke me and others. The power had come back on, and we had not known which switches were still on when we went to sleep. I rose and began flipping off switches to stop the full glare of electric lights. George was up, too, turning off lights in the common area. Soon I was back in bed. The rain continued, but now it was only a quiet, gentle patter.

Economic Justice

In his book *One World, Ready or Not: The Manic Logic of Global Capitalism*, William Greider described the vulnerability of nations like Nicaragua who rely on the World Bank and countries like the U.S. for capital. With little power to negotiate interest rates or terms, the borrowers are subject to the requirements of lenders including policies like privatization and deregulation. Not all partners in international trade agreements come to the bargaining table with equal power. Greider writes, "The developing nations, whatever they may wish for, do not always have a free choice on these questions. Many are simply too weak and disorganized to set their own terms."[6] In an earlier book, *The Case against "Free Trade": GATT, NAFTA, and the Globalization of Corporate Power*, Greider suggests some guidelines for more just trade agreements. He writes:

> For a start, the United States ought to reject any new trade agreements that do not include a meaningful social contract—rules that establish a baseline for standards for health, labor law, working conditions, the environment, wages . . . Indeed, companies ought to post community bonds when they relocate—guaranteeing that they will not run away from their obligations to develop roads and schools and the other public investments.[7]

I agree with this analysis and appreciate this articulation of reforms needed in trade agreements to better international exchange policies. Economic ideology can seem overwhelming, but transnational collaboration pushes partners to study the ideological fault lines of economic theory.

For example, JustHope partners encounter problems that illustrate political and ideological battles over socialism versus capitalism. In fact, Marxist scholars continue to add important voices to discourse about gross inequalities in wealth distribution. Raised in a culture that feared and rejected anything associated with Marxism, I was slow to recognize that Marxist theories are as varied as forms of capitalism. Over time, I discovered the passionate concern for the poor that motivates many Marxists. Despite vehement rejection of totalitarianism, Stalinism, and repressive social control, I find some defenders of economic socialism convincing. For example, I agree with Zillah Eisenstein's critique of corporate global capitalism. Eisenstein writes:

> Some 800 million people are starving across the globe. Women and girls represent approximately 60 percent of the billion or so people earning one dollar a day or less. However, in countries labeled democratic, a new kind of excessive wealth exists in which billionaires are allowed to amass as much as they can with few

---

6. Greider, *One World*, 264.
7. Greider, *Case against "Free Trade,"* 214.

limits. New levels of arrogance emerge just as the nation-state is being overshadowed by transnational corporations.[8]

I agree with Eisenstein that this phenomenon of inequality is obscene. Hence, I hope some middle way between democratic socialism and carefully regulated capitalism can be found. For many who have not previously considered the U.S. economy from the perspective of the two-thirds world before, the cognitive dissonance can be bewildering. The discourse concerning advantages and disadvantages of different economic systems has been stymied by rhetoric and political dogmatism. Liberation theology invites openness to these issues and their consequences of social justice. For example, as part of the Reclaiming Liberation Theology series, Néstor Míguez, Joerg Rieger, and Jung Mo Sung wrote *Beyond the Spirit of Empire* arguing that market capitalism fosters economic injustice.[9] According to their analysis, policy makers of capitalist economies view the poor as "flawed consumers." Environmental activists are viewed as enemies of progress. Campesinos are viewed as pre-moderns; thus, like the poor and environmental activists, they are viewed by neoliberal capitalists as "enemies of the state."[10] North Americans may balk at links between socialism and liberation theology.

Yet, when we see movements for fair trade and even socialism in light of gross income inequality, we begin to question neoliberal economic policies. The lie of neoliberalism is that unfettered expansion will result in boundless material wealth and prosperity. Given the strain on the environment, we need new solutions to economic puzzles.[11] Many who travel to Nicaragua with JustHope come with little awareness of the World Bank or international trade policy. They have not seriously investigated the claim that prosperous nations perpetuate poverty in other nations through unregulated global capitalism. Liberationist thinkers like Rosemary Radford Ruether have worked to educate North Americans about the resistance to neoliberal capitalism in Nicaragua and elsewhere. Ruether corresponded with Sister Joan Uhlen about her work in Nicaragua and supported this ministry in Chacraseca. Ruether writes:

---

8. Eisenstein, *Global Obscenities*, 1.

9. Míguez et al., *Beyond the Spirit of Empire*, 92.

10. Míguez et al., *Beyond the Spirit of Empire*, 92.

11. Kotsko, *Neoliberalism's Demons*, 137. See also McFague, "God's Household"; Cobb, *Sustainability*, 111.

Although it cannot be proved from these data that these declines in economic growth, education, and health were directly caused by the policies of the World Bank, the researchers declare that there is a prima facie case that these policies played a major role in causing these declines during the period when structural adjustment rules were imposed . . . Hence, structural adjustments had the effect of creating a net extraction of wealth from the poor countries to the rich countries or rather, to international banks.[12]

Capitalists often dismiss social enterprise that promotes collective work and ownership of the means of production as unrealistic or untenable. However, the ability to generate creative, meaningful work that fosters strong relationships with other people and the environment challenges the practicality of neoliberal capitalism. Ironically, economic socialism can protect types of freedom. More and more scholars are arguing that unfettered capitalism is built on dominance rather than freedom. For example, Brian Milani writes: "Dominance-based civilization can no longer survive, simply because it now threatens humanity's survival."[13] Milani suggested a new concept of wealth that is sustainable for the planet. He writes, "The new concept is wealth as regeneration—qualitative wealth—the (inner) development of people, the (social) development of community, and the restoration of all living systems."[14] This kind of reimaging of economic justice and sustainable living is fruit of transnational interchange.

Theologian John Cobb agrees, "American Christians must question the validity of sending aid to people elsewhere to alleviate problems of which they are a partial cause."[15] Cobb describes free trade as "a system of bondage of all to the few multinational institutions that control the flow of capital and goods."[16] The call to confront wealth distribution and materialist needs can challenge current academic focus on identity and postmodern theory. As Jennifer Bickham Mendez writes, "I gained new appreciation for socialist ideals."[17]

Feminist ethicists and political scientists have made similar observations about the unjust impact of neoliberal capitalism. For example, V. Spike Peterson observed ways that geopolitical elites benefit from

12. Ruether, *Christianity and Social Systems*, 229.
13. Milani, *Designing the Green Economy*, 185.
14. Milani, *Designing the Green Economy*, xv.
15. Cobb, *Sustainability*, 25.
16. Cobb, *Sustainability*, 51.
17. Mendez, *From the Revolution to the Maquiladoras*, 24.

neoliberal policies at the expense of the developing economies. In her article, "International/Global Political Economy," Peterson writes:

> Deregulation has permitted the hyper-mobility of ("foot-loose") capital, induced phenomenal growth in crisis-prone financial markets, and increased the power of private capital interests . . . Liberalism is selectively implemented: powerful states continue to foster their interests while developing countries have limited control over protecting domestic industries, goods produced, and jobs provided.[18]

That view is expressed across various disciplines. Joseph E. Stiglitz, winner of the 2001 Nobel Prize in economics, writes not as a theologian or ethicist but as an economist. He claims that liberalization often "fails to live up to its promise." Austerity measures, privatization, and market liberalism are promoted as the rational policies by neoliberals who claim to defend freedom. But research shows that those policies often perpetuate poverty, contribute to escalating environmental degradation, and diminish state sovereignty. Stiglitz writes, "While I was at the World Bank, I saw firsthand the devastating effect that globalization can have on developing countries, and especially the poor within those countries."[19] He criticizes neoliberalism that is characterized by unfettered markets and promotes a global economy that is not restrained by state power. Rather than think of socialism and capitalism as two polarized options, JustHope partners are seeking more liberating alternatives.

Perhaps most importantly, interchange between JustHope partners sparks imagination for new possibilities of rich life without overconsumption and obsessive, material consumerism. Partners from the U.S. often return from Nicaragua with new appreciation of minimalism and simpler living. They gravitate toward movements of sustainable living, alternative economies, and critique of capitalism. For example, Charles Eisentein writes about reclaiming "the creation of connections," saying, "The time for the mind-set of wealth preservation is over."[20] More people are finding that it is possible to be oppressed by too many material possessions. This does not mean that we can ignore the reality that others have been made poor and kept poor through global economic systems in ways that leave them with fewer material resources than they need.

---

18. Peterson, "International/Global Political Economy," 206–7.
19. Stiglitz, *Globalization and Its Discontents*, 61.
20. Eisenstein, *Sacred Economics*, 395.

Nonetheless, excessive accumulation of material goods is also damaging. To divest from excessive property can be liberating. Eisenstein writes, "Lest you think I am doing some noble thing in practicing nonaccumulation, let me assure you that when I began to live in this way, I had no sense of self-sacrifice, but rather of lightness and freedom."[21]

Similarly, David Korten writes about what he calls the "Happy Planet Index" as a tool for measuring economic success. He argues that happiness is the result when we choose beneficial economic resources instead of destructive ones. He writes, "We can find hope in the fact that the institutional and cultural transformation required to avert economic, environmental, and social collapse is the same as the transformation required to unleash the positive creative potential of the human consciousness and create the world of which humans have dreamed for millennia."[22] I agree with his claim and share his experience. The opportunity to learn from partners in Nicaragua can open our eyes to ways our humanity has been distorted by our economic systems. As Korten says, "The culture and institutions of the Wall Street Economy cultivate and reward our capacity for individualistic greed, hubris, deceit, ruthless competition, and material excess. They deny, even punish, our capacities for sharing, honesty, service, compassion, cooperation, and material sufficiency."[23]

Not all forms of capitalism promote the extreme neoliberal commitment to deregulation and privatization. Not all forms of socialism promote the extreme eradication of private property and all private enterprise. Although liberalism is often criticized by postcolonial thinkers, there are liberal theorists who have insisted on equalization of power dynamics in the market. For example, philosopher John Rawls, famous as a liberal exemplar, recognized the problem of unequal power to negotiate. He writes:

> The criterion of reciprocity requires that when those terms are proposed as the most reasonable terms of fair cooperation, those proposing them must also think it at least reasonable for others to accept them, as free and equal citizens, and not as dominated or manipulated, or under the pressure of an inferior political or social position.[24]

---

21. Eisenstein, *Sacred Economics*, 375.
22. Korten, *Agenda for a New Economy*, 187.
23. Korten, *Agenda for a New Economy*, 91.
24. Rawls, *Law of Peoples*, 136.

JustHope partners often come to see the way inequalities in the international power systems prevent fair negotiations in global trade. New ways of solving economic problems and international cooperation for sustainable trade patterns require collaboration of diverse voices representing a broad spectrum of wisdom and knowledge.

5

Sustainability in Educational Programs

The morning light was still soft when I stepped onto the porch. I was surprised that I didn't see puddles or streams of water after all the rain the night before. I realized that the soil was all volcanic sand that didn't hold water. The plants and trees looked washed and vibrant, but there was no other sign of the downpour. During our morning devotional time, Leslie invited us to reflect together on the spiritual and theological tools and practices that connect with the concept of sustainability. What sustains community and partnership? What sustains the work of seeking justice and right relationship? As I explored that question I thought about habits and routines of meeting in circles with others for mutual support. I thought about listening circles where safe and brave space is established for education that includes honest conversation. I wondered about the loneliness that propels us toward community. Was I becoming more skillful at sustaining relationships that matter?

Before breakfast, we reviewed our agenda for our second full day in Chacraseca. Part of our group would attend the weekly meeting of ACOPADES, while others volunteered in the local elementary schools. Paula and Martin happily anticipated observing the way the leaders in Chacraseca made decisions together. Leslie would stay with that group for their meeting on the porch of the Peace House. In the afternoon, our group would reunite to focus on JustHope educational programs, including a visit to the cultural center where we would learn about the scholarship program and backpack initiatives before a visit to the local church.

Rose, Laura, and I prepared to spend the day volunteering in an elementary school observing and supporting the work of a JustHope team from Denver, led by a teacher trainer, Michelle. That team had arrived the previous afternoon, and we would meet them at breakfast. We felt fortunate to be in Chacraseca at the same time as this returning group of educators. Leslie had told us that Michelle was a long-time volunteer with JustHope who had responded to requests from teachers and administrators in Chacraseca to collaborate on improving their schools. Nicaraguan teachers had invited Michelle's group to share planning and teaching strategies. As a previous kindergarten teacher in Houston, Rose was excited to talk with others who shared her passion for education. She hoped that in the future, she might return to Chacraseca to work with Michelle's team. That team was staying at the Annex, another building across the labyrinth from the Peace House.

When our team gathered in the dark, humid dining hall for breakfast, our translators Julio and Francis arrived. We passed around dishes of food remarking on the previous night's storm as we ate breakfast. Michelle's group had not come yet, so our team had time to hear from Nimia. As an elected sector leader and member of ACOPADES, Nimia would be part of the ACOPADES meeting that morning. I had asked her to share her story, and this was a good time. She joined us; Julio translated her words. She said:

> *I have lived in Chacraseca all my life. There were many economic, educational, and social problems when I was younger. I have been working with JustHope and ACOPADES since the beginning. The partnership that ACOPADES has with JustHope started many years ago. I worked with Sister Juanita and Sister Elizabeth as they organized everything. They called people from all the areas to meetings to talk about how the community could be developed better.*
>
> *The first projects were schools, then the health center. They looked for people who needed scholarships to study. After that, they built a meeting place, Casa de Paz. Each sector worked one day a week. Yes, I helped build it with my own hands. We mixed concrete and laid bricks. We had to carry water in buckets from this well by the church. It was something beautiful because we were united. Sister Juanita and*

Elizabeth taught us how to work in groups for all the good of the community. All the buildings that you see now are the fruits of the seeds Sister Juanita planted.

That was the dream of Sister Juanita and Sister Elizabeth: to have schools, the ability for kids to go to college, better houses, and health care. It is something incredible because her dream came true. We are living it with the groups that come to support the community. Before, people couldn't read. Now, there are people from Chacraseca who are primary school teachers and administrators. Now, Chacraseca has people who have studied because of scholarships.

My first memory of Sister Joan was about thirty years ago. Father Donald Mendoza invited the sisters. Sister Juanita fell in love with Chacraseca. She came to organize meetings of pastoral committee. She called a lot of people to help. She was an angel for Chacraseca.

When I was a child, we had a small school with a roof made of tile. It was only for elementary; they didn't have high school. We had one teacher and about fifteen kids of all ages in one room. It was hard when I was a child. I was the oldest of seven kids. There were times I could not go to school because I had to take care of siblings. That made me sad. Sometimes I only went one or two days a week. I didn't have a childhood. I was always working. It was hard. But that was the life that I had. I liked school; when I went, I learned.

In the 1980s when the Sandinistas won, all the university students went to the country to teach people to read. This was a literacy campaign. One of the girls came to Chacraseca for a year and taught us every afternoon. At that point, I learned to read and write. That was something beautiful.

I learned to cook when I was a girl. My mother taught me, so I could help. I didn't like to cook, but I had to do it to take care of my sisters and brothers.

Now I cook for the groups like yours. In order to have breakfast ready for you by 6:30 a.m., I wake at 4:00 a.m. and have fifteen minutes for prayers. Then I shower, dress, and come to the kitchen here before 5:00 a.m. We work here until 4:30 in the afternoon, and then I go home and make supper for my family.[1]

---

1. Interview with Nimia, May 2016. Translated by Julio Delgado, transcribed by Donna Greene.

When Nimia finished sharing these words, Leslie said to our group, "Donã Nimia has been an important teacher for me in this community. She is a wise, strong leader." Then Leslie turned and said to Nimia, "Paula and some of the others here are interested in how you make tortillas. I told them you sometimes offer tortilla making classes for groups. Would you be willing to do that this week?"

"Yes, I want to be part of that!" Martin said. Others chimed in in agreement.

Nimia beamed with joy lighting up her face. "Sí," she said. "I would be happy to teach you." We agreed on a time on Thursday before lunch for tortilla making lessons.

We thanked her for sharing her story and looked forward to hearing more from her later in the week. Michelle and the other teachers arrived and began to eat breakfast. After quick greetings, our team finalized morning plans and broke into two groups. Most of our group headed back over to the Peace House to prepare for the community meeting.

Rose, Laura, and I joined Michelle's educational team as they finished eating. Leslie introduced us all. Before going to the school, we would organize supplies they had brought. When everyone was ready to work, we moved across the road to sort materials. The JustHope office was in another small, metal building beside the Peace House that everyone called Leslie's apartment. We had not been in the building before, but we knew that Leslie slept there. When we stepped into the dark, hot space, Laura laughed and said, "So this is Leslie's apartment?" Leslie smiled. I grinned and asked, "Did you think she had air conditioning?" I noticed Laura raise one eyebrow as she looked around at the cot in the corner between the piles of supplies.

The room looked like a dusty storage building stacked with bulging duffle bags and cardboard boxes. There was not much room to work, but we joined Michelle and her group sorting through a box of children's books donated from communities in the United States. Some of the books were in Spanish, others in English. The skillful educators quickly stacked books appropriate for the various age groups. Rose pointed out several she had used in her class in the past. Michelle explained that most of the children do not have a book of their own at home, and their families may not have a book at all. Her team collects boxes of books to leave with teachers.

Leslie said, "The kids are excited to take turns looking through picture books, even if they can't read yet."

Michelle and her colleagues began to discuss the lesson plans for the day. We could see that this group of teachers had invested painstaking reflection preparing math, science, and art projects that could be offered despite language barriers. These professional educators from the United States were dedicated to supporting Nicaraguan teachers by sharing new methods. As we listened to their plans, we began to share their excitement.

Rose said, "My teaching often relied on copied pages and the use of material resources that might not be available in this context. I am impressed that you have clearly thought about plans that don't require supplies like that."

Michelle said she learned that the hard way the first year she came. "Even the most basic things like paper and pencils are hard to come by here," Michelle added.

Michelle's teachers from the United States were learning at an existential level how dependent their models are on material resources. They knew that it was not helpful to suggest teaching strategies or techniques that can't be sustained without necessary supplies like paper copies or books. All of us began to recognize what audacity we had assuming we had answers that could be helpful. Francis confirmed what we imagined. In Nicaragua, teacher training often replicates the methodologies that seem outdated and ineffective to North American teachers. Copying lines and rote memorization are the most common practices in typical classrooms in Chacraseca. A few students continue to college; less than half graduate from high school. The vast majority of students will grow up to work in the fields or factories.

Laura asked, "I am curious about how the Nicaraguan teachers have received your training in the past. I imagine it could feel patronizing as if outsiders were criticizing how they usually did things in their classrooms."

Michelle replied, "Remember it was teachers in the community here who asked for more teaching techniques. They know that teachers in the U.S. share ideas and strategies. JustHope has been working for years to build schools and fund teachers. Now it is time to work with the teachers who are asking for more training. This is a new venture."

"I am glad you are thinking about those dynamics. Making sure our partnerships are as mutual as possible and not patronizing is a priority. Keep an eye on that issue this morning, and let's talk about it afterwards," Leslie said. "I will be with the rest of your group for the community leaders' meeting, but I will see you at lunch."

Next we loaded on the van with boxes of books and supplies, ready to go. We waved goodbye to the rest of our group, who were lounging placidly in rocking chairs on the porch of the Peace House. Leslie pulled up a rocking chair to sit with them, preparing for the meeting that would begin soon. Julio stayed at the Peace House to translate for the meeting of community leaders. Francis went with our group to translate. Juan Pablo was ready and waiting as we boarded the van with Michelle's team of volunteers.

Laura, Rose, and I got better acquainted with some of the other teachers as we rode on the van. We formed connections quickly through our shared appreciation for education. We enjoyed the colorful scenery during the ten-minute drive to the school. But when the van pulled up in front of the school, I felt my heart sink at the bleakness of the building and grounds.

Rose turned to Francis and asked quietly, "Are the other schools like this?" Francis nodded. We stepped from the van toward the dingy, cinder block building with its faded paint walls, tin roof, and open-air windows covered with iron bars. Rough, wooden doors of each room stood open. The playground was a yard of bare, dark earth void of the lush, green grass in the surrounding fields. Children of various ages, most of them dressed in the uniform navy-blue pleated skirt or pants with impossibly white shirts, popped out against the drab setting.

Rose's face brightened, and she smiled as we all appreciated the contrast between the lively, laughing faces of the children and the sad facility. The inescapable dust coated the building, making it seem to blend into the dirt yard with scattered shrubs and tropical trees. As we approached the classrooms and glanced inside, we saw that worn chairs and old desks were practically the only items in each room.

We noticed that there were three classrooms and another dark room at one end of the building. Rose, Laura, Michelle, and the other teachers speculated together about age level grouping in each room. One aged latrine flanked a corner of the building. Francis moved with us stepping from the school yard to the covered porch, ready to assist with translation. Class had not started for the day yet. No one came forward to greet us. Were the teachers aware that we were coming today, I wondered? Michelle cheerfully took charge. After a quick look around and a brief exchange of greetings with some of the children, we began unloading boxes of books and supplies from the van. Juan Pablo said goodbye; he would return to pick us up around noon.

With the help of Francis as translator, Michelle entered a room and explained that the JustHope volunteers were available to work with teachers as requested. There seemed to be three adults on the school premises, one in each of the classrooms. One Nicaraguan teacher, Anita seemed to have known to expect this visit, but it seemed doubtful that any of the teachers were expecting us that morning. Since none of us spoke much Spanish, Francis went to each teacher seated behind her desk and explained that we were there to volunteer. It felt chaotic and awkward. Michelle directed a couple of us to each room. A pair of teachers from Michelle's group explored the building and grounds. Francis and Michelle spoke with each teacher, then directed Rose and me into a classroom for kindergarten and pre-K. The teacher, who looked quite young, seemed self-conscious that we were there. Smiling at her, we sat down at a table with some of the kids. Laura went with Michelle to another room.

Rose and I looked around the room where eleven children were seated at two, small tables. Francis translated as the young teacher explained. One table was for the six kindergartners. The five pre-school kids were grouped at the second table. I sat with the youngest children, and Rose looked happy and comfortable with the kindergarten children. We smiled and tried our few Spanish phrases with the kids then sat in silence as the teacher began the day's schoolwork. Francis left us to help in another room. I did a quick visual inventory of the supplies in the room. The teacher had a small table to serve as her desk. A simple, handmade poster presenting different colors was taped to one wall coated with dust. It looked faded, as if it had been hanging for several years. There were no books, no art supplies, no paper, no blocks. On a shelf out of the children's reach, there were five plastic bottles filled with objects that must be for play or counting: small stones, a string of rusty bottle caps drilled with a hole, a variety of dull, broken pencils. Every item looked worn, rusty, and dull.

Rose said to me quietly, "I wish you could see the bright, clean, well-stocked classroom where I taught in Houston!" She looked a little stunned. The teacher gave the children paper and stubs of pencils and directed them to copy short words she was writing on the board. As I sat watching, I thought of the abundance of supplies that are often wasted in the U.S. Could we organize a school supply drive? I watched the children struggle to manipulate a pencil and copy letters. The kids were so cute that I longed to interact more. I smiled and nodded over their work. I kept thinking about how to get resources to these teachers. Then, I realized I was resorting to that impulse to fix problems with money and material resources. After about half an hour of observing in silence, Rose and I stepped out, since we could see no way to assist.

"I cannot imagine teaching those children day after day with no supplies!" Rose said. "How in the world do they manage? The kids are adorable! I was amazed at how long they sat at the tables."

"Did you see the little girl with the long braids at my table? She was able to copy almost all the words. Let's go see what Michelle is doing with the older class," I suggested.

In the next room, we found Michelle getting along well with Anita, the teacher of the oldest group. It turned out that Anita had been part of the request for training; she oversaw the other teachers. She and Michelle were using Francis's good translation services, as well as hand gestures, to communicate and collaborate. Each student had one of the colorful books from the collection we had brought. They were taking turns reporting about the book. I noticed that Laura was not in the room and assumed she had been directed to another class. Michelle invited Rose and me to assist with an art project in the classroom for first through third graders who had moved out to the covered porch where the air was a little cooler.

Rose and I exchanged appreciative looks as we felt the cool breeze. As we sat on the floor with the children and watched for ways to offer help, we were soon charmed by the kids' warmth and openness. I knew very little Spanish, and although I often felt self-conscious attempting conversation with adults, I felt braver with the children. Slowly, the interactions began to feel like healthy connections between the teachers and children despite the language and cultural barriers. We enjoyed helping the kids learn to weave strips of paper together. The morning flew by.

It was almost time for lunch. Francis had been floating from one classroom to another assisting. She came to us and explained that kids were allowed to go home or stay for lunch. Two of the teachers prepared to leave the school, saying goodbye to other teachers and students. Although a few students left for home, many began gathering around the school kitchen. Like meals at homes in the neighborhood, the usual fare was rice, beans, and tortillas cooked over the wood fire.

Laura joined us. She motioned to me and Rose to come look at the lunchroom and led us to the end of the school porch, to a kitchen where two Nicaraguan volunteers had prepared breakfast and lunch for the school. Laura ushered Rose and me into the dark, smoky lunchroom and raised her eyebrows as she looked pointedly around the workspace. Then, as children began to crowd in line for food, she waved us out to the porch. She pointed to a scruffy chicken wandering through the school yard where a few barefoot children were playing. Laura spoke with intensity in her voice, "Can you believe the lack of sanitation in this school? I know this is like every traditional Nicaraguan kitchen, but there is no hot water for washing hands. Did you see that woman who was cooking as she rinsed plastic cups and plates, using only a worn brush and some soft soap? Was the water in the plastic bucket safe even before the woman dipped her hand in a plastic bowl and sloshed the rinse over the dishes? Did you see the flies that buzzed around the tables where damp dish clothes covered the food in plastic bowls? Look at the dust clinging to the concrete block walls, the dilapidated wooden tables, and the children running in and out through the open doors. Couldn't they at least clean the place up?"

The sun was hot, and hardly a breeze stirred. Before Rose or I could answer, Juan Pablo pulled up in the van to pick us up and take us back to the Peace House. It was time for us to rejoin our team. We said goodbye to Michelle's team of teachers who would continue working at this school all week. They seemed happy and fully engaged, just getting started on their plans. We waved goodbye to kids who continued to eye us with curiosity. We got in the van and rode away.

As we rode back to meet the rest of our group, Laura snapped open her small travel-sized bottle of hand sanitizer and offered to share as she rubbed her hands with an ample coating of the gel. I realized I had already seen Laura do that several times since breakfast.

Laura said, "My mind keeps returning to thoughts of disease or parasites. I used the latrine in the school yard. In the damp, dusty corners of that building I saw lots of small insects buzzing around. I couldn't tell if they were gnats or small mosquitoes. I wonder how often children in the school spread contagious diseases. What would happen if a child fell and sustained an injury in the play yard? It is at least a twenty-minute drive over rough dirt roads to the nearest hospital. Besides, there is no ambulance in the community. I know there is that clinic that has a doctor present most weekdays, but that is several miles away from the school down long, dusty roads. Who would a teacher call if a child was injured and needed emergency care?" Laura was obviously agitated. We listened but didn't have much to say in response.

Eventually Laura fell silent.

A few minutes later Rose said, "Which is the most urgent need here: jobs or education? I am convinced that these kids need reading, writing, and arithmetic, as well as history and other studies, but it seems sort of hopeless. I believe education provides access to dignity and liberation. I feel overwhelmed with this small glimpse into the dynamics of the educational system in Nicaragua."

"But just think of all the wasted resources back home that could be used and appreciated here," Laura said.

Rose replied, "That was my first thought, too. I started thinking of systems to transport supplies to these schools in Chacraseca. I don't think that is feasible or sustainable. Remember what Leslie said about sustainability?"

As I listened to the conversation, I appreciated Rose's insight. I was chagrined to think of my own tendency to assume the solutions required material resources, money, and the power of financial wealth. Our dependency on economic prosperity was on full display. This visit to a Nicaraguan school invited deeper engagement with a new type of resourcefulness. How can we live more sustainably in harmony with the planet instead of placing our confidence in material goods and solutions?

I said, "The kids we saw today were the lucky ones who were able to come to school. Others are home helping their families or working. Remember what Nimia said about missing school to watch her younger siblings? I have been trying to imagine what it is like to be a grandmother here. I am guessing that Nimia must be near sixty, close to my age. How incredible that she learned to read and write when she was an adult during that famous literacy campaign after the Sandinista revolution! Can you imagine what it might have been like to have been a young adult then, already the mother of four or five children? If she had started having kids when she was a teenager herself, like most of the girls in her community, that is about how old she would have been during those years."

Rose said, "I was trying to imagine what it would have been like if neither of her parents could read or write, and they struggled alongside her and the rest of the family to learn to read. I wish I could meet volunteers who worked in that literacy program in these rural areas to teach reading and writing. It all sounded inspiring when I read about it."

We already felt as if we had a full day, but when we arrived and rejoined the rest of our group back at the Peace House, we were excited to hear about their experience in the community meeting. They were going for lunch, and we washed up quickly to join them. Each time we left the

Peace Hose, we had to lock it up. Janeth had explained that the computer and other items in the office, as well as our own property, could be a temptation in this community with such a high level of poverty. In the past, office materials had been stolen. So Janeth asked us to lock the Peace House any time that all of us left. She had given us one key for our group to share for locking and unlocking the front doors. We had agreed that whoever was out last would lock. Just as I was ready to leave the Peace House, I saw that all our classmates had left except for Bill.

"Bill, I am going to lunch. You are the last one here; you are in charge of the key," I said passing it to him.

"I will be right behind you in a couple of minutes," Bill said.

I walked across the dusty road to the community center where Nimia and Estella were cooking. I noticed Laura talking with them and looking at a large tub of water by a deep concrete sink that was the source of water for washing and rinsing dishes, just like the system at the school kitchen. Sweat trickled down the side of Laura's forehead in the heat of the building even though she was not working close to that fire where caldrons of beans and rice bubbled. I wondered if it had just dawned on Laura that all of us had been eating on plastic dishes washed and rinsed by hand without hot water. I looked more thoughtfully at the concrete counter where a large knife that had been used to cut melon still rested in a pool of juice. More than a few flies and gnats buzzed around. I noticed a frown line between Laura's eyebrows as she looked around at the rustic kitchen.

"I guess there is no way to prevent bugs from coming through the open doors and windows," Laura said frowning as I joined her. Nimia smiled and greeted me as she continued cooking. Laura said, "I'm not sure I can eat anything." I nudged her toward our teammates at the long rectangular table covered with a plastic tablecloth. Laura sat down and flipped open the top of her hand sanitizer bottle again. Using a generous squirt of sanitizer, she offered to share it. Nick used a little, as did Elizabeth. Laura sighed as she put the bottle away. She took a big swig from her water bottle.

"I'm not even sure I should try drinking the fruit drinks they made us. There is no way I can eat anything. My stomach hurts."

Paula and Martin began passing plastic plates, forks, and cups with a heavy, full jug of cold fruit juice. Soon big bowls covered with dish cloths were ready. George was excited to see watermelon. Rice and beans were no surprise. Julio and Nick heaped steaming spoonsful of chicken stewed with tomato as they discussed soccer. Before long the talking faded out as we ate lunch. Bill ambled in and sat down.

"Bill, please give me the key, I want to go lie down," Laura said. She had not eaten at all.

"Oh, darn. I forgot to lock it. The key must be there on the table by the door," Bill said.

Julio stopped eating and responded, "Bill, let's all remember how important it is to lock the Peace House when we leave." He raised his voice so everyone at the table could hear.

Bill shrugged. Laura rolled her eyes and walked away. Once again, I found myself considering options for helping learn about the challenge of living in community. Bill asked that the bowls of food be passed to him and complained that the main dishes were empty. Everyone else was finishing up. Lunch had started twenty minutes earlier.

After a few minutes Rose asked, "How was the community meeting?"

Paula said, "It was super cool. We sat in the back corner so Julio could translate. He just whispered to keep us understanding what was happening. They started the meeting with singing."

Martin continued, "They talked about the cost of water and how the price of electricity affects the price. The pumps that run the system are really expensive, and the system doesn't make enough money to replace pumps when they burn out. I didn't realize that the government doesn't provide any utility services here. The community has to maintain the water system in rural areas like this."

Paula expanded, "The water system was the main thing they discussed. Some thought they should raise the price for water; others objected. They also talked about plans to build latrines and a new house this summer. There was a report about the college scholarships and how various students were progressing." Then Paula asked about our morning at the school.

Rose answered, "Those Nicaraguan teachers inspired me. They are working so hard with so few resources." She continued to describe the rough condition of the school and the lack of supplies. Her enthusiasm was evident in the animated way she talked about the children. We shared highlights from our day with Michelle and her group of teachers.

"Did all the kids wear uniforms?" George asked. "We have seen kids in uniforms walking to school. It seems odd to me."

Rose said, "Yes, most of the kids were wearing uniforms. There were a few who did not have them. The uniforms seemed strange to me at first, too."

George agreed. "Having attended public schools myself, I guess I have a certain mental resistance to uniforms that I had not consciously examined. When I think of school uniforms, I think of privileged children who attended expensive private schools."

Rose continued, "Yes, same for me. I think I may also have disdain for uniforms because uniforms prevent children's ability to express their individuality through choosing their own clothes. When I was growing up, I felt sorry for children who had to wear school uniforms for that reason. It is likely that I got the message from my parents or culture that children who had to wear uniforms were stuck in the past. Maybe this came from something like anti-Catholic sentiment in my Protestant community."

"Exactly," Nick chimed in. "I wasn't sure whether my parents were trying to convince me not to be jealous of kids who wore uniforms or really did pity them. But, over the years, I developed an appreciation for the ability of a uniform to eliminate class difference and hierarchy between those whose families could afford more expensive and fashionable brands versus families without that monetary wealth."

"Good point," Paula agreed. "Wow. What a relief it would have been to be spared the harrowing competition and pressure to conform to dictates of teen fashion trends! Seeing children from such economically poor communities wearing school uniforms baffled me at first, too. I am also amazed at the ability of those families who live in homes with dirt floors to keep those uniforms dazzling white despite washing clothes by hand in concrete sinks."

Rose said, "I know. I can't imagine. As we talk about this, I realize it helps to examine my critical attitude about school uniforms."

We stacked up our empty plates and agreed to talk more about the morning later. We had half an hour for a quick rest before our afternoon activities. Leslie, Julio, and Francis were enjoying rocking chairs on the porch when we returned. A man named Horacio sat with them visiting. He works around the Peace House and is a volunteer with ACOPADES. His face was familiar as one of the daily circle of new friends. Francis helped me ask Horacio if he would be willing to answer questions and share his story with our group. He seemed happy to accept our invitation for later that day. We visited and rested, glad to have a little free time.

About an hour later, our group regathered and walked to a nearby building, called the Cultural Center, where JustHope offers art, music, and dance classes for children and youth. There we met JustHope staff person Abimiel, who teaches music. He also oversees the scholarship program. He explained that he was preparing for the monthly check-in meeting with scholarship students. He was setting up metal folding chairs in a circle, and we joined him, adding chairs for ourselves. Soon a few young adults arrived and joined us.

As we waited for the meeting to begin, I looked around the large room and freshly painted walls. I remembered a year earlier when this area had been the rubble and ruins of a previous building that had been abandoned for years. JustHope teams worked with local leaders to construct the building. I had come with a team from Harvard Avenue Christian Church in Tulsa whose sweat and hard work set the foundation and helped raise the walls. I had painted metal ceiling beams with others on the team, and it was fun to look up and see the metal beams in place. Like other concrete block buildings, this one was hot. Fans stirred the air from open windows, but we were all sweating despite sitting still.

College students began to arrive. Soon Abimiel started the meeting with Francis translating. Ten scholarship students were present that day. Several others were unable to make the meeting because of work schedules. The students introduced themselves and talked about their studies. Armin said he was nineteen years old and was studying tourism and English in León at the University. Marian, also nineteen, was studying to be a nurse. She explained that she worked at the clinic to fulfill her required volunteer service. Rudolpho, age twenty, was studying engineering. Each student talked about their appreciation for the opportunity to continue their education and become professional workers to serve their community. Abimiel explained that the students come to this meeting once a month to show their grades, verifying that they are still in school, report their volunteer hours, and confirm that they are making progress. The leaders of ACOPADES set up this arrangement for monthly support and accountability. Students talk about how their studies are going, receive their monthly scholarship money, and support each other.

To receive a scholarship each student agrees to work weekly volunteer hours. Some work in the clinic, others in schools; one works at the hardware store. The students explained the costs required for their education: bus fare to León, school supplies, school fees, and books. Tuition at the national university is free, but it is not easy to gain entrance. Abimiel added that even at the University teachers don't have access to copying exams. Students must pay fees to pay for the copy they use. Francis added that this is also true in the high schools. The fees add up quickly.

As the students shared their experiences, our group listened with interest. I found myself reflecting on public education back home. I often complain about our educational system, but I saw many privileges of educational access as I reconsidered. I looked forward to hearing from our group about how they viewed this comparison. As our meeting with the scholarship students continued, a couple of older elementary school-age boys, looking shy, came in the building and walked back to an area near the musical instruments. Abimiel explained that after the scholarship meeting, the children's folk dance and music class would perform for us. The children would begin arriving soon. As the final part of this meeting Abimiel called each scholarship student individually, checked their grade sheets, and gave them some cordobas. One by one they received their funds; soon the meeting ended. We all stood and exchanged appreciative words and support as the college students began to leave.

Before we left the cultural center, Abimiel told us about another JustHope education project organized to provide backpacks for each child in primary grades. ACOPADES named school supplies as a high priority among the needs of their community. JustHope raised funds for three hundred backpacks that year. Each backpack includes paper, pencils, notebooks, a pair of shoes, and a school uniform. The community also identified the need for dance, music, and art lessons as a priority; thus, JustHope pays Abimiel and other staff to provide programs after school.

"How many JustHope staff are there?" Bill asked.

"We have nine full-time staff in Nicaragua," Abimiel said. "There are also two who work in the United States."

When our discussion with Abimiel ended, he invited us to return to the cultural center on Friday for a presentation of music and dance that the children would perform for us. He turned to join the kids for music lessons. We walked back to the Peace House for some free time.

Before supper our group reconvened on the porch. Michelle and the team of teachers joined us to hear Horacio tell his story. We moved the rocking chairs outside making a large circle for this conversation. The sun was low; the temperature was lowering. When everyone had gathered, Julio translated as Horacio shared.

My name is Horacio Morales, and I was born in Chacraseca. I live in the sector called Raul Cabesa. My mom had fourteen kids. I am oldest. Now, I have five children of my own and six grandchildren. I am just struggling to survive. One of the things that has amazed me has been seeing this Peace House being built.

When I was eight years old, the community of Chacraseca was very different. Then, two sisters, Sister Joan and Sister Elizabeth, came. We had no idea what their intentions were at first. One sister said we had to organize ourselves. That was a very important step for the development of the community.

When I was a kid, only about two thousand people lived in this community. We had no electricity, no potable water. When I was a kid, there were only two schools in Chacraseca. I would go barefoot wearing shorts. My dad would get me notebooks that I carried in a cardboard bag. Then, many kids had to walk about two miles, or even more. When little girls are walking, they are at risk. We wanted to build more schools closer to the homes. When I see kids, I see innocent human beings. They deserve education and protection. Teachers see that. Teachers work hard to educate the children.

Sister Joan and Sister Elizabeth had a dream to have a house where people would meet to pray and organize. This land was sold by a man to the sisters. People came in good faith to work. We gave of our time by sector to come help the foreman. That is how this Peace House got built. Sister Joan and Elizabeth received a lot of help from the U.S. It took months of work and organizing, to build this. When the construction was finished, there was a celebration service. All these years, leaders meet here every Tuesday. Because of this Peace House, groups from the U.S. could come share with us.

Now, because we are organized, we have schools in all the sectors. We have scholarships for students. They get some help to get backpacks. Parents would like to help their kids even more. But they don't have the resources. Children need scholarships. There are more kids that need help, but at least there are three hundred kids who get scholarships. Parents have to make lots of sacrifices to buy uniforms. If a family has three kids, they may not be able to buy uniforms for all of them. I see that some kids are poor, but they are smart. They want to study.

Families have to pay for copies and all the papers for schoolwork. The school has paid for the paper for the test. The school can't pay for copies, so families have to pay. For an elementary school child to go to school, a family has to pay thirty-five dollars a year. They pay one hundred dollars a year for a student to attend high school. Families also have to pay for transportation to high school. The government only pays for the teacher salary. Teachers have no money for supplies. When the broom breaks, or when a desk breaks, there is no money to fix that.

Now, we have beautiful schools. We have two high schools. Some students even graduated from college, thanks to the solidarity of people like you. We even have some youth that are studying medicine, journalism, and engineering. I rejoice to have professionals like that from Chacraseca. There are some youth who only got half-way through college because there were not enough resources.

These changes are possible because we organized. We feel grateful to see you here. You come with good intentions for the development of this community. I also think of the housing programs. Back in the 1970s, often the huts would catch on fire. When that happened, people would lose everything. Then our houses were made of palm trees. Now, houses are safer. I thank God because through ACOPADES, I got a house. We can have more of a comfortable life.

I have worked here with ACOPADES and people like you who come in solidarity. I have seen people with great hearts. It is not for everybody. Other communities in Nicaragua admire Chacraseca because there are people coming here to help.

One time, I talked with this young guy about his work building the latrine. He was a pastor from the U.S. I asked him, "How are you impacted by your work in Chac?" He said he felt something in his heart he had not imagined before. He gave me a hug. He has come back many times. I never thought I would find someone who was such a good friend.

We love you a lot with all of our hearts. It is hot here, but now you have to take that human warmth back to the U.S. Don't stop coming back. We will be expecting you with a lot of love.[2]

After our group thanked Horacio, we assured him that we would visit with him more during supper soon. We looked forward to seeing him after our next meeting. We had an opportunity to tour the Chacraseca church building and meet the priest who served that community as our final experience of the day.

2. Interview with Horacio, May 2016. Translated by Julio Delgado, transcribed by Kathleen D. McCallie.

Father Pablo welcomed us into the hot sanctuary. Since the parish was humble and the altars were sparse, our tour did not take long. Paula and I lingered over the simple stations of the cross on the walls surrounding the rustic, wooden benches of the sanctuary. Then we set up a circle of chairs outside in the shade, hoping for a little breeze while we talked. Leslie said, "Father Pablo teaches at a seminary in Managua. He lives in León, but his ministry in Chacraseca has made a tremendous difference in the community." Father Pablo was generous in sharing about his work and interested in hearing about the studies of these seminary students. His devotion and love for the people was clear. He described the baseball teams he organized for teens, opportunities he offered for girls to assist in serving as acolytes, and the "meals on feet" ministry for delivering food to people who were unable to leave home. He credited the people with the developing ministry. Students asked about details of his work and the life of the congregation. After some time, the priest asked questions of us.

"When you saw our sanctuary, what caught your attention?" Father Pablo asked the group.

At first the students seemed somewhat reluctant to name the things that seemed most unusual to them. "The use of images and icons like those in your sanctuary is not a practice most of us grew up with," I ventured. Father Pablo nodded in understanding.

Bill said, "I am surprised that the statues have such fancy clothes."

I was aware that our Protestant formation positioned us to approach this conversation with judgmental assumptions. I hoped we were sensitive to our presuppositions. Somewhere along the way, I had been told that Roman Catholics worship idols. I had long since replaced that prejudicial misconception with an appreciation for the use of images and icons as helpful tools for prayer practices. Yet I was mindful that heated conflict between Catholics and Protestants persisted in many communities.

"And perhaps you wonder about the colonial legacy of venerating the white skinned images," Father Pablo said. "That bothers many of us, too. We have many saints; not enough look like the people in this community. But we just celebrated the annual day of the Black crucifix," he said.

Martin said, "I saw the icon of the Black Christ. Could you tell us more about that, please?" he asked.

Father Pablo said that the community celebrates an annual day of lifting up a saint known as El Señor de los Milagros, whose story originated in what is now Guatemala. He said, "Parades lifting up the saints often include drumming and firecrackers, even in these dirt streets of

Chacraseca. Old cultural customs are interwoven with the church traditions." Father Pablo suggested we could research to learn more about Cristo de Esquipulas del Sauce.

"The colonial history is complicated. The Spanish brought the faith, but some local customs and wisdom survived," the priest said. "For example, look at that tree there. Do you see those hard, green fruits on the ground? That is a Jicaro tree. See how the leaves are shaped like a cross? Before the Spanish first came, the tree was used for medicine and ancestral remedies. The fruit ripens and smells like apples when it touches the ground. The Spanish thought the tree was holy because of the shape of the leaves."

"I grew up Catholic," Paula explained to Father Pablo, "but most of my classmates are not accustomed to the traditions of icons in the sanctuary."

"Are there many Protestants in this community?" Elizabeth asked.

"In one sector, the Assemblies of God congregation is so strong they won't allow Catholics in at all. There is a Jehovah's Witness congregation and a Seventh Day Adventist congregation, too," Father Pablo explained. .

I thought about the meeting of ACOPADES leaders that morning and wondered how conflict over religious identity affected efforts to build up the community

"Nimia told us that over half of the people in Chacraseca are single women head of households. Are there many men who attend mass?" George asked.

The priest smiled thoughtfully. "More women than men attend regularly," he responded. "Is that different in your community?"

"No, it is the same in my congregation," George said, grinning.

The conversation continued, ranging from questions about seminary education to daily spiritual practices. Father Pablo was generous with his time and seemed to welcome the opportunity to talk about his ministry. Finally we ended our conversation with the priest because we needed to eat supper and prepare for our nightly reflection group.

That evening we had lots to talk about.

Evening Reflection

"I want to hear more about the ACOPADES meeting. I got to hear a little about it at lunch, but we were not all there for that discussion." I said when we circled up after supper.

George's passion was evident in the tone of his voice. "It was awesome!" he said. "This porch area was transformed into a meeting space. Leaders set up about thirty chairs in rows. They created a little table with fresh flowers and songbooks. I was moved to see Antonio, who I had only thought of as the groundskeeper and gardener here, lead prayer and singing at the beginning of the meeting. He and Nimia led that part of the meeting, then Juan Enrique led the business meeting. He had a big white board on a tripod where he had listed the agenda items for discussion. It was very well-organized and collaborative."

"There are seven elected members of the Board of Directors for ACOPADES, plus subcommittees with five elected members from each sector," Bill said.

"What types of things did they discuss?" Laura asked.

"The water system has a pump that needs repair," Martin said. "That was one big item of business. But then they had a police officer come address some issue about a person's pig being stolen. The whole meeting was like a cross between a city council meeting and a congregational business meeting. It really was intriguing," Martin reflected.

Nick asked, "Who owns the Peace House and cultural center?"

Leslie said, "ACOPADES owns the land and buildings for the hardware store, the Peace House, the cultural center, Stitching Hope, and the annex. In other words, the community owns the property in common. But ACOPADES is the legal entity that owns the deed."

Rose asked, "Was there anything else that happened in the meeting?"

George said, "They talked about projects for culture and sports, housing, health, and education, also."

"They called on Leslie to give updates about the JustHope construction project of building houses and latrines," Nick said. "They took time to welcome us formally and thanked us for coming."

Rose asked, "Could you understand what was going on in Spanish?"

Martin said, "My Spanish is good enough that I followed most of the conversation, but Julio was translating quietly for us, too. In some ways the meeting is like community organizing meetings I have attended back home."

SUSTAINABILITY IN EDUCATIONAL PROGRAMS 115

"What were the schools like?" Martin asked.

Laura spoke up first, "The school was very depressing. I told you all that I am a U.S. 'city girl.' The bugs and dirt were only part of the problem. The building was filthy and hot. The kitchen was horrible. There were no school supplies. It was shocking," she said.

"Michelle and the teachers with her team were impressive," Rose said. "But it was surprising to see how little the Nicaraguan teachers have to work with. The kids were adorable, though."

Our conversation continued, reviewing insights and impressions from the day.

"Could we talk about our group plan for locking the Peace House when we leave each day?" George asked. "I have my expensive camera here, and I need to be sure it is secure."

"Agreed," Martin said. "Bill, when you left this place unlocked and came for lunch, you put our stuff at risk. More importantly, the Peace House computer and office equipment was not secure. We need to pay more attention to locking up."

"I apologize," Bill said. "I just forgot."

Laura cleared her throat and spoke up, saying, "While we are on the subject of group housekeeping, we need to figure out a better system of washing dishes. I wonder if we can buy some antibacterial disinfectant and a new cloth or something to wash dishes while we are here," Laura added. "I can't stand the way we are using that filthy, old brush. And maybe we should be heating the water before washing dishes with it. My stomach has been hurting, and we don't want to pass around germs."

As Laura spoke, a couple of people nodded their heads in agreement. Others leaned back as if considering. I thought again about the challenge of living as a group in close community.

Martin spoke up in response, "Maybe we can think together about how obsessed our culture is with germs. I think it is much better for the environment not to use all that antibacterial chemical stuff."

I could see the tension simmering between Martin and Laura. I knew that the stress of cultural shock, the discomforts of being away from home, and the close living situation strained interpersonal relationships. Resolving challenges like this one was part of our work as a team. This is part of the work of community practice that illustrates our need for spiritual growth. I was glad when Leslie spoke up next.

Leslie reminded our group of the reality that for hundreds and hundreds of years, people in this community had been living without running water at all, much less hot water and antibacterial dish soap. The majority of people in Chacraseca live in houses with dirt floors and do not have refrigerators or hot water. The kitchen facilities at the Peace House look extravagantly rich compared with what is available in most homes in Chacraseca.

"Look, I know I can be obsessive about germs," Laura said sounding defensive and angry. "I am trying to keep an open mind about this." Her voice became strained as if she was choking back tears. We sat in silence a few minutes. I was thankful that Martin was allowing Laura time to explore her feelings.

"I haven't been sleeping well either," Laura said. "I am missing my own bed and my own kitchen, I guess. This trip really is an educational experience," she finished in an exasperated tone. A few seconds later she exclaimed, "It broke my heart to see those kids at the school today. There was one little boy who didn't have a uniform or shoes. He was so skinny that it made my stomach hurt just looking at him. How are these kids supposed to have any chance in life if they can't even learn to read and write? All they can hope for is picking crops or farming with a machete!"

Listening to Laura's voice choke with tears and sorrow, I was thankful that she was recognizing the way her own emotional process added to her focus on details of washing dishes and sanitation. This was a rich learning moment.

"You have to have faith and focus on the positive," Nick said quickly.

I was not surprised when Nick rushed in with his comment rather than allow our group to sit with the discomfort of hearing Laura's reflection. Unfortunately, this often happens in groups, especially with groups of people with an impulse to fix others. I was sure that some of the students had observed the dynamic that had just taken place. I allowed more silence as a gentle response to Nick's comment rather than countering his suggestion. I wished I knew a way to invite Nick to recognize that his impulse to avoid the pain Laura expressed was a move of avoidance driven by his own discomfort. I was frustrated with his trite, moralistic advice. At the same time, I felt sympathy for Nick. It was clear that he was experiencing challenges to his world view, too. As an educator, I often try to allow the discomfort to be a tool of learning. Once again, I was glad when Leslie spoke up after a few moments of pregnant silence.

"Maybe we need to just acknowledge Laura's feelings and let her feel them," Leslie responded. "What does it mean to have faith in this situation? What does collaboration look like right now? What about sustainability?" she asked. More silence followed.

"I am sure I have lots to learn about living in community," Laura said. "Maybe I'll sleep better tonight."

"Today had some tough moments," Rose said. "There don't seem to be answers to the question of how to be good partners in a situation of such gross inequality." "The steps we can keep taking are reaching and listening while we try to learn the skill of collaboration as partners."

"I hope we can care for each other through this class. It is definitely more intense than I imagined. How can we even be good partners to one another?" Elizabeth said.

"We could just take our toys and go home," Leslie said. "Or we can ask ourselves what type of partnership can be sustainable."

We had been in Nicaragua three days.

Popular Education

JustHope educational programs are not just for Nicaraguans. Educating North Americans is an essential part of the mission. Unlearning and recognizing our need to learn can be painful, especially if we operate with the assumption that our society is better educated than others. Many people in the United States grow up never doubting they will graduate from high school and college. Their families expect this, assume it will happen, and support their progress. Other people do drop out before they graduate from high school, but some support and assistance are often available to prevent that. The expectation that a high school diploma should be available to all is common in the U.S. Inequality in resources for poor versus affluent public schools persists in most cities in the United States. However, even the worst schools in the U.S. have access to material supplies, teacher training, and support for education that are worlds better than many rural communities in Nicaragua. JustHope partners seek to ameliorate these needs with scholarship programs and teacher training. JustHope also invites North Americans to open to learning from Nicaraguans.

Connecting groups of educators from North America with teachers in Nicaragua has been a vital part of the mission of JustHope. Teaching is a vocation that calls forth creativity, passion, and love that connects partners around the world, and watching volunteers connect through the work of education is inspiring. Many children in Nicaragua have some opportunity to attend public school, although they may have to walk or travel miles from their rural homes to do so. In an economy where many people struggle at a subsistence level, children are often needed at home to provide care for younger siblings, prepare food, work in the gardens, or even help with crops or livestock. In addition to those challenges, there are costs associated with attending school as well as supplies and uniforms. Especially for families with multiple children, the fees can be prohibitive. Over the past decades, JustHope has worked to provide scholarships and support so that most children in Chacraseca can attend school. Now, the focus is on providing better teacher training and resources. In the United States, most people take for granted the availability of publicly funded schools for children through high school education. Although the Nicaraguan citizens value public education and vote to fund it, national debt and structural adjustments result in lack of funding for teachers in Nicaragua. In many communities like Chacraseca there are not enough teachers. The teachers who work there may not always be paid, and they may not have adequate education themselves.

Many people in the Nicaraguan countryside still recall with fondness the famous literacy campaign that won loyalty and approval for the Sandinistas in the 1980s. The dream of gaining the benefits of education and active participation as a citizen with self-determination was manifest in art, poetry, and recovery of cultural traditions like folk music and dancing. However, the debilitating effects of the Contra War and the economic pressures of grinding poverty eroded the gains in education. Without consistent access to books or writing materials, many people eventually lost confidence and interest in reading. As the decades passed and economic troubles persisted, adults who had learned to read late in life watched their children stumble through their own attempts at education. In Chacraseca, most kids have a chance to finish elementary school, but not all. Many adults there have little formal schooling, but that does not mean they are without education or wisdom.

To learn how to collaborate with Nicaraguan partners, North Americans must learn new skills like listening. Popular education models emphasize listening attentively. Nicaraguan educators seek transformation of the whole person as well as the society.[3] We can learn to see listening as a form of tacit knowledge and essential wisdom. Instead of thinking

---

3. Jones, "Liberating Praxes," 197.

of ourselves as highly educated in comparison to Nicaraguan partners, North Americans can be open to discovering what Nicaraguans can teach. Mutual, collaborative education can happen if participants recognize their own embodied ways of learning. At its best, JustHope offers education for both Nicaraguans and North Americans.

What Counts as Knowledge Worth Learning?

When I ask JustHope partners from the U.S. why they travel to Nicaragua, they often respond by saying they want to help; they care. What if learning to truly care requires spiritual practice? Claims that North Americans care about Nicaraguans are patronizing and disrespectful without recognition of the rich, embodied wisdom Nicaraguans offer. Consider how complex learning can be. Learning to care includes practicing skills of perception, recognition, or relational awareness as a type of embodied knowing. Pia C. Kontos and Gary Naglie wrote about the "Tacit Knowledge of Caring and Embodied Selfhood," calling for an "expansion of the tacit knowledge paradigm to include embodied selfhood as a source of caring practices."[4] They drew on the thought of Polanyi and the relationship between "knowing how" and the primordial experience of embodiment. Applying this theory in their work on the sociology of health, they were interested in embodiment and practice of providing care. Their work points to the potential to connect embodied tacit knowledge with learning to care. They said, "Our exploration of the communicative capacity of the body to facilitate sympathetic care is intended to provide new insight and direction for future investigation of the body as a site for the production of tacit knowledge."[5] Traveling to Nicaragua makes it possible to engage our bodies with the land and to learn from Nicaraguan partners. This collaboration is a skill or know-how that can't be learned from reading or research alone. Hope for development of more humane communities drives the collaborative, educational process of JustHope partnership. What can we learn together about solutions to global challenges?

The education JustHope can foster requires self-awareness, cultural analysis, and humility with commitment to lifelong learning. In his 1998 book, *Seeing Like a State: How Certain Schemes to Improve the Human*

---

4. Kontos and Naglie, "Tacit Knowledge," 689.
5. Kontos and Naglie, "Tacit Knowledge," 700.

Condition Have Failed, James C. Scott attributes injustices in human development to epistemological problems. Scott recalls the concept of mētis, as a form of knowing that is under appreciated. He said this type of knowing is exemplified when a scientist "recognizes the 'art' of farming and the nonquantifiable ways of knowing."[6] His analysis illustrates a common mistake of those attempting transnational partnership. For example, rather than approaching Nicaraguan farmers through the lens of the Western gaze, assuming they need something outside experts can teach them, partners might urge a stance of curiosity about mutual knowledge production respecting the expertise of Nicaraguan farmers. Scott writes, "Mētis, far from being rigid and monolithic, is plastic, local, and divergent." If we cultivate appreciation for this type of knowing, the potential for learning expands. Scott claims, "Any experienced practitioner of a skill or craft will develop a large repertoire of moves, visual judgments, a sense of touch, or a discriminating gestalt for assessing the work as well as a range of accurate intuitions born of experience that defy being communicated apart from practice."[7] Contextual, embodied awareness can contribute to knowledge production. "The power of the practical knower depends on an exceptionally close and astute observation of the environment."[8] Yet, Scott expresses concern that embodied, tacit knowledge is not adequately appreciated. He writes, "What has proved to be truly dangerous to us and our environment, I think, is the combination of the universalist pretensions of epistemic knowledge and authoritarian social engineering."[9] Our world needs a type of education inseparable from caring.

Sonia Kruks makes a similar point about the lack of attention to tacit knowledge in feminist theory. She claims, "Intersubjective embodied experiences—the ways we tacitly 'know' the experience of others through our bodies—warrant far fuller consideration than they generally receive (or indeed can receive) within the discourse-oriented, post-modern, paradigm that now predominates in feminist theory."[10] When partners in Nicaragua share their distress or sorrow about consequences of severe poverty, an embodied learning encounter is possible. Put another way, their communication about their lives provides a shared experience if

6. Scott, "Thin Simplifications and Practical Knowledge," 332.
7. Scott, "Thin Simplifications and Practical Knowledge," 329.
8. Scott, "Thin Simplifications and Practical Knowledge," 324.
9. Scott, "Thin Simplifications and Practical Knowledge," 340.
10. Kruks, *Retrieving Experience*, 234.

North American partners are learning skills of true listening. I do not mean that JustHope partners can know what a Nicaraguan's experience of poverty is like. However, we can learn something of what it is like to recognize a person sharing testimony about their experience of poverty. Being present to see, hear, and witness this testimony makes possible a new kind of knowing that is different from reading about poverty. Showing up and staying connected long term in such encounters is educational and transformational.

Furthermore, recognizing the benefits and problems with conceptual frames or perspectives can enhance collaborative knowledge production. Transnational partners aspire to be teachable, but too often those of us from the U.S. carry unrecognized assumptions of superiority. That imperious gaze and cultural elitism infects our ideas in ways we fail to recognize. Elisabeth Camp's work on both the advantages and problems with "frames" illustrates this dynamic. She states, "frames are representational vehicles with the function of expressing perspectives. Perspectives in turn are open-ended dispositions to interpret, and specifically to produce intuitive structures of thought about, or characterizations of, particular subjects."[11] But she was quick to point out how such frames can distort as well as make sense of our experience. She claims, "The fact that frames, perspectives, and characterizations can make genuine contributions does nothing to dislodge the point that they can also manipulate cognition and occlude understanding."[12] In a similar vein, Wayne Riggs explores the epistemic virtues of "Open-Mindedness" noting the "epistemological entwining" of ideas and concepts into "perspectives."[13] We may scrutinize and reject a propositional knowledge claim, but still be stuck with perspectives connected with rejected belief. In other words, beliefs are enmeshed in systemic patterns and structures, so they are not always easy to excise. These systems or frameworks are much like what Richard DeWitt described as worldviews or interconnected beliefs that interlock like pieces of a jigsaw puzzle.[14] Unless JustHope partners recognize the effects of their inherent conceptual frames, they are less skillful than they could be at caring and collaborating. Education requires the commitment to creative open-mindedness as a practice that respects the tacit knowledge of a potential partner in knowledge production.

11. Camp, "Perspectives and Frames," 18–19.
12. Camp, "Perspectives and Frames," 18–19.
13. Riggs, "Open-Mindedness," 148.
14. DeWitt, *Worldviews*, 7.

Cynthia Townley, in her book, *A Defense of Ignorance: Its Value for Knowers and Roles in Feminist and Social Epistemologies*, makes a similar argument. She suggests ways that something like open-mindedness is an important tool for skillful learning. She reflects on the ways that epistemic humility can function like a safeguard against being too quick to intervene in the lives of others. Townley appreciates the ability of those who are teachable, who are open to the insights of others. She warns against the type of dogmatic posture of those who are so enthralled with their own insights that they are unable to listen or see alternative views. Thus, she encourages learners to attend to the processes and practices of seeking knowledge rather than to the content of specific knowledge claims. The relational dynamics of sharing knowledge are enhanced by appreciation of ignorance if ignorance means something like what Riggs calls open-mindedness.[15] Townley writes, "Most significant is the shift of emphasis away from increasing knowledge to questions central to human practice, including an emphasis on the community in which epistemic interactions occur, with the distinct perspective that a focus on ignorance allows."[16] Townley credits feminist theory and praxis with her insights. Interdependence of those who would be knowers fosters insight and awareness of the benefits of ignorance. She claims, "The emphasis on epistemic dependence at the heart of my analysis is indebted to feminist critiques... I acknowledge the political dimensions to epistemic practices."[17] Awareness of the need for open-mindedness is a foundational value in feminist thought. Ironically, education requires unlearning, as these feminist and liberationist pedagogical tools illustrate.

The idea that there are universal truths to be taught through best practices of education is controversial and often rejected by postcolonial thinkers. However, the value of international interchange offers counterbalance to the focus on local, identity-based insight. I suspect that the closest we can get to universal truths are relational truths to be held loosely with humility and readiness to change our minds. Our dialogical exchanges need to cross borders and seek the widest inclusion possible. Liberation theologian Jon Sobrino writes, "I would ask all universities, and specifically those of the First World, to be universal, to see the whole world from the perspective of the Third World majorities, and not only

---

15. Riggs, "Open-Mindedness," 175.
16. Townley, *Defense of Ignorance*, 114.
17. Townley, *Defense of Ignorance*, 89.

from the exceptional islands of the First World."[18] The focus on education that JustHope partners share embodies this type of learning.

JustHope partners can gain greater self-awareness about impulses to dominate, to insist on being right, to push for perfectionistic ideals, and to react to avoid emotional distress. This type of learning is spiritual formation. Most people from the U.S. must undergo transformation to discover that Nicaraguans have as much to teach as to learn through transnational interchange. Mutuality and solidarity go both ways as Nicaraguans patiently bear with learners from the U.S. JustHope partners are attempting to do a difficult thing: to collaborate across cultural, linguistic, and economic chasms. This work engages spiritual discernment motivation. Building relationships across these types of borders requires patient teaching and learning. Education is key to the mission of JustHope.

18. Sobrino, *Spirituality of Liberation*, 172.

— 6

Collaboration in Health Care

When we actually went out and did what we said we were doing, which was listening to the poor, we discovered that we weren't listening enough. So, when we went and listened more, we heard them say, "I can't get to the clinic, the hours are inconvenient. I don't have someone to take care of my children while I am gone to clinic. I don't have enough to eat. I don't have a donkey to get me there." ... When we started addressing these structural problems, as opposed to things that were related only to individual patients or to the culture, mortality rates dropped ... Imagine, even after several years of reading and thinking, there's still more you can learn about how to structure a program by actually listening to people.[1]

—Farmer and Gutiérrez

Alarm clocks were unnecessary thanks to the early morning light and accompanying birdsong. The small, crowded bedrooms in the Peace House provided little in the way of privacy. Bill was digging through his duffle bag in the common room as he waited for his turn in the bathroom.

---

1. Farmer and Gutiérrez, *In the Company of the Poor*, 184.

"I am having trouble finding my deodorant," he muttered in a flustered tone to no one in particular. Laura and I were already dressed and sipping coffee in some rocking chairs nearby.

"Be sure to find that deodorant, or I will loan you mine!" Laura joked.

"It is hard living out of a suitcase for so many days," Bill said. "I've been sleeping on a bottom bunk and using the top bunk as a shelf. George and Martin are doing the same. I wonder how larger teams managed to share the space when people have to sleep on the top bunks, too?"

"Just think," Laura replied, "Most people here in Chacraseca often live their whole lives with less personal space than we have at the Peace House. And we have the flush toilets and indoor showers! I am reviewing my previous assumptions and expectations regarding what is necessary for adequate housing space," Laura said.

"Well, I just hope I have time to shave before breakfast," Bill grumbled.

Elizabeth, wrapped in a bathrobe, walked through the common room while brushing her teeth, headed toward the kitchen to use the sink. We were getting used to seeing each other as housemates.

On Wednesday, we would be exploring one of the major JustHope program areas: health care. We planned to go to the beach for supper that evening. Our workday would end earlier than usual to allow for this schedule. Our plan for the day was to connect with a JustHope medical team from Wichita. Since he and his wife both worked in healthcare, George was especially excited about this opportunity. He was curious about the team from Kansas and imagined that he and his wife might be part of a medical team like that in the future. The team of JustHope partners from Wichita were a group of medical professionals who had come to volunteer for a week, doing clinics each day in different areas. They were staying at a hotel in León and would meet us at the work site.

George, Paula, and Martin were the first who were ready to go after breakfast; they urged others to get moving. As our group bustled out to leave, Leslie reminded everyone to fill and bring their water bottles. Juan Pablo had the van door open, waiting for us. We had all agreed that we would leave by 7:45 to meet the medical team. By 7:45, everyone was on the van except Bill. Avoiding the hot van until the last moment, George stood by the van door trying to chat with Juan Pablo despite the limits of their language barrier. Bill must have still been in the Peace House. Moments passed. George stuck his head in the van and asked, "Should I go look for Bill?"

"Let's give him a few more minutes," Martin said. The challenge of living in community was on full display as irritation grew.

Someone sighed loudly in an expression of frustration. A few minutes later, Laura said, impatiently, "Let's go; it is hot in this van. Where is Bill?" No one responded. More awkward moments passed. The morning was already uncomfortably warm. I was sweating.

Finally, I asked, "Does someone want to go find Bill?"

"Bill, let's go! We are waiting. Where are you?" Martin screamed out the van window in the direction of the Peace House. A few more minutes passed, and George went to look for Bill. Moments later, they hustled toward the van together, with Bill locking the Peace House door on the way out.

"Are you okay?" Laura asked Bill.

"Sorry about that," Bill said. "I lost track of time."

"He couldn't hear us because he was sitting in front of the fan shaving," George laughed.

No one else laughed with him. I made a mental note to be sure we discussed this strain on the group during our processing time that evening. This type of interdependence and group community dynamic is an essential aspect of the learning for a team. Most of us are used to radical autonomy rather than the cooperation required to work collaboratively as a group with consideration for how our choices affect teammates.

We drove almost an hour down winding dirt roads, enjoying the slight breeze coming through the van windows while wondering about the day ahead of us. Dogs barked and roosters crowed as we passed dewy trees and tropical plants glowing in the slanting morning sun. We were intrigued with the various houses we passed along the way. Some were larger than others and freshly painted; others were nothing more than black plastic tarps stretched around poles or tree limbs. We caught glimpses of brilliantly orange and red flowering trees. Occasionally, we passed a person on the road, a woman carrying a large basket on her head, a motorcycle carrying a couple and two children. Bill said that he was noticing lots of paper and plastic trash along the roadside. Rose said she had noticed it, too. The van ride provided more opportunity to see life in the countryside. Eventually, Juan Pablo turned into a driveway towards a building where a few vehicles and a large group of people were gathering.

Dust wafted with the smell of diesel as our van rolled to a stop in front of a rough looking building constructed from concrete blocks and aluminum. The temporary one-day clinic would take place in this community building that is used for a school when there are teachers available. The building appeared dingy and inhospitable to the North American volunteers, but as the sun climbed, the shelter from the oppressive heat and glaring sun was welcome. The heat and humidity were already vexatious; despite this, forty or fifty Nicaraguans stood in line, looking both hopeful and determined, flashing shy, curious grins as we piled out of the van. Although we had traveled a long way over bumpy, dirt roads to reach this location, we realized that many of these Nicaraguans had walked long distances to get here this morning. We met the medical team from Wichita and their leader, Dr. Roberts. He and Julio seemed like old friends. They introduced us to another doctor, a pharmacist, a nurse, and a few other members of their team who were setting up. We began to help unload heavy trunks of supplies. As we got organized, Dr. Roberts told us he had been coming each year with JustHope since 2010. We asked him how we could help most that morning.

Our team members had various skills. Although George was the only member of our team who was a medical professional, others of us could help set up and assist with logistics. Some had the physical strength to carry heavy trunks and boxes of supplies. Local leaders helped move plastic lawn chairs and tables to accommodate the improvised medical services. We pulled tables together and began unpacking boxes and bottles of medications on the tables that would serve as the pharmacy. The Wichita team came prepared with a good system of small plastic sacks and labels printed in Spanish with directions for the most common prescriptions. We took direction from the pharmacist who told some of us how to package pills. Several workers would spend the day counting out pills and labeling them to be given as doctors directed. The pharmacy area was organized under a shady tree, to be ready for the first patients to bring prescriptions for medications. The doctors had clipboards with lists of the medications available for free distribution that day. A Nicaraguan doctor and nurse arrived, and Dr. Roberts greeted them warmly.

They devised three consultation areas with a few chairs at each station. Each U.S. doctor had a translator and sometimes a nurse to assist. We hung up sheets to fashion rooms that would provide some privacy for patients who needed to be examined more intimately. Our team members helped wherever we could.

Soon the doctors were ready to begin seeing patients. Francis, Nick, and a sector leader worked out a process for signing in patients and sending them to the consulting areas. Before long patients began coming to the pharmacy requesting medications with paper prescriptions. As we watched patients make their way from the doctors' stations toward the pharmacy, Francis came to translate for the pharmacy. She explained that it would have done no good for people to see the doctors if the team had not brought the medications. Most people could not afford to purchase the needed medications even if they had a prescription. Laura helped stick labels on sacks, instructed by the pharmacist. Rose and I watched people leave with sacks of medications that would last about 30 days. Rose asked how long it might be before people in this area saw doctors again. Francis said it might be three or four months. We grew more and more aware of the difficulty of depending on a temporary clinic. We watched women shepherding their families of multiple children, leaving with packets of pills for each child and themselves. Volunteers in the pharmacy knew that because illiteracy is high among this population, some adults might have trouble reading the instructions. We found ourselves hoping that the mothers would be able to keep track of which medication was intended for which child.

Translators worked closely with each doctor, communicating with patients about symptoms, treatment, and how to take the medications. In this remote, rural area of Chacraseca, it was almost thirty miles to the hospital in León. Even the permanent clinic in Chacraseca was more than ten miles away. We heard stories from some of the Nicaraguans who had walked hours in hopes of being seen by a doctor that day. People waited patiently, taking turns to sit in the few chairs available for those waiting to see doctors.

Although I continued working in the makeshift pharmacy, I was curious to hear how George was feeling and thinking about the process. He had been quite enthusiastic about JustHope health programs.

George's Reflection Journal

It was only after we returned to the U.S., and I read pages from George's journal reflections that I realized what a potent experience he had that day. I was thankful he was willing for me to include his writing from that night about his encounter. He wrote:

> *Dr. Smith, a doctor from Wichita, invited me to sit at her station just inside the first corner of the building and observe her work. The room was swelteringly hot, but at least we were not in the sun. Julio sat with*

us offering translation. I was intrigued by the first few patients who described problems like neck and stomach pain. Dr. Smith, who had been to Nicaragua with JustHope on two prior trips, explained that she wished she was not so dependent on Julio's translation. I sympathized and agreed. Her next patient was a woman with two small children clinging close to her and an infant she held in her arms. She had heard from a neighbor that the medical clinic would be offered that day. After walking more than an hour with her children, wearing their best clothes and plastic shoes, they had already been waiting several hours in line. I wondered what her options would have been to seek care if the clinic had not come to her area that day. She began to describe her symptoms to the doctor through the help of Julio. She asked the doctor to examine each of her children, and talked about problems they had as well, although none of them appeared ill to me. The doctor wrote out prescriptions for the woman and each of her children. After she left, I asked Dr. Smith about this because I was surprised that the doctor provided medicine for children who did not seem sick. She explained that since few people could afford what we consider common, over-the-counter medications for childhood illnesses, she was willing to write prescriptions that would meet future needs. Even a woman whose children are not currently sick would want to take advantage of the opportunity to take home Tylenol or decongestants. These medications could prevent more serious diseases from developing in some cases.

Over the next hours we saw some people who were quite ill, and others who seemed to have less serious or urgent complaints. I noticed patterns in the types of ailments that doctors were seeing in patients. Many people had parasites. The water and sewage systems were inadequate. I knew that without systematic changes, the short-term supply of parasite medicine would not be a permanent solution. High blood pressure, diabetes, and back pain were common as well. Julio and Dr. Smith remarked on the strain people caused by carrying baskets, buckets, and heavy bundles balanced on their heads. The consequences of systemic poverty manifested quickly. I realized that I was accustomed to being able to help people and solve common health problems. I began to grow frustrated with seeing cases that could easily be addressed in my hometown with plentiful, inexpensive, over-the-counter medications. I wondered why the Nicaraguan government couldn't do a better job of providing health care for these people. As the day wore on,

I found myself increasingly impatient with the heat, the insects, the harsh sun beating down and the poverty surrounding me.

A teen-age boy came limping from a wagon with an ugly gash on his leg. The swelling and coloration indicated an infection that could be serious without treatment. As Dr. Smith removed the soiled strips of cloth from the wound, I thought again about how often I tended to take for granted access to everyday antibiotics and first aid products back home. Dr. Smith invited me to clean and bandage the boy's leg as she wrote prescriptions for antibiotics. Glad to do something useful, I went to the pharmacy and asked for clean dressing materials I needed. As I returned with the supplies, I smiled at the frightened looking boy and his mother, hoping to reassure them. With Julio's help we chatted as I cleaned and dressed the wound. I asked what the boy would have done if the clinic had not been available in his area that day. They explained that the family would either attempt to treat the injury at home or pay for transportation to the nearest clinic or hospital in León. I realized that for families struggling to afford food, the cost of treating an injury could be devastating. Cleaning and dressing the leg was painful, but the kid was stoic. I was confident he would be better in a few days.

After a few hours, a woman came with an infant who looked to be about a year old. This was the sickest person we had seen all morning. The baby had had diarrhea and high fever for several days and looked dehydrated and limp. The mother looked anxious and frightened. The doctor examined the child quickly and asked how far away the woman lived. She said it took more than an hour to walk to her home. I was thankful for the hydration packets that were available in the pharmacy, but I knew that without access to safe water, the problem was serious. The doctor asked me to go to the pharmacy and get a packet of hydration salts.

I walked over toward the shade tree pharmacy. About a dozen Nicaraguans were crowding around the table, waiting for medications. Some of our team members were assisting the medical team volunteers who were counting out pills and labeling packets. A translator was explaining the directions for each medication to a person receiving several items. I felt impatient as I walked around behind the table looking for the hydration treatment. Everywhere I looked, people were crowding around tables that were piled with stacks of medication. There was not enough table space. The area seemed chaotic. The buzz of the crowd speaking Spanish irritated me. It occurred to me that I felt frustrated because I was frightened for the sick infant and for the baby's mother. Elizabeth helped me to find the packets I needed. The pharmacy had a few bottles of water available for mixing medication. I took one and headed back to the waiting doctor.

The doctor read the instructions on the package and told me that she had never used this before but had read about it. I had never seen it used either. I helped mix the hydration salts in the bottle of water according to the directions. Then I had to go in search of a cup to give the infant the liquid. Once again, I needed to pass through a crowd of people waiting to see the doctors. Everywhere, people were speaking Spanish that I was unable to understand. I interrupted volunteers at the pharmacy again to ask for a cup. I knew that my emotional agitation was a response to the critical situation of the seriously ill infant, but I still felt irritable with the people who seemed to be in the way. When I joined the doctor again and poured a small amount of the liquid into the cup, she held the cup to the listless child's mouth for a sip.

The infant barely tasted the salty solution and jerked away, clamping his mouth shut. As Dr. Smith explained to the mother the importance of making the child drink this fluid, the mother began to shift uncomfortably on the plastic chair. She tried to force the child to drink. The child squirmed, spit out the liquid, and began to cry. We each tried to get the kid to swallow a sip. No luck at all. How would we get the infant to drink? I knew the liquid probably tasted salty and unappealing. I found myself becoming angry, thinking that the child needed to go to the hospital or somewhere to receive intravenous fluids. Not knowing what else to do, the doctor had Julio explain that the mother should continue trying to get the child to drink the fluid. The rest of the team was beginning to stop for a lunch break. We would need to see the infant again in the early afternoon. The anxious mother took her infant and children and moved to a bench in the shade of a tree.

I started thinking maybe I could get a hotel room for her and the child in León for a few days to make sure they had clean, safe water as the infant recovered. My thoughts were running away. Could I help raise money when I went back home to make sure this community all had access to safe water? Childhood diseases like severe diarrhea could easily be prevented. It seemed unbelievable to me that this community wasn't preventing cases like this.

Francis and Julio were explaining to the people waiting in the still growing line that the volunteers would take a break to eat lunch and return to see more people soon. Stepping from the shade out to the hot sun beating down, I realized that I was hungry. I joined the others from our team, but I was still distracted from worry about the infant. I was sick and tired of trying to understand Spanish. The few words I had learned and my pitiful attempts to communicate seemed futile. We walked the distance of a few blocks to a nearby home of a community leader. Under some trees outside the house, our group sat at a plastic table and lawn chairs, but there were not enough chairs for all of us. We took turns eating in shifts because there were not enough plastic plates or forks for everyone to eat at the same time. I waited to let others eat first. I wasn't sure I could swallow food even though I knew I needed to eat. I sucked down water from my own bottle and waited. Lunch was a better meal than what most in the community could afford on a regular basis. Paula asked about who purchased the food, and Leslie explained that JustHope paid for the groceries, and leaders in this neighborhood cooked. Each plate included a piece of chicken in addition to the ubiquitous rice, beans, yuca, tortillas, and vegetables. When the first round of us finished eating, Nicaraguan women took the plastic plates, cups, and forks and rinsed them quickly as the rest of us sat down. I thought about the system of washing dishes without hot water and remembered the cases of illness I had seen that day.

I looked at the food on the plate in front of me and still wasn't sure I could eat. A tight, hard lump in my throat seemed to be making it difficult to swallow the dry tortilla in my hand. My own internal dialogue seemed irritable and even judgmental to me. Surely these people could improve the way they cooked and washed dishes, I thought. It was a relief to be sitting at a table with a group speaking English. I realized that I was surprised at some of my own thoughts. I felt resentful toward Julio and Francis at the end of the table who continued to speak Spanish with each other. I acknowledged to myself that some of my frustration could be a response to my first taste of being immersed in a culture where English-speakers are not the majority. I noticed that I felt myself gravitating to the other white members of the team. I felt embarrassed and ashamed as I wondered if some of my discomfort was about race as well as culture or language. When Rose asked me if I was all right, I recognized how much I was struggling emotionally. I began to explain to Rose about the young mother and sick infant. I didn't feel like talking much, but I appreciated being able to explain about how frustrating it was.

I felt angry with Dr. Smith, who seemed able to enjoy her lunch while I was obsessing about the dehydrated infant whose mother couldn't get him to drink the rehydration fluids. Although I did not want to think or feel this way, I admitted to Rose that criticisms of the Nicaraguans running through my mind might be connected with this sense of helplessness I was feeling. I found myself thinking of ways to fix what seemed to be problems in the Nicaraguan community. I couldn't understand how the lack of resources and development could be anything other than consequences of something I could help fix.

I said to Rose, "There are lots of ways to get resources donated to help these people. I know how to raise money. I could contact pharmaceutical companies. I have colleagues who could afford to donate money. If only the people here had access to the systems from our community back home!" I exclaimed. "But I am afraid this infant is going to die. We have the hydration fluid, but the baby won't swallow it." My voice was charged with strong emotion. My body was tense.

After the team had finished lunch, we returned to the clinic and began seeing patients again. The crowd of waiting people was smaller than it had been in the early morning, but others had been arriving all morning. I saw the mother with the dehydrated baby waiting nearby. Rose followed me to check in with the mother. Although Rose was not a medical professional, she had plenty of experience with young children and infants. We could see that the infant still had not swallowed the salty solution in the paper cup. Rose called Francis who had been working with them at the pharmacy all morning and asked for help. Rose had Francis ask the mother whether the infant usually drank from a cup or a bottle. The mother replied that the infant did not drink from a cup well yet and still used a bottle. Francis went in search of an empty baby bottle. I thought that surely the infant was old enough to be drinking from a cup in a situation like this. Before long, Francis returned and filled the bottle with the rehydration liquid. The baby began sucking it down. Rose and Francis smiled at each other, and the mother seemed to relax, too. I was amazed. With all my medical information and expertise, I hadn't thought of a baby bottle.

The afternoon wore on, and eventually, every person who had been waiting in line was able to talk to a doctor. At one point, I had seen Dr. Smith go over and talk with the mother whose infant had been so ill. With the help of liquid Tylenol and hydration, the infant looked better already, and the fever was lower. Dr. Smith and Julio talked with *the mother about care and prevention in the future. They urged her to seek alternative sources for safe water and to be mindful of watching for changes. Tears stung my eyes as I wondered about the future for that infant, whose symptoms could have been treated so easily back in the U.S. I watched with concern as the mother left, carrying the infant to begin the long walk to her home. Eventually, the pharmacy finished filling the last prescription. We began packing up trunks of supplies and loading them on the vans to leave.*

During the rest of the afternoon, I struggled to process my anger and frustration. During free time, I laid on my bunk thinking. Hours later, as I heard other team members sharing snacks and laughing together, I still felt grim and moody. When I tried to relax and rest, I found myself overwhelmed with a sense of unfairness. The stark contrast between the resources and opportunities available to me since birth and the situations of people born in Chacraseca floored me. Instead of feeling gratitude for my good fortune, I felt anger that people here had such bitter struggles with poverty. Such an intense jumble of feelings and thoughts welled up inside of me that I felt exhausted. I tried to pray. That seemed stupid. Finally, I decided to write in my journal to get some of this on paper. At least I can fulfill my assignment to write these journal pages. Reflective writing helps me sort out my feelings. Thinking back on the day, I can see that culture shock is real. My impulse to try to fix everything with money also surprises me. I know that some JustHope teams work at temporary day clinics like Dr. Smith's team did with us today. I would like to come back with a medical team to do more of that type of care in the future.

That writing from George's journal reflections described our day better than I could. His self-awareness and insight in those pages he wrote were exceptional.

In contrast to the remote areas that only have occasional temporary clinics like the one we observed that day, the center of Chacraseca is served by a permanent clinic that is open five days a week. We were all interested in touring the medical clinic two doors down from the Peace House. Our team visited the clinic and met Dr. Dora, who travels from León to work there each weekday. She told us the ability to provide consistent care, including immunizations, prenatal vitamins, check-ups, and first aid makes a big difference in the health of the community. The Nicaraguan ministry of health pays her salary and provides a few medications. JustHope stocks the clinic there with most of the needed supplies and medications. Although the clinic building looked rustic and poor in our eyes, we realized that it was a great asset compared with the improvised day clinic we had just witnessed.

Thanks to the persistent leadership in the community of Chacraseca and sustained partnerships with JustHope and other NGOs over many decades, this permanent medical clinic is open year-round. Dr. Dora expressed appreciation for the consistent availability of medical services and pharmacy stocked by JustHope, supplementing the meager medications and supplies provided by the Nicaraguan government. The clinic there was built about a decade ago and has been operating consistently thanks to the partnership of the Nicaraguan health ministry and the JustHope volunteers. Health outcomes have improved dramatically during that time. Although this is a vast improvement for those who live within walking distance, emergencies or health crises sometimes occur when the doctor is not present. There is no ambulance in Chacraseca. If an accident results in a serious injury, a neighbor with a motorcycle, jeep, or pickup truck must be found to transport the patient to the hospital.

While visiting the clinic there, we met Sarah, a nurse from North America who was volunteering for several months with the local doctor in Chacraseca. She told us about an experience from the previous week. A young woman did not show up for her appointment close to the due date of her expected delivery. Sarah and Dr. Dora walked several miles to check on the woman, who was at home with a toddler. They asked how the woman planned to go to the hospital in León for the birth. She explained that her brother, who lives nearby, would drive her on the back of his motorcycle over the rough, dusty, unpaved road that spans the twenty-minute ride to the hospital. This week, when Sarah and the doctor checked on her at home again, the young mother was back after the delivery of the new infant. Sarah said that the dark, hot, dusty house did not look like a safe, healthy place for anyone to live. It was hard for her to imagine bringing a new baby there. Yet, hearing about the ride on the back of a motorcycle during the process of labor was also unimaginable.

In the clinic building, we also met the dentist, Dr. Samson, who lives in León and works in Chacraseca several days a week. He proudly showed us the dentist's chair where patients recline for examination and treatment. This chair had been donated and shipped by another dentist from the U.S. that came to volunteer with Just Hope. Dr. Samson was clearly delighted with the chair, although it looked well-used and old to me, like something I remembered from a dentist office during my childhood many decades ago. We asked him what problems he sees most often.

"We have a problem here because of sugary drinks," he said. "I would like to work more on prevention." He thanked us and praised JustHope volunteers, like a team from Tulsa Community College that had brought volunteers trained in dental hygiene and dentistry.

After visiting the clinic in Chacraseca, the team from Wichita left to return to León. Our team enjoyed a brief free time before our reflection circle. I noticed George stayed in his room. Some team members tried to check email, and a few were able to get a strong enough signal if they found just the right spot to connect. Others took cold showers that felt so refreshing they didn't even resent the lack of warm water. I stretched out on my bunk for ten minutes of silence, thinking over my experience of the day.

Because we planned to visit León and have supper at the beach, we shared reflections in mid-afternoon. We all had plenty to think about, and we realized that we had many questions. How did the people out in the remote rural area we had visited that morning learn about the clinic that day? How was the decision made about where the clinic would be set up? What do doctors do if they encounter a patient who needs surgery, x-rays, or treatment beyond what is available that day? How could we contribute to future efforts to improve the lives of the people we had met? Most importantly, we wondered what it had been like for those who had just received medical care at these clinics.

Daily Reflection

When we formed our rocking chair circle on the porch for our group process time, we relaxed into the comfort and familiarity of being together as North Americans who spoke the same language. We laughed awkwardly over how nice it was to communicate without a translator for a little while. I invited everyone to share reflections on the events of the day. I had noticed George struggling throughout the day and hoped he would talk, but he sat in silence. I was glad when Bill began to share about his reflections on the day.

"I was thankful for the opportunity to see some of the farming practices as we drove to the work site today," Bill said. "Some of the crops, like the sesame seed and the cotton, look too dry, and I can see how poor the soil is around here," he continued. "I did have an uncomfortable moment during the day when I was trying to talk with a man about my age who had just gotten some medications at the clinic. Julio translated for me, and I tried to ask the guy about his farm, but he did not say much," Bill said. "It felt like there was a barrier between us. I wondered if that was due to language, culture or even race. I thought about that moment when we arrived at the airport in Managua, and I noticed that we were surrounded by a sea of people speaking a language I did not know. I had to admit, I also noticed that I was not accustomed to seeing so many faces that were not white," Bill shared. I saw Bill glance sheepishly at Rose, perhaps aware of her identity as a person of color.

As an educator, I realized that talking about race and racism so openly in a mixed race group was unusual for many students, especially white students. This was a potent moment with great potential for our learning process. I wanted the class to explore dynamics of racism and systemic injustice that related to race, and I knew this would be challenging.

"Thank you for your openness in addressing the topic of race," I said to Bill. "Those of us who embody white privilege often operate without consciousness of how race dynamics function. I would like for us to continue exploring these issues of how race and racism influence our experience here." I asked the class to sit in silence a few more moments, considering possible examples of race relations or racism they had encountered during the trip.

As a white teacher, I have sometimes felt bewildered when anger and conflict emerge in a classroom during learning about racism and anti-racism activism. My students are mostly mid-western, white and have limited experience with intercultural dialogue. Typically, they will pastor in small communities that are predominantly white. They may be uncritical about power dynamics and triggers that can occur during intercultural dialogue. They are often theological liberals who feel guilty and somewhat helpless about racial injustices. However, it is not unusual for them to have some defensiveness or even resistance about facing white privilege. At the same time, each course typically has one or two students of color. I strive to avoid increasing the burden on those students of color when we discuss racial conflict. Furthermore, my own embodiment as a white woman invites reflection within these systems of learning communities. I frequently make missteps, and the impact of my words is sometimes harmful, despite my best intentions to act as an ally in anti-racism work.

My goals are to discover, practice, and promote teaching and learning that dismantles systemic patterns of white privilege during intercultural dialogue. If I am successful, students will practice identifying triggers and expanding options for self-awareness and self-regulation as qualities of leaders and competencies for intercultural dialogue. This context where all students are experiencing an unfamiliar culture provides an interesting opportunity to discuss intercultural dialogue and anti-racism activism. North American students immersed in a Nicaraguan community where whites are not the majority have a new perspective to expand insights about race dynamics. Pastors and community leaders need competencies for intercultural dialogue. These skills are likely to be even more valuable and necessary in the future. I hope students will gain new self-awareness, confidence, and skills for more just participation in intercultural dialogue. I was thankful that Bill steered the conversation this direction.

Nick was the next to speak. "I have noticed my own emotional dynamic of heightened consciousness about racial difference in the interactions since we arrived," he said. "I live in rural Kansas now, and I am accustomed to being surrounded by white faces for the most part. But I went to college with many international students. My roommate in the dorm was from Argentina. I frequently experienced classmates and friends having conversations in other languages. This reminds me of how lost I sometimes felt. As a white person, I grew up wanting to understand and even work to correct injustices related to racial bias. I was raised to believe in racial equality. I think of myself as someone working for equality and fairness. I value cultural diversity, but it is difficult to be surrounded all day with people who don't speak my language. When I take time to reflect deeply, I know I have feelings of vulnerability and frustration. I'm not sure how much is related to race versus language," Nick said.

Martin responded, "Yes, I am politically and ideologically committed to the idea that each culture has beauty, dignity, and unique characteristics that must be appreciated on their own terms. At the same time, I have found myself comparing benefits of our culture back home with life here. For example, today I kept feeling critical about all the young women bringing so many children to the clinic. Where are the fathers? I need to think more about whether implicit bias or roots of racism are part of my reactions. I realized today that I had been reacting to the discomfort of culture shock by obsessively planning and considering ways to spend money from the U.S. to provide material solutions. I have been surprised to discover that my first reaction to being immersed in another culture was to make judgements and assume Nicaraguans would want to be more like North Americans if they just knew how. Even more painful is the realization that my discomfort of being in the minority for this brief encounter brought to mind how little internal work I have done comprehending white privilege and systemic racism. At the same time, I am horrified by any conscious thoughts or feelings that my own culture is superior," Martin said. "Maybe it is just that my own culture is familiar."

Rose said, "I had an interesting experience today that made me think about race in a new way. While we were working in the pharmacy, one of the women who came to get medicine asked me if I was Nicaraguan. She said I looked Nicaraguan. It surprised me! About an hour later, another person asked the same thing. I am not even sure how I feel about it. Since we arrived I have been reminded of ways I have been born into systems of privilege as a U.S. citizen even though I am a Black woman."

"I appreciate your vulnerability in talking openly about this," I said. "It is interesting to wonder how culture, race, and economic privilege are entwined."

Bill said, "There was a moment today when I realized suddenly that the three of us from the team were the only white people in the building. I thought this must be what it feels like to be surrounded by people of another racial identity. I never understood at a gut level what it is like to be a minority."

Rose looked down at the floor. I suspected that she might be weighing choices about how to respond. I guessed that, as a Black woman who grew up in Texas, she could have told a number of stories in response to Bill's last statement. However, Laura spoke up quickly.

"Recently, I have been involved in anti-racism work that is helping me recognize some consequences of my white privilege," Laura said. "I suspect that those of us who are white may carry a sense of self assurance and internal confidence even when we are not numerically in the majority. My experience has been that, as a white person, I move through the world with a sense of entitlement and tendency to overlay my privilege on others even if I am immersed in a diverse community or culture. Maybe what I mean to say is that I am pretty sure I don't know what it is like to be a racial minority even though I have an experience like we had today."

I was impressed with the way Laura seemed to be making an effort to modulate her tone of voice. She made some points that I hoped the class could absorb and consider.

George responded to Laura with a defensive tone in his voice. "Laura, I guess I have been on an emotional roller coaster all day and discovering things I had not expected. In some of our seminary classes, the curriculum included discussion of race relations and white supremacy. I have worked as a professional with people of different races for years. I am still surprised to see I have deeper layers to work through on these issues."

"Do you find that people do not often discuss race dynamics in your circles at home?" I asked.

"Except for our classes at seminary, I haven't ever been in groups that discussed racism or race dynamics," George said. Other students nodded in agreement.

"That is part of how privilege works," Leslie said. "Privilege is invisible. Those of us with white privilege may not have thought much about it or discussed it openly."

"I have heard Julio say that racism as it exists in the United States is not an issue here in Nicaragua," I said. "However, I have also heard that in the eastern part of Nicaragua there is more racial tension, even conflict."

I appreciated this opportunity to reflect with this group about systemic racism. I shared with the group my wish for opportunity to talk more about race with our Nicaraguan partners. In my dialogue with JustHope staff and translators in recent years, I have heard other Nicaraguans make the claim that race is not a problem in Latin America the way it is in the U.S. Although I agree that the history and the dynamics in the U.S. are different, I appreciate the insights of Amy Chua, who documents a pattern she observed throughout Latin America. She claims, "A tiny, light-skinned, market-dominant minority has always had a stranglehold on economic and political power," and this illustrates bias "deeply internalized by suppressed color hierarchy." She pointed out that Latin Americans hold the belief that their societies enjoy racial harmony in contrast to the racial conflict in the U.S., and this has "long been a source of pride."[2] She wrote:

> Throughout Latin America, centuries of ethnic degradation and discrimination, not to mention disenfranchisement and violence, have left deep, lasting psychological scars. A dashing blond, water-skiing Bolivian recently assured me that "in my country everyone is mestizo, everyone has some Indian blood," then later in the same conversation asserted, with equal

---

2. Chua, *World on Fire*, 69.

equanimity, that "no member of the upper class would even think of marrying a Quechua."[3]

I have observed similar dynamics in Nicaragua. Race relations might be one area of possible collaborative learning and healing for partner trips. However, part of such work requires unmasking and dismantling white supremacy and patterns of neocolonial dominance. I told the group that I had made plenty of mistakes but wanted to continue learning to be an ally in anti-racism work. Rooting out the seeds of supremacy and racism is ongoing work that requires lifelong commitment. As Adrienne Marie Brown writes, "White supremacy is a virus that distorts every lens of the mind, making it impossible to see the vulnerable, mundane, same same same body."[4] These are key issues that challenge collaboration. Healthy individuals and healthy societies require attention to these issues of equity and justice. Intersectional approaches in critical race theory exemplify praxis that integrates action for justice with relational truth.[5]

"I bet talking about racism and racial justice issues is challenging for all of us," Laura said. "Before we try to dialogue with our Nicaraguan partners here about race, I would think we might need to do some of our own work first. The anti-racism workshops I participated in required that those of us with white privilege work with each other first to get in touch with our own process without adding to the burden of historical injustice. That has helped me recognize some of my own patterns."

"Intentional anti-racism work could really enhance awareness of JustHope partners," I said. "Do you think diversity training should be part of the preparation?" I asked the group. "Maybe all JustHope partners need to talk about decentering whiteness and dismantling systems of white supremacy."

"I don't know that I could have prepared for the experience ahead of time. It is fascinating how unfamiliar it feels to talk openly about racism," George said. "Another darn learning experience!" he joked. Others in the circle nodded sympathetically.

"Working to become an anti-racist ally is a commitment to life-long learning, listening, and changing," Laura said. "I had an eye-opening experience today, too."

---

3. Chua, *World on Fire*, 71.
4. Brown, "Touching White Supremacy," 191.
5. Collins, *Black Feminist Thought*.

Laura began telling the group about a conversation she heard between a translator and a nurse that day. At the rural day clinic, Laura had been assisting one doctor and nurse in the afternoon. A young mother came in with one small boy who looked about one year old. When they asked her if she had other children, she replied that she had two others who had died. When asked about the name of the baby boy, she just shrugged. When the translator asked the question in another way, the woman explained that in her neighborhood near the free trade zone in Managua, people don't name their children until they are about a year old because so many die during the first year. Although the translator was translating the conversation to Laura and the nurse, who was also from the U.S., Laura had checked with the translator later to make sure she understood the conversation correctly. Laura said she was stunned. The woman was in the area visiting her parents, who lived on a farm, but said she would have to go back to work in Managua next week.

When I asked what other images or experience we could recall from the day, Bill said, "One of my memories from today is something I saw as our van passed bicycles, an ox pulling a simple cart piled with fire wood, a horse hauling a wagon with aluminum canisters of fresh milk, and numerous walkers on the road before pulling up in the community waiting for the doctors. It reminded me a little of stories my grandparents told about life on the farm when they were young. I thought about how my back would ache when I helped with chores on the farm years ago."

Nick said, "Yes, I noticed that many of the people complained to the doctor of neck and back pain. No wonder they have that kind of pain carrying those heavy loads on their heads. I saw an older woman carrying a huge bundle on her head out in the middle of nowhere as we drove along. I bet everyone needs pain relief."

Rose shared that she had worked with the pharmacy team all morning. "The industrial size bottles of ibuprofen and the other most common pills were huge. We divided the tablets into small plastic bags with 30 or 40 in each, then labeled each bag. I spent all morning counting out pills. When we emptied the first of those big containers, we started to pile the trash in a sack. But one of the women who was watching us and waiting for her prescription waved at us and asked if she could have the big empty bottle and the white cotton that had been in the top. Then when we took a break for lunch and walked down the block, the woman who had taken the empty bottles came out and took me by the hand, inviting me to come see her house. I couldn't speak Spanish, and she couldn't speak English, but she was proud to show me her house. I was amazed to see that the only things in her house were a bed made of some old lumber and a plastic table and one plastic chair. Almost the only thing in the house was the little packages of pills on the table and the empty pill bottle with the cotton. It made me realize how valuable a clean storage bottle with a lid and clean cotton could be. I felt crazy that I had been prepared to simply toss that stuff out as trash."

Paula started and stopped herself a few times, as if she was nervously trying to decide whether to make a comment. She obviously felt self-conscious as she carefully articulated her question. "Has anyone else wondered about obesity here? I know there are severe levels of hunger for some, but it looks as if some of the people we meet here are overweight."

Bill jumped in immediately, "I'm glad you raised the question. I have wondered about it, too."

Leslie did not react immediately, and George responded, "Sometimes malnutrition can result in a high carb diet that still lacks sufficient protein or essential nutrients. So it is not uncommon for people to be overweight and become diabetic in communities where there are shortages of food. But some of the bloated bellies we saw today were from parasites."

"Ew," Paula said.

Then Leslie explained that diabetes is a serious health concern because cheap calories come from white rice, sugary fruit drinks or soda pop, tortillas, and beans. Especially for those who experienced food insecurity and scarcity as children, weight gain is not surprising on this high-carb diet. "So, we do see people who look heavy, but we still see many, especially children, who do not have sufficient food for healthy development. Hunger is also a great threat to the most elderly in the community."

"I am still trying to figure out how the day clinic we saw today got organized," Rose said.

Leslie explained how the system depends on sector leaders keeping in touch with neighbors in their area for communication. When a clinic is offered in a rural area many sector leaders and neighbors work to organize the services and volunteers.

We continued to think over the long day. Then, I told the class that I wanted to try an exercise of imagining ourselves in the shoes of someone we met that day. "We will spend a few moments in silence while we think and imagine," I said. "Then I want you to speak in first person voice, as if you were a Nicaraguan at the clinic today. Tell about the day as if you were that individual. We can't presume to know what their experience was like, but we can try to get closer to understanding."

After some moments of pregnant silence, Martin spoke first. He said, "I am trying to imagine that I was that teenage boy with the bloody leg." Martin leaned back and closed his eyes trying to speak as if he was the boy. "This is how I imagine it. I lived my whole life on a farm down miles of dirt roads where the nearest town is almost fifteen miles away. I feel stupid and embarrassed because I cut my own leg in an accident with my machete. It hurts like hell, and after a few days, it is getting more painful and may be infected. For many generations, my family has managed to barely make a living, but food is often scarce. I know that a trip to the medical clinic in town would require money for transportation, not to mention more money for the clinic and even more for medicine. I become more afraid, seeing my mother look worried as my leg is swollen and more painful day by day. I imagine that my mother places a cool hand on my forehead as she studies my face with a worried look. She is sure I have a fever. Fortunately, she heard from a community leader in the neighborhood that some volunteers will be setting up a one-day health care clinic with nurses and doctors who have even brought medicine to dispense. She will ask our neighbor to take me in his wagon, so I can get health care help next Friday. The community leader said anyone can be seen for only one dollar. Even that dollar will deplete my family's resources, but the cost is much more manageable than the alternative. It is no exaggeration to say that a person could die from a bad infection. I have heard my mother and grandfather discussing a story about a neighbor who died from an infected cut. I feel scared.

Our neighbor is the leader of our sector, and he said there will be a clinic in our area this week on Wednesday. My leg has continued to look more infected. I can barely stand on it. My grandfather has been applying some herbal and saltwater mixture to clean the wound, but I don't think it is getting better. I wondered if someone could take me by motorcycle the ten miles to the center of Chacraseca to see the doctor there, but that would cost money my family doesn't have. I have to wait until Wednesday.

My grandfather tells a story I have never heard before about a time when he was a child. His brother accidentally cut his ankle with a machete while chopping yuca. It was so bad that he could not walk at all. It was hard to stop the bleeding, and everyone knew he had to go to the hospital in León. He had to be taken in the back of a neighbor's ox cart because there was no other way to get him to town.

While it was still dark on Wednesday morning, my mother helps me climb into the back of our neighbor's wagon. The jolting wagon bumps over the rough road and jarred my painful leg, but as I listen to the clopping sound of the horse's hooves, I appreciate the ride. My mother pedals her old bicycle beside the wagon during the ride to the old community building. She wants to be early in line to make sure I get care. When we arrive at the building, a few other people are already gathering. We join them in line. The time drags by as we wait. A few hours later, the line has grown, and the day is getting warm. Most people are sitting on the edge of the porch in line, although a few are standing. Because of my leg, someone brought me a plastic chair to sit in while we wait. I am sitting down, but I feel embarrassed because many elderly people continue to stand. Several leaders from our sector who are part of the Chacraseca leadership committee answer questions about how to line up and how the clinic will be organized that day.

When we hear the engine noise of a large van coming that way, my mother and I are relieved. We watch quietly as about a dozen people with expensive looking clothes, hats, and shoes begin to unload the van and set up. A little later, another van pulls up with more gringos who are speaking in a language that I guess is English. They seem cheerful and energetic, loud, and forceful in their movements.

My mother and I are curious about these gringos who look so busy as they set up the tables quickly. We watch them carry large, heavy trunks to an area under a nearby tree, where tables are organized with medicine. We wonder what kind of things they have that might help me. Finally, the first patients begin to file up to each doctor's table. When it is my turn, I lean on my mother as I slowly move toward the table. Maybe I feel a little embarrassed that I draw such comfort from my mother's presence. I have never talked with gringos before. I am glad that a translator who speaks good Spanish is there to help communicate. The doctor watches as I unwind the strips of cloth around my leg. She frowns looking at the wound and says something to the younger man with him who goes toward the pharmacy tables. He comes back with some packages, and I wonder what they will do next. My mother's hand rests on my shoulder in reassuring silence as they begin to use soft, clean, white cloth with some liquid they pour over the cut. My leg stings, but I know I need this help. The translator explains that the doctor will give me pills that will help with the pain and heal the infection. They tape a clean pad covered with ointment over the wound, and I think the pain eases a little. The translator explains what the doctor is saying. They do not think I will have to go to the hospital unless my leg gets worse. Taking the small paper with the doctor's writing, my mother and I walk to the pharmacy table and wait in line to get the packages of pills. I don't feel better yet, but my mother seems satisfied that I will not have to go to the hospital. I try to keep the new bandage clean as I perch on the bike in front of my mother, who begins the long ride toward our home." After Martin stopped speaking, our group sat in silence several minutes.

"Great job!" I said. "I like the way you put yourself in that role." I was pleased that Martin had managed to imagine vividly and articulate his insight well. This exercise of imagination seemed worthwhile. The group sat in silence a few moments waiting to see who else would attempt the task.

Laura spoke next. She said, "I imagine that I am a local sector leader in a remote area of the farmland around Chacraseca. I have to deal with a network of dirt roads that is often impassable due to the torrential seasonal rains, but it is the only pathway for transportation to the more densely populated center of Chacraseca. My neighbors struggle to have enough time and energy to complete their subsistence farming, much less manage to provide wellness checks for their children or elderly relatives. Although many women do travel to León to give birth, they often make arrangements to travel days or weeks before the due date to avoid being stuck far from health care assistance during labor. Having the clinic near the Peace House has been a big improvement, since the doctor is there during weekdays. But, from time to time, some accident or emergency happens when the only option is a trip to the hospital in León. When I gave birth to my children, I rode behind my husband on a motorcycle to León.

I have mixed feelings about the North American volunteers who come to provide assistance. On the one hand, I am proud of my government and know that my country wants to provide healthcare for our own people. I know that many Nicaraguan doctors and nurses can't find work because there are not enough jobs for them. I wonder if the volunteer services provided by these foreigners contribute to the lack of opportunities for Nicaraguan health providers. On the other hand, I know that our government struggles with inadequate financial resources to fund the healthcare that is needed. MINSA, the Nicaraguan Ministry of Health, has developed systems to regulate volunteers from outside the country who come to offer medical assistance. I remember when I was a child, and a group of volunteers came who were medical students that had not completed their training yet. Some people in the community murmured that they felt like animals in a laboratory being used for testing and training. How could we trust that these volunteers really knew what they were doing at all? Some people in my community thought some of them might not even be licensed to practice medicine in their own country. But I also heard people complain about all the bureaucracy and forms that made it difficult for volunteers to obtain approval to come offer services and bring medications. I can see that there had to be some control over these teams of volunteers bringing multiple trunks of medications across the border. I also heard rumors that sometimes people brought medications that were no longer safe or effective according to the expiration dates printed on the packages. Did the volunteers in the pharmacy know enough to ensure the safety of the instructions and packaging of the medicines they dispensed?

I imagine that after I attended the meeting of ACOPADES and heard there would be a medical team coming to my sector, I visited almost every home of my neighbors to tell them about the opportunity. I was frustrated that some asked if the doctors would be Nicaraguan or American doctors. I knew that people valued the chance to see American doctors, but that felt unfair to doctors from our own community. Still, I knew that this visit from American doctors would motivate people to show up. After the day was all over, I felt thankful for the help in our sector." Laura ended her story. Our group sat in silence a few moments.

Elizabeth spoke next. She said, "I am imagining that I am one of those doctors from Wichita. I am not used to seeing people with minor ailments. I know that for most people in the United States, routine health care challenges from minor injuries to childhood illness are often managed by over-the-counter treatments. Access to simple first aid supplies to prevent infection or control fever keep small problems from escalating to life-threatening situations. It is difficult for me to imagine the inability to access supplies that my regular patients often take for granted. In fact, I am frustrated to see that in Nicaragua, even poor nutrition exacerbates preventable health care problems. I know that the World Health Organization reports that Nicaragua continues to suffer from some of the worst disparities between rich and poor, especially in rural areas. I am glad that JustHope links volunteers from the United States with community leaders requesting health care services. I am excited to be part of a one-day medical clinic in remote Nicaraguan communities to provide medications and consultations for people who would otherwise have to travel hours on dirt roads to see a doctor. I wouldn't want to do this all the time, but it is cool to be a JustHope volunteer with the medical brigade to do the traveling instead, riding hours over roads that may be washed out in places. I wouldn't say it aloud, but it felt kind of heroic to make such a difference in these people's lives." The group let those words hover in thoughtful silence. I noted the success of this exercise of imagination.

"Thanks for your good work reflecting together," I said. "We can continue to explore these and other issues in the rest of our time together. Remember, you will write reflection papers to integrate your thoughts and learning when you get home," I said.

"Is there anything else we need to discuss now?" Leslie asked.

"Hey, friends," Martin said, "Before we close our reflections, can we come up with some plan to hold each other accountable to show up on time for group meetings or scheduled times to leave?"

"It sounds like you are talking to me," Bill replied testily.

"We just need to take care of our group time to be respectful of our hosts and driver," Laura said.

"I will just speak for myself," Martin said. "I feel frustrated when I am waiting with the group past a time when we all agreed to meet. If we all agreed we needed more time, I could enjoy a little more alone time myself. But I need a sense of trust that all of us respect each other's time."

"Maybe we could take turns being the group herder each day. One person could be in charge of reminders and counting or going to look for anyone who is missing when it is time to go," Rose suggested.

"That sounds smart," Bill said. "I will take the first turn doing that tomorrow."

"Sounds like a plan." Martin smiled.

"If we are going to make it to the beach for supper, we need to be on the van by 3:15," I reminded the group.

Beach Break

It did not take long for us to regroup and meet at the van ready for our trip to the beach. I could tell the group was happy to have a fun break, and I felt excited, too.

George said, "It smells like tourists in here," as he climbed into the van this time. The scent of suntan lotion filled the air. The mood of the group was festive and light, but we were aware that not everyone in

Chacraseca could run away to the beach for the evening. "I feel a little guilty going to the beach, but I am ready for some play time and a break from the intensity of the heat and challenge of learning about myself." The rest of us laughed appreciatively.

Leslie said, "Nicaragua has beautiful beaches, and I want you to see more of the countryside and culture. It will be good to have a little rest and relaxation this evening. We asked you to bring some extra money for supper tonight, since this meal at the beach is not included in our plan. Has everyone got a towel, swimsuit, and money with you?"

"I am not planning to get in the water," Elizabeth said. "I just want to wade a little. Do we need bug spray there, too?"

"Yes," Leslie said. "There are mosquitos everywhere."

We continued to chat as we headed away from Chacraseca, jolted by the bumpy road. We had to slow down in some traffic as we passed through part of León, but soon we were on the highway to the beach. The two-lane road didn't have much shoulder, but we saw plenty of people walking, riding bikes, or on horseback traveling beside the speeding highway traffic. After about forty-five minutes, we began to smell ocean moisture in the warm air. The terrain was flat, so we didn't get a good view of the water until we were close to the beach.

Juan Pablo pulled up and stopped near the door of one beachfront restaurant called Costa Maya. We disembarked and happily heard the waves as we walked through the open-air restaurant past simple bathrooms and changing rooms toward tables under a spectacular cabana roof.

"Look at the pattern of the woven ceiling! Are those palm leaves?" Rose exclaimed. We marveled at the beauty of the rustic, natural construction of the cabanas. "I wonder how many people know how to make that type of roof now?"

Juan Pablo, who had parked the van across the street and was now joining us, saw our interest.

"Many houses used to have roofs like that," he explained. "It is a traditional type of construction."

The restaurant had tables on a tiled floor, but also others on the sand. About half of the tables were taken, but our group found a long, large table on the sand and piled our backpacks in chairs. We agreed to take turns sitting with our bags at the table while others got in the ocean. A waiter began taking orders for beer and cold drinks. Leslie said she would stay at the table for a while and encouraged others to enjoy the beach.

"Be careful, the undertow and the surf can be really rough here at times," Leslie warned.

Martin and Paula were the first to reach the shore. The course, volcanic sand was hot. The waves were crashing and churning the sand. George, Rose, and Bill were laughing like children as they splashed around ankle deep in the ebbing and flowing waves. I was almost knee deep in the water when a strong wave knocked me down completely. I enjoyed feeling like a little kid, loving the ocean. After the sweltering heat we had experienced for days, the water was wonderful. I could tell the intense sun would threaten serious sunburn if I was not careful. Our group roamed in and out of the waves, up and down the coast where a few Nicaraguans enjoyed the beach. After some time, I walked back toward the shade of the restaurant, rinsed off some of the sand and salt at an outside shower, and rejoined part of our group who were enjoying drinks and reading the menu.

We were in tourist mode, but it was impossible not to view the experience with new eyes in light of our encounters the past few days. Leslie helped everyone order supper and organized communication with the waiters. The mood was relaxed. I recognized that the group had been working hard and engaging in challenging reflections while undergoing culture shock.

Three Nicaraguan children approached our table with baskets of necklaces and items made of shells they were selling. One young girl sidled up to Rose and placed a necklace of colorful shells around her neck. The little girl said, "Two dollars?" in rough English. Rose was charmed with the girl and looked tempted.

Leslie gently asked the kids to come back later. "We can look at their crafts when we are getting ready to leave. Otherwise, we will get swamped by more and more requests to buy." Leslie firmly asked the kids to come back later. "I know these kids because we have been coming here for many years. They know we will give them the leftover food from our supper." Leslie said.

"These prices are not all that different than restaurants in the U.S.," Bill said, studying the menu.

"Most of the people in Chacraseca could not afford to come here," Leslie replied. "There are higher prices for Gringos, though."

"That doesn't seem fair," Bill objected. "The prices should be the same for anyone."

"Should they?" Martin asked. "I wonder what Juan Pablo thinks about us spending so much money on this meal tonight."

"One meal costs about what his family spends on food for a week," Leslie said. "Think about it: fifteen dollars for a fresh, seafood dinner sounds like a bargain to us. For those who work in the sweat shop earning two dollars a day, it would take more than two weeks to earn the money for this one dinner. Most families in Chacraseca would never come here for a family meal."

I felt thankful for the conversation about economic justice and equity, but I also recognized my own longing to take a break from thinking so much about privileges I so often took for granted. I guessed I was not alone in this resistance to consciousness raising. I smiled laughing at my own resentment of learning like this.

Soon, everyone was seated back around our big table, refreshed from swimming or wading, cooled by the breeze, enjoying the sunset over the water. Waiters began to bring out platters of shrimp, fish, or chicken with French fries and salad.

"Is it okay to eat the salad?" Laura asked.

"I do," said Leslie. "At this restaurant they are used to tourists. They wash the vegetables with bottled water."

We were amused to see the white rice that accompanied each meal, even those that included French fries. Paula asked for catsup and was glad they had it. Our group settled into silence as we enjoyed the meal. We shared tastes of different dishes and appreciated the good food.

George voiced what most of us seemed to be thinking, "How can we enjoy this meal thinking about our friends in Chacraseca who don't have enough to eat?"

I was glad George named this question that we all harbored. There are no easy answers to the question. It represents the larger issue of how we live in a world of gross inequity, working for change but finding ways to sustain our long-term efforts for justice. The prevalence of the question and our struggle with the question points to a deep sense of injustice and solidarity with others that keeps me convinced of the reality of something like God. We long for the wholeness and flourishing of all life not just our own.

The time at the beach allowed each of us to relax. After dinner I enjoyed moments of solitude walking slowly on the shore with time to reflect. I thought about ideas I hoped to discuss with the group later. The day's focus on health and wellness brought to mind problems with health in the U.S. I had been thinking about Ray Bradbury's dystopian novel,

Fahrenheit 451, with glimpses of a world where people often overdose on drugs attempting suicide. That society turns to pharmaceutical solutions to manage all emotions, but suicide is not allowed. Society intervenes through "firefighters" making routine rescue calls to interrupt attempts at overdose. Decades ago that futuristic fictional world sounded alarming and hard to imagine. How terrible it would be if life was so painful that suicide prevention had to be a routine part of public service that the community provided! However, recently I saw the connection as I listened to a radio program about the growing epidemic of opioid addiction and overdose in the U.S. In 2016, "more Americans died of overdose ... than in the entirety of the Vietnam war" and the numbers of opioid overdose deaths are expected to continue climbing even higher.[6] Doctors, therapists, and care providers make valiant efforts to reverse the trend. Imagine Bradbury comparing that type of health care need with the needs we saw at the rural clinic in Chacraseca.

I thought of some underlying root causes of addiction that seem so prevalent in the U.S. including spiritual hopelessness. One leader from Chacraseca said she believed that North Americans are suffering from an affliction of the spirit. Despite our material wealth and access to expensive, high tech medical treatments, we have growing problems with mental health. A crisis in meaning, an epidemic of despair and hopelessness affects our culture. Soren Kierkegaard called it "sickness unto death." People reach for pain relief because the worries of this life seem unbearable. It is as if people are asking who cares and why does life matter anyway? Depression and despair gain the upper hand too often. The only antidote may be stronger relational bonds and community. But our affluent society does not seem conducive to fostering strong relationships.

Many of us have learned about the theory of Maslow's hierarchy of needs. We were taught that health care, nutrition, and basic physical needs must be met before persons can turn to spiritual and supposedly higher mental challenges. In Nicaragua, we meet people who have lived in communities where food insecurity and lack of reliable access to healthcare are generational realities that are never fully met for long. Ironically, a sincere satisfaction, a meaningful sense of community, and a deep spirituality seem to be possible regardless of those unmet physical needs. In fact, it could be argued that overabundance of material wealth causes new needs and appetites that have the capacity to be as debilitating

---

6. Lopez, "In One Year," para. 1.

as hunger and poverty. Could JustHope partnerships offer learning and experiences of mutual health and wellness? I thought about a friend who returned from a recent trip in Mexico and reported that someone had asked her, "Why are people from the U.S. so unhappy?" The question stuck with me.

The controversy within the United States about whether the government should provide health care as a recognized human right is controversial and polarizing. However, few would dispute the need for health and relief from pain as universal goods. The capability to respond with compassion to those who are suffering and the ability to provide healing to those who are ill or wounded is valued in every community. Yet, the more our freedom from illness and suffering increases, the more complex our responsibilities become in relationship to choices regarding health care services.

Groups of health care professionals travel to Nicaragua with various religious groups and organizations. Many would be shocked and offended to be accused of being neocolonial or problematic in any way. Often, volunteers with medical groups think of themselves as heroic, virtuous, and worthy of praise. Helicopter medicine is a term that describes a practice of dropping in a remote community, offering medical care, and then pulling out the same day, without addressing systems in the context. JustHope strives to avoid that type of action that can make North American volunteers feel great but perpetuate dependency and unstable care.

Part of what we can learn from our JustHope partnership experiences is that we need to explore what we mean by health in the first place. Intercultural encounters and dialogue provide opportunities to talk about our human experience of pain and also of what constitutes a good life. Although the rural lifestyle of those living in remote areas of Nicaragua has appealing qualities like being closer to nature and consuming fewer resources, few would choose the lack of access to goods and services like dental and health care. It is important to acknowledge that the material prosperity that meets the need for medical care simultaneously introduces questions regarding what causes pain and what constitutes health in the first place.

— 7 —

Model Farm Mutuality

THE SOUTH-FACING SIDE OF the Peace House is a pleasant place to sit and enjoy the early morning breeze. First light begins before 5:00 a.m. in the morning, so I had plenty of time to enjoy the tranquility there before breakfast. Bright butterflies and birds glide over the labyrinth and sail among the treetops. Sister Joan's influence remains visible in a leafy labyrinth constructed with shrubs just beyond the porch. Today the gravel paths were shrouded with thick spider webs that discouraged me from trying walking meditation. The view beyond the swaying trees offers glimpses of a distant field across a quiet road. Monday, I had noticed those workers cultivating with machetes in that field, too far away to be heard. I couldn't tell if they were planting corn or yuca, but the field must have been about five acres large. It looked like impossible work for the two men bending over the rows of plants. At first, I thought they couldn't really be working that entire field without machinery. But after watching them toil day after day as the week wore on, I gleaned a little insight about farm labor in Nicaragua. Inch by inch and row by row, the fields are cultivated, planted, and harvested. Thursday morning, the men were bent over their patient, persistent work again, chopping deftly with their machetes, sweating away as I sipped my morning coffee in the shade.

This was our day to visit JustHope's model farm. I looked forward to seeing the newly constructed pavilion and hearing about the expanding plans for the farm. I thought about the gift of being in a farm community, immersed in the beauty of nature. I hoped students remembered discussions we had about tendencies to romanticize and objectify rural partners through consequences of our imperious gaze, illustrated in the pre-travel readings about peasant studies. I reflected on the day's theme of mutuality, one of the JustHope values. What could mutuality mean when the work of farming and agriculture, so elemental to our universal human need for food, was not freely chosen by workers who were born into cycles of poverty perpetuated by patterns of global wealth distribution? Nicaragua has rich land. Farmers only need about six acres to feed their families. Yet corporate industrial agriculture is swallowing up more and more land, while many farmers are reduced to day labor in fields they do not own.

That evening we would have the option of participating in homestays for one night. Bill had decided to opt out and stay at the Peace House. From the beginning of our class, Paula, Martin, George, and Rose had been committed to participating in the home stay, but Nick, Elizabeth, and Laura were still unsure. Leslie had explained the process thoroughly. We would share our daily group reflections in the afternoon. We would eat a quick supper at the Peace House, and then the van would take us to meet our host families in time to see their homes before dark. I was enthusiastic about the experiences I had in the past homestay visits, but I assured everyone there was no pressure to participate. I mulled over the upcoming day, aware that our week in Nicaragua was more than half over.

First George, and then others joined me on the porch. Mostly we sat in silence, writing in journals, reading devotional material, soaking up the beauty of the gardens and countryside. Before long we began discussing the day ahead. As we shared the freshness of the morning and savored our coffee, more members of our group joined us. When Laura arrived, she reluctantly told the group she had decided to stay at the Peace House with Bill that night instead of going for a homestay. We all agreed that each person needed to take care of themselves. We would support each other regardless. Part of me longed for the quiet, rest, and solitude I could have if I skipped the homestay myself. Intensive trips like this require introverts to stretch beyond comfort and postpone needs sometimes. It is wise to allow each person to pace themselves and know their limits. The group was cheerful as we headed toward breakfast.

We talked over our associations with farming as we ate tortillas and gallo pinto that morning. "These beans are so delicious," Rose said. "They aren't quite like the pinto beans I am familiar with, but that is the closest thing I can come up with. Is it because they are fresh that they taste so good?"

Paula said, "These beans are a little different, but they remind me of beans I grew up eating at my grandparents' farm in Arkansas. I enjoy the fresh tomatoes and cucumbers, too."

We wondered aloud about exactly where the rice we ate that morning had been grown. How had it been harvested? Had the beans been picked by hand?

"I remember the rows looked so long, I thought we would never get to the end. The plants were so tall that I felt I was in a tunnel in the shade between the rows," Paula said.

"Some of my happiest memories are of picking peaches with my grandparents," Bill said. "I can almost taste the sweetness of the sun-warmed fruit with that juice dripping down my chin. I love farm life."

"The sights and smells here have brought back early memories for me, too," Nick said. "I was thinking last night and realized I am usually cut off from nature. I have the windows closed, the air conditioning on, and I rarely spend time away from asphalt or concrete. There is a kind of nostalgia about a simpler time from my childhood connected with helping my grandparents garden. Of course, I know it wasn't simple for them. I was a kid without the pressure of trying to feed the family from the land."

"Yes," Paula said. "I think of myself as a gardener, but I can't imagine being totally dependent on what I could grow to feed myself. I garden as a hobby. I don't think I would like farming as a full-time job year after year."

"We North Americans have complex relationships with the history of farming and rural community," I said. "When my parents were born, their families lived off the land farming and hunting. Their generation was the first to break that cycle. I grew up appreciating gardening, but also with pressure to distance myself from rural farm life. In my family, success is associated with moving away from rural Oklahoma to urban life. We probably were not fully conscious of the assumption that staying on the farm signaled personal failure. We have a nostalgia about farm life, but also a sense of unease about our country roots."

"My family were all city people for generations," Laura said. "I wouldn't know the first thing about how to grow food." She chewed thoughtfully.

Bill said, "I am excited about the opportunity to see JustHope's model farm. I have been looking forward to this day on the schedule all week. The farmers in my community in Oklahoma will want to hear about this."

Martin agreed, saying, "I am curious about how the principles and practices of permaculture are being implemented in this context. I have researched organic gardening techniques even before the recent trend in sustainable gardening. Last year I attended some classes in permaculture back home. I am intrigued to explore this topic in Nicaragua."

After breakfast we prepared to leave. Elizabeth and Nick both told me they decided to participate in the homestays. I confirmed details for those arrangements with Julio, whom I found by the van ready to go. Martin was chatting with Juan Pablo in the van as our group gathered to leave for the day.

"Is Bill rounding people up to leave on time?" Rose asked, smiling.

"I reminded him that he was responsible for herding us today," Elizabeth said. "I think they were all coming when I left a few minutes ago."

Soon we were on our way in good spirits. As the van rolled down the road toward the model farm that morning, Martin remarked about a woman we passed who was lighting a small fire. He said, "I notice people raking and sweeping up fallen leaves or twigs like that each day. It is as if they are scouring the area to keep it clean like a floor. I am frustrated to see people set fire to small piles of organic rubbish every morning to keep the areas around the house neat and tidy. The fine, sandy soil seems to need the organic mulch that those leaves and sticks could be providing." The smoky scent of burning leaves hung in the warm, damp air.

Paula replied, "Have you noticed it is women and girls who we have seen doing that chore? I admit that I wondered about composting instead of burning the leaves, too. I've seen the way they fling a handful of water to settle the dust after they sweep. I guess they do that to prevent dirt blowing in the open windows or doors of the house. I wonder how many hundreds of years women have been doing that chore in this area," she mused. "Maybe the leaves attract too many insects if they just leave them."

"I have been troubled by that, too. It bothers me to see them burn organic matter instead of composting," Nick said.

"Is that our imperious gaze or assumption that we know better how they should be living?" George asked. No one responded in the thoughtful silence that followed his question.

We drove past a man who was already sweating while swinging a machete, deftly chopping a weedy clump of unwanted grass. Bill said, "I notice how skillful these guys are with the machete. We have seen people use them to cut the grass, chop vegetables, prune the trees, remove the weeds, and open a coconut." We passed another farmer wielding a machete and a boy riding a bony horse while shepherding a few cattle toward a place to graze. All these were reminders of the daily agricultural work that started early.

George said, "I have been wondering what it might be like to spend day after day, year after year doing this kind of farm work. It depresses me to think about it, and I can barely imagine the monotony."

Bill said, "I feel a twinge of guilt realizing that I am enjoying the leisurely van ride and heading to a meeting to observe and learn rather than work myself all day."

Eventually the van reached a road with steep banks on either side, as if the road was at the bottom of a riverbed. In fact, the road was about ten feet lower than the pasture level on either side of it. Leslie explained that, according to Doña Nimia, before Hurricane Mitch in 1998 the road was level with the surrounding fields. Then the torrential rains and flooding transformed the dirt roads to rivers in some places and scoured out deep trenches in this earth that caused the sunken level of the road. It felt somewhat like driving through a tunnel, although the sky was visible overhead. The team looked at the holes in the earthen banks on either side of the road. The colorful guardabarranco, the national bird, live in these holes, hence the name, "guardian of the banks." We hoped to catch sight of these colorful beauties in their nests, but none were to be seen that morning.

Soon the van turned up a steep drive, and Julio announced that we were at the model farm. A covered pavilion stood on a hilltop, overlooking rolling farmland. A group of men and one woman were waiting to greet us. Sharing greetings and quick introductions, we expressed enthusiasm about the farm. We stepped into the shade of the pavilion with gratitude for the protection from the glare of the sun and took seats in a circle of plastic chairs to hear the presentation.

"This is the farm committee," Julio said. "This is Pedro Luís, Augustine, his son Miguelito, and Doña Lucia. Also, I am glad to introduce Austin, who works here at the farm as part of the JustHope staff." One by one, the leaders shared the story and the concept of the model farm. Seeing the success of the women's microcredit program, the farmers had approached JustHope about a new idea. They were concerned about increased drought and high temperatures in their area. Climate conditions were changing. They explained that if you only have a few acres of land and your family depends on agriculture to survive, you can't really afford to experiment or innovate with new crops that might work. Farmers tend to stick with what they know worked in the past. Yet they heard about farmers from other regions and even around the world sharing knowledge and discovering new possibilities. They wanted to initiate a project to help farmers in their community.

So JustHope was able to purchase a farm consisting of less than ten acres of land, about the size of a typical family farm in the area. The plan was to divide the farm into four sections to develop four projects. One portion of the land would be used to generate income by growing a crop like yuca that is already known to produce well. A second section of the land would be used to innovate, by planting new experimental crops or using new methods. The third section would be used to replicate successes discovered through innovation. Given the changes in rainfall and temperatures from year to year, it took time to see what new methods could be dependable. Then the fourth section of the land would be used for programs to educate neighbors. This structure where we sat for our meeting was on the educational section of land. Located on the summit of the hill, the space had a dramatic view and a strong breeze.

While we were hearing this presentation, another farmer drove up on a motorcycle. He came to pick up some moringa seeds. Austin stepped away from our circle to fetch a sack of moringa seed from the storage room on one side of the pavilion. I was happy to watch this exchange. It demonstrated the difference the model farm was already making in the community. Pedro Luís explained that he was now growing moringa on a portion of his own land. He reported that he had made more money from that crop last year than he had ever made before in one season. He showed us the hard, dark brown seeds. We learned that the fast-growing, drought resistant moringa, grown in India and parts of Africa, had high nutritional value in every part of the plant.

Austin said, "The leaves from the moringa make good feed for cows. The plants add nitrogen to the soil and prevent insects." He said the farmers hoped to try a project of raising pigs that were fed solely on the moringa plants. Austin continued, "We also hope to grow avocados. It takes four years to establish the trees, but then they produce for approximately twenty years."

The men pointed out a concrete cistern to collect rainwater. We asked a few questions before walking out to see more of the farm.

"Are you able to irrigate from the cistern?" Bill wanted to know.

"The cistern needs work. We have repaired it once, and it still leaks when the water reaches a certain level," Augustine explained. "There was once a well here, but we discovered the cost of repairing it would be more than putting in a new well."

"Do you plan to put in a well?" Bill asked quickly.

"A well would cost about twenty thousand dollars," Pedro Luís replied. "That is a lot of money."

Paula interjected, "I bet we could help organize a way to raise those funds."

Pedro Luís said, "The problem is that we could make a beautiful farm here if we had a well, but that is not a solution that can be replicated by most families in our community. We are trying to explore sustainable methods that work for our neighbors."

"What are the expenses for the farm?" Rose asked.

"We learned the hard way that we have to pay for security," Augustine explained. "We had purchased the first set of moringa trees and planted them, only to discover that they were stolen in the night. That was a big disappointment. Poverty in this area is so severe that people can be desperate."

"So, our main expenses for the farm are security, seeds, labor to plow and plant, and fertilizer," Pedro Luís said. "The JustHope staff has been researching workshops for permaculture and innovative crops. Today we invite you to volunteer some of your own labor to assist us in our fertilizer development."

Austin brought out a series of five-gallon plastic buckets and explained the process. In an effort to invent organic herbicides and pesticides made from local products, they were experimenting. The popularity of fresh fruit drinks resulted in a plentiful supply of citrus fruit peels and rinds. Would it be possible to use that waste to make compost that could rival the expensive organic products for sale? Austin said, "We are trying various recipes, keeping copious notes on the results. You could help by putting in a little time and effort today. Who is willing to help?" he asked.

We all agreed to work at this project, and Austin explained the process. First, he dumped some buckets of rotting fruit peels that had been waiting for attention. He instructed us to pick out plastic or paper trash and sort the fruit into categories depending on how rotten it was. Rose and Laura got busy sorting one pile, while George, Martin, and Paula worked on another. Bill and Elizabeth followed Austin's instructions for measuring vinegar and the sorted fruit peeling into clean buckets, as he made careful notes. We would take turns working at these tasks and going in small groups for a tour of the crops in the field. Soon, flies were gathering to the smelly, sticky fruit waste. As we worked together, we imagined friends from home who would be intrigued with the model farm.

This love of growing food and working for food justice transcended national borders and united us across cultural, political, and even language divides. It was delightful to see people from the United States and people from Nicaragua sharing their enthusiasm for gardening and growing food. As we worked, we continued to hear about efforts for the model farm. Austin described changes in Nicaraguan agriculture over time. Once tropical jungles covered thousands of acres of land that are now used for farming. Colonial plunder stripped ancient hard wood trees from the mountain sides centuries ago. The environmental degradation of lakes from industrial pollution was happening at the same time deforestation and invasive mining proliferated. Austin spoke of the love Nicaraguans have for their land. That love was obvious as the leaders of the model farm committee talked about their own farming practices and hope for the future of farming.

Bill said, "Jesus told lots of stories about farming, maybe because many of his followers were intimately familiar with planting seeds and watching them grow. Farming is about trusting the process, slowing down, detaching from the results, marveling at the mystery of new life springing up from the soil."

Austin said, "Many guys my age have left to find work in Costa Rica or even the U.S. It is hard to find work here sometimes. The life of a farmer is not easy."

"I read a book about immigration called, *The Right to Stay Home*," George said. "The writer said that global corporations like it when workers feel insecure because then people are more vulnerable and desperate."[1]

Austin nodded in appreciation for this mutual understanding.

Bill said, "Farming has been hard in the U.S. at times, too. When my parents were kids, they nearly starved to death on the farm. It is better now. Where I live now most people think farm life is the best way to live."

Pedro Luís smiled at this. He said, "I told my neighbors that I hope I live five more years to see how beautiful the model farm becomes, God

---

1. Bacon, *Right to Stay Home*, 287.

willing. We always say, 'God willing,' because God is the light of everything we do."

After we completed our contribution to the fertilizer experimentation and toured the farm, we gathered for a final circle with the farmers. We stood together under the shade of the large trees and enjoyed a breeze on the hilltop. Austin encouraged us to share the story of the farm with people in the U.S. who have an interest in permaculture and food justice. Before we left, Pedro Luís invited us to stop by his farm to see his moringa fields. Juan Pablo maneuvered the van over the rough terrain and down the steep hill into the washed-out road. Pedro Luis rode with us, pointing out neighbors' homes along the way to his farm. When we pulled into his dusty drive, he proudly welcomed us and led the way to the barn.

As he showed us his forest of moringa and explained his crops in various other fields, Pedro Luis urged us to come see the bumper crop of squash he was currently harvesting. We watched while he nonchalantly placed a wooden yoke and fastened leather harnesses on a pair of massive grey oxen to pull his wooden cart to the field. We walked out in the field following the intimidating oxen, as Pedro Luís negotiated the muddy ground while wearing his plastic flip flop shoes. The fragrance of the rich soil filled the air as the ruts opened behind the oxen, cart, and farmer. Pedro Luis pointed out the colorful, abundant vegetables visible as he used his machete to cut the large gourds from the vines and pile them in the cart. A few of us picked up ripe squash and added them on to the cart trying to be helpful.

Bill said, "That is impressive skill you have with the oxen. I think that talent for training and using the strength of oxen is mostly lost on our farms in the U.S."

Pedro Luis looked astonished and asked, "Do you mean that if I visited farms in the United States, I would not see farmers out working in the field with oxen like this?"

Bill and George exchanged looks as if to say, "How could we possibly explain this?" Then Bill said, "Most farmers in the U.S. use tractors even on small farms now."

I marveled at the comfort and skill of Pedro Luis as he guided the enormous oxen back toward the barn pulling the loaded cart. We thanked Pedro Luis and said our goodbyes.

When we returned to the Peace House around 11:00 a.m., Leslie reminded us that our cooks had invited us to join a lesson in making tortillas. Embracing this opportunity, Elizabeth, Rose, Laura, Paula, Martin, and I crossed the road toward the kitchen.

Tortilla Making Lesson

We looked around with new curiosity at the steamy room we had walked through all week to eat our meals. The concrete sinks along one wall and the shelves built along the opposite wall were the only things in the large kitchen except the massive stove in the center of the room. The stove was about three feet high and three feet wide, but it was at least seven feet long. It was like a long, scorching, narrow bed made of concrete blocks with a roaring fire inside. The iron griddle and huge pots boiling and sizzling on the stovetop looked alarmingly dangerous. Nonetheless, the competency of our dauntless cooks was obvious.

Doña Nimia and Doña Estella gleefully waved us over to the bubbling vat of swollen corn which looked something like thick pudding made of hominy that was breaking down to mush. Our teachers explained that the corn is soaked and simmered for many hours before being ground to the mealy dough used for tortillas. In order to show us the steps in the process, they had prepared some dough beforehand to speed up our lesson. A nice bowl of dough covered with a damp cloth was ready for us to shape. Doña Nimia demonstrated first by taking a handful of dough about the size of a small apple in her hand. She used a circular, plastic pattern that might have been cut from a bread sack to round out the thin tortilla as she patted it out expertly. Then she peeled the plastic away and held the thin, round tortilla in her palm before laying it down on the hot griddle. Within a few seconds, the tortilla puffed up. Reaching out with deft, skillful touch, she quickly picked up the tortilla and flipped it over, using her bare fingers. How did she do that without getting burned? Just a few more seconds, and she lifted the corner of the finished tortilla and transferred it to a plate.

With varying degrees of confidence, we each attempted to make a tortilla. Estella and Nimia guided and encouraged as we scooped handfuls of warm dough and tried to pat them into thin rounds as our teachers had done. We laughed and practiced, noting how much more difficult it was than Nimia and Estella made it look. The sultry air and searing heat from the stove left us sodden with sweat, but we were having fun. We took turns taking pictures of our humorous, fumbling attempts. While we worked together, Elizabeth asked Nimia how she had learned to cook. We enjoyed hearing her talk about her mother and grandmother who taught her. We shared stories and watched hopefully to see if our tortillas would puff up as they are supposed to do while cooking.

The taste of the tortilla fresh from the griddle was even better than those we had been enjoying with our meals each day. The experience of cooking together and bonding in the kitchen reminded each of us of early childhood experiences of learning to cook. I felt a tender connection with these Nicaraguan women as I thought of cooking lessons at my grandmother's side. Soon the bowl of dough was empty, and the women shifted their attention to dishing up the rest of our lunch.

"From the corn we saw growing in the fields today, to the kitchen and table, I wouldn't have missed this for anything!" Rose said.

"I agree," Paula said. "This was one of the highlights of the trip for me."

Cultural Center Presentation

Just after lunch, we walked to the Cultural Center building to watch a presentation from the dance and music classes. Abimiel and the kids had been preparing this program for us, and many of their parents and grandparents also attended. This time when we climbed the steps and entered the newly constructed building, Julio and Abimiel were adjusting the speakers of the large sound system. Kids bustled in carrying colorful costumes. Excitement filled the atmosphere of the room with happy energy.

Some older teens were testing the microphones. Several girls in colorful folk-dance dresses with swirling skirts walked through on the way to a room in the back that must have served as a dressing room for staging. Horacio came in smiling at us and taking a seat. We saw Janeth, Maria Jenia, and Nimia already seated in rows of plastic chairs lined up for the audience. As we took our seats, a couple of women from the Stitching Hope building next door came in smiling and nodding as they joined us. More kids walked through looking freshly combed and excited or maybe nervous.

A group of half a dozen boys were setting up stools and drum sets beside a large marimba. A large puppet character of a woman with blonde hair and a pink face stood at least twelve feet high in the corner of the room. Soon Abimiel began the program, welcoming us and explaining that the cultural center had been a dream of the children who used to have dance classes on the porch of the Peace House. Now the classes have been expanded to include music and art lessons as well. The audience had filled up with other adults and children, perhaps siblings of the performers, as well as friends and neighbors. After a dramatic pause, the performance began.

Three girls in colorful costumes and three boys wearing traditional hats and campesino clothing stepped from the back room and took their places as the music began. The band of musicians kept up a lively beat. I recognized the tune as a familiar Nicaraguan folk song. The dancers swirled and tapped their bare feet, clearly enjoying the music.

Julio joined in singing some of the numbers. He translated as Abimiel introduced various numbers, explaining the stories behind each song that featured different kids dancing and singing. Sometimes the audience sang along. I watched Nimia's face beam with pleasure as she joined in singing what must have been one of her favorites, "Children of the Corn." Although I could not catch all the words, the delight of the local audience was obvious as they sang familiar lyrics and tunes.

One number included a performance of Gigantona and Pepe Cobazón, and the audience cheered when the towering puppet from the corner came to life as it was animated by one of the kids who ducked under her ruffled skirt. Another puppet appeared from the back room, a short man with dark hair and eyes, an enormous head, and funny flapping arms. Julio explained that these familiar characters symbolized the interaction of the Europeans with the Nicaraguans. Gigantona was a tall gringa with a beautiful face, but she was hollow and stiff. Pepe Cobazón fawned on the giantess, striving for her attention. His large head indicated that he had the brains, but he was still drawn to something about her. They danced and twirled to the music. When the song ended and the boys inside the puppets revealed themselves, the audience cheered.

After the final song, all the performers lined up and stepped to the microphone one by one to introduce themselves. They stated their age and grade in school. Some shared hopes or goals for the future. We were amazed to discover that the band learned to play their instruments in less than the span of a year since the completion of the cultural center. Earlier we had learned about the scholarship program in that center. Now we understood more about the diverse programs Abimiel led.

We walked back across the hot, dusty road, ready for a little break before our reflection time. Since we were organizing ourselves for the homestays that evening, we circled up on the porch for our reflection time early in the afternoon.

Rocking Chair Reflections

Laura and Rose were leaning back with their eyes closed, allowing the full stream of air from a box fan to wash over them. Bill plugged in another fan and aimed it at a different corner of our circle.

"Each of these rocking chairs is slightly different, isn't it?" Elizabeth asked.

Juan Pablo was tilted back in one chair looking as if he might be napping. The heat made us all a little sleepy. Julio sat next to Juan Pablo, ready to join our conversation.

As we started our reflection time, I passed out a page with lyrics of a song we had heard the kids perform, "Somos Hijos del Maiz" (Children of the Corn), written by Carlos Mejía Godoy.

"This song has become one of my favorites," I said. "The poetry of the lyrics reflects some of the themes of liberation theology and the struggle for justice in Nicaragua. Did you notice the adults singing along with the kids when they played this song? I have asked Julio to talk a little about the meaning of this song in Nicaraguan communities."

"SOMOS HIJOS DEL MAIZ"
(Children of the Corn)

If they take our bread, We will be obliged, To survive as our grandparents did, with the corn fermented in the blood of the heroes.

With corn planted from before forever—From before they bloodstained our land: the crows, the pirates, the cross, the sword, and the capitalists!

We are children of corn, builders of furrows and dreams. And although we are a small country, We already have counted over a thousand winters.—A million hand blooming, In the endless task of planting seed, from April to May, tilling, sowing, tapping, tapping, shelling and storing up for war and peace!

(list of names of traditional food items made with corn) Chicha de maiz, chicha pujagua, chicha raizuda, pelo de maiz, EL

ATOOOOOL—Chingue de maiz, nacatamal, Atolillo, PER-RERREQUEEEEE! Tamalpizque, totoposte, marquezote, chocolate, cosa de horno, pinolillo, pinol tiste, bunuelo, chilote, elote, posole, chilote, tortilla, wirila, atol duro, empanada.

Forged in the oven; The unstoppable sustenance of the village
The irrepressible nourishment of the people.

This is the way we will be renewed; This is the way we will be made new,

This is the way we will be rejuvenated,

This way we become . . . New![2]

Julio began by explaining how the lyrics refer to Nicaraguan experience of colonialism and imperialism. "Invading armies tried to starve the people out," he said. "But our connection with the land and nature sustained us. This is a song of pride, resistance, and resilience of the pueblo, the people. The song includes names of local foods developed from corn when people had nothing but corn to eat. The people were creative and made delicious dishes from corn," he explained. "The chorus repeats these food items in rapid succession almost like a fun tongue twister. People often laugh as they race through that list. There are parts of the song that sound like the voices of vendors calling out to sell their wares in the street or market: 'el atool' . . . and 'perreque!' Maybe you noticed how we shouted out those words like sellers."

Our group sat in silence a few minutes studying the lyrics.

"What words or phrases stand out as you read these lines?" I asked.

Laura said, "I can see how it is difficult to know how some of these lines should be translated. Some of it doesn't really make sense. What is this part about 'hands blooming'?" she asked.

Rose responded decisively, "That is one of my favorite lines. At first it didn't make sense, but then I pictured people broadcasting corn seed in the field, walking as they reached in a bag and tossed out the seed. Their hands would look like a flower unfurling its petals when they threw a handful of seed. Can you see what I mean?"

"Wow," Laura said. "A million blooming hands, in the endless task of planting . . . I see that now. It is a beautiful image."

2. Godoy, "Somos Hijos del Maíz." Translated by Julio Delgado and Kathleen D. McCallie.

Bill asked: "When the song begins with the phrase, 'If they take our bread...' who do you think the singer refers to as 'they?' Do you think it is the same group as the ones who 'bloodstained our land'?" He glanced sideways toward Julio, who said nothing and shrugged.

I was aware of the opportunity to think together about how national identity could be a point of conflict. Bill expressed a feeling of defensiveness about being a U.S. citizen in light of the history of intervention in Nicaragua. I wanted the class to explore this tension.

"When was this written?" Elizabeth asked.

"This is one of the revolutionary folk songs written around the time when the Misa Campesina was being written. Probably during the 1970s or early 1980s," Leslie said. "During the Contra War, one of the tactics was to destroy crops to starve the enemy. Both sides did that at times. The issues of hunger were severe."

"The ending of the song is powerful," Rose said. "I like the concept of grain crops growing new season after season as an image of regeneration. Maybe that can help me with my struggle to make sense of the theological concept of being born again."

"When I think of the phrase 'children of the corn,' I associate that with Native Americans. In one of our seminary classes we learned about George Tinker's work on Native American Liberation Theology.[3] We talked about the images of the corn mother in that study. I wonder how that is connected? Does that make any sense?" George asked.

"Yes. But remember, the people here are like all Latinx people in this hemisphere, descended from Spanish colonists but also from Indigenous people." Laura said. "Children of the corn denotes connection to the land and nature in my mind."

"The borders between here and the U.S. are relatively recent in history," I added.

"This phrase stands out for me: 'Corn fermented in the blood of the heroes,'" said Paula. "I get the feeling of strength for the revolutionary heroes and martyrs being fueled by energy from the land, rain, and sun through the corn."

"I keep seeing and smelling that huge vat of boiling corn that Estella was cooking to teach us how to make tortillas," Martin said. "Just think how many centuries people have been boiling corn and smelling that steamy aroma."

---

3. Tinker, "Jesus, Corn Mother, and Conquest," 84.

"Here is the line that stands out in my mind," Bill said, "'To survive as our grandparents did...' I am fascinated by all the different food products made from corn."

"Yes," Julio said. "In the market in León, women sell these traditional foods made from corn: el atool, nacatamal, atolillo, perrerreque, tamalpizque, totoposte, marquezote, chocolate, pinolillo, pinol tiste, bunuelo, chilote, elote, posole, chilote, tortilla, wirila, atol duro, and empanada. These are all traditional dishes made from corn. Through the years when people had nothing but corn to eat, they invented all these variations on ways to eat corn. See the way the song recalls our history of being colonized and dominated? It was as if our ancestors said, 'Alright, you try to starve us out. We have nothing but corn. We will show you. We will get creative.' All these dishes made from corn were invented by people trying to survive."

Martin said, "Listen to this line: 'With corn planted forever from before they bloodstained our land: the crows, the pirates, the cross, the sword, and the capitalists.' I hear the reference to colonizers and imperialists. I find it interesting that the church is implicated as well. I remember how playful the song sounded. I watched Nimia sing along. Her face was shining with laughter and delight. The depth of political analysis of systemic injustice in the song is fascinating."

Nick said, "What I notice is a striking kind of strength of the rural people rising up in resistance to the efforts of colonialism and imperialism to dominate or wipe them out. Rising up like sprouting corn, the strength of the people seems to come from the land. I hope we can circle back to some of our earlier discussion about the term, 'campesinos,' that is translated as peasants. I agree that the term peasant is problematic, but there is a wonderful pride and fortitude in the people who identify so strongly with the land and the corn. This song gets at that dynamic."

"Would you say that the farmers we met today were peasants?" Bill asked.

"I think they would call themselves campesinos, but I don't think peasants is a good translation," I said. "This is a good illustration of the problem of translation and intercultural dialogue. I am not sure there is a good English word that works well," I said. "What would you call rural folks from your own community?" I asked. "Farmers, country folk, rural folk? Would you call people from your community peasants?"

"No!" Bill said. "I don't think there are peasants in the U.S. Maybe that is your point. That guy who came to the farm this morning to pick up seeds looked as if he had a hard life," Bill said. "He reminded me of my own family's connection with farming. My father grew up picking cotton in a part of Texas where the land is poor, and the rain is unreliable. For my father's generation, success was equated with getting away from the farm. I learned that being 'countrified' was not something to be proud of. My father would have been offended if someone called him a farmer or country boy. I was born and raised in Kansas City, long after my father moved to town and started his own business. My father always had a funny mixture of pride about his farming background but also some awkward embarrassment," Bill said. "He didn't want us to grow up picking cotton and experiencing food insecurity as he did during his own childhood. But, on the other hand, my father seemed to look down on us as if we were too soft or citified. My parents worked hard so that we never knew hunger, but they seemed frustrated that we didn't appreciate what we had. It was complicated. I wondered today about the generational attitudes here as more young people are moving to live in cities."

"That tension between city people and rural people seems to exist here, too," Laura said.

"Yes, I see that tension between the JustHope staff who live in León as opposed to those who are from Chacraseca or rural areas," I said.

Julio agreed. "Many of us who have lived our lives in town have not had the experience of working in the fields day after day," he said.

Leslie thanked Julio for his help with the song and said we needed to turn our attention to preparation for the home stays that evening. The JustHope staff had made arrangements through ACOPADES for three host families to be ready to receive us in their homes that evening. A translator would spend the night at each house, too. Leslie said that she just slept in her clothes and only took her toothbrush and water with her, because the van would pick us up before breakfast the next morning. We talked through the process and then ate a quick supper. Then, we started to prepare to leave for the homestays. Bill and Laura looked relaxed as they rocked in rocking chairs in front of a fan while the rest of us bustled around stuffing things in our backpacks.

Home Stays

"Be sure to take toilet paper and a flashlight," Leslie reminded us. Our translators arrived. Since few families had an extra bed, Juan Pablo helped us load folding cots on the van. We each took a full water bottle and a backpack.

Leslie would stay with George and Laura at the first house, which was painted brightly and looked new. The black earth yard was swept clean, and a few chickens wandered around undisturbed by a couple of dogs watching from the shade. Juan Pablo helped George and Laura unload three cots as Leslie introduced the host family. We waved goodbye and drove on to the next house. Roberto would stay with Paula, Martin, and Nick at this second house.

Only a short drive from the first house, this home was also made of concrete blocks, but it looked older. The paint was coated with dust. Other houses stood close by, and a few people peeked from various porches as Nick, Martin, Paula, and Roberto gathered their cots and backpacks. We watched them greeting an older woman and several kids as we drove away. Rose, Elizabeth, and I would stay with Francis at the third house. It was almost dusk as we arrived at the home of Veronica and her family. Veronica was a young mother with two small children. She welcomed us to her home and explained that her husband was at work. Thanking Juan Pablo for his help with unloading our cots, we said goodbye to him, and he left to return to the Peace House.

Veronica was somewhat shy, but she was clearly excited to have us as visitors. She was enthusiastic about showing us her little farm. Since she had gotten a microcredit loan, she had recently bought a pig. She proudly showed us how she fed the pig. Rose asked about the chickens ranging freely around. Veronica explained that her husband's parents lived in the house next door. Her mother-in-law raised the chickens. Since it was growing dark quickly, Veronica showed us where to find the latrine. There was a light bulb hanging outside near the latrine. Veronica explained that light was there because sometimes bats bite her pig at night. Rose, Elizabeth, and I exchanged glances, trying not to react. I thought of the fat, pink and white pig in comparison with my own pale skin. I wondered if I would have to get up to use the latrine in the middle of the night.

Veronica showed us where to set up our cots out on the covered porch of her house. Francis translated as Veronica explained that she and her husband had been living with his parents for the first four years they were married. Then they built a plastic house on this spot when their first child was a few years old. They lived in that house for five years. The leader of their sector told them about the housing program of ACOPADES partnering with JustHope. They applied for a home, and last year volunteer teams helped build this house. It was clear from Veronica's expressions and tone of voice that she was proud and thankful for her wonderful new house. Veronica showed us a picture of her family with a smiling group of JustHope volunteers.

As we sat talking on the porch, her children came in from playing outside. Her daughter, Fatima, was ten years old. Her son, Justo, was five. They shyly invited us inside to see their house, a single room with their two small beds and a larger bed for their parents. Although the house seemed tiny to us, we understood what an improvement it was for them. In her winsome way, Rose engaged both the kids as she admired the Mickey Mouse bedspread and cartoon characters on their bed sheets. Elizabeth peered appreciatively at the photo on the wall. Veronica turned on the old television set and the kids settled in their beds to watch. We moved outside toward plastic chairs on the porch again. I was aware of the intimacy of being invited into her humble home and touched by her gratitude for the advantages it provided. Clearly, we were all thinking about houses with their differing styles and sizes. Veronica looked at us and asked candidly, "How many rooms are in your house?"

For a few seconds, I was a little startled. The gulf between my experience and hers loomed between us. I realized that I didn't even know how many rooms were in my house. I had not thought much about it. What a revelation to recognize my oblivion to the privilege of having enough space that I didn't need another room! I may have blushed as I began counting rooms in my house. How awkward I felt reporting that there are ten rooms in my house! I didn't want to tell her that I lived alone in such luxury.

Elizabeth said her house had five rooms. Rose explained that she lived in an apartment with four rooms. I imagined the thoughts each of us were likely having as Francis translated. Veronica did not react visibly as we answered. I could only imagine what she felt. She seemed curious about us and completely accepting. Our exploratory questions and responses ranged from asking about weather at our homes to discussing favorite foods. I was thankful for the opportunity to visit.

Although Leslie had told us that families often go to bed very early in Nicaragua, Veronica continued our conversation for hours. The first hour, we learned about her own story, growing up in another sector and meeting her husband through a cousin. She wanted to hear more about our homes and our families, too. Then her daughter came out on the porch and reported that her brother was asleep. Veronica went to turn off the television set and encouraged her daughter to join our conversation. Rose asked Fatima about her school, and Fatima replied that she liked reading and poetry. Veronica bragged that Fatima had recently learned a popular poem by the national poet, Rubén Darío. We asked to hear the poem, and we were amazed at Fatima's skill in reciting what must have been two or three pages. Although Francis did not translate every line, she told us that the poem was about the beauty and strength of Nicaragua and her people. To see this young girl recite the lengthy poem so skillfully in the context of the poor, one-room house surrounded by dusty fields and farms was remarkable. I marveled at her ability and wondered what opportunities her future might hold.

Fatima went to bed soon, but Veronica wanted to talk more. Her husband worked at the factory until past midnight; she warned us that he would pull up on his motorcycle while we were sleeping. Elizabeth asked more detailed questions about raising pigs.

Veronica became more open with her questions as the night wore on. I was tired and hoping to sleep soon, but our conversation felt like a rare, intimate type of sharing. She asked how we got our hair so shiny. She said she didn't like her hair. I thought her thick, straight black hair pulled back in a ponytail looked great. But she talked about how our hair was cut in ways that made it have good shape and style. I imagined her thought process as she cautiously asked things like: Were you afraid to ride in an airplane? What is it like to fly in a plane? My limited awareness of her own experience slowly expanded as she probed with more questions. She asked how often we see our mothers and siblings. Had we ever driven a car? Did we own a car? We asked about her daily routine.

She described her days as mostly the same, cooking, washing clothes, taking care of her pig. She said now that her son goes to preschool, she is alone much of the day. Elizabeth asked her if she had friends who visit. Veronica said that her sister lives in León, and once a week Veronica goes to León to spend a day. She brightened up as she talked about this. Francis asked if Veronica liked to watch television, and she said no, that the programs were not very good. Eventually, Veronica was ready for sleep.

Rose, Elizabeth, and I were thankful to prepare for rest. When Veronica snapped off the electric light, the house and yard were pitch black. Rose had been smart enough to bring a flashlight in her backpack. We went together through the dark yard to find the latrine behind the house again. We giggled about the bats, trying to decide whether to turn on the light. None of us could remember whether the light would scare bats away or attract bats to the area. We whispered and tried to be quiet. We hurriedly used the latrine and returned to the welcome shelter of the porch, where we joined Francis, brushing our teeth and spitting water from our water bottles onto the ground. We doused with bug spray one more time and stretched out next to each other on our cots. The night was so warm that we did not need the single sheets we had brought. I lay for a long time thinking over highlights of the day. Sometime later, I woke suddenly to the roar of a motorcycle and the flood of headlights approaching the house. Veronica's husband drove right up and parked just a few feet from our cots. We barely woke enough to wave, and he went inside, after flipping off the headlight.

The dawning light or the birdsong and roosters woke me soon. Rose and Elizabeth continued to sleep peacefully, and I wondered if they had been awake most of the night. My skin felt sticky and my face oily from yesterday's heat, but the morning was delightfully cool and breezy. As I went to the latrine, I saw that Veronica was already raking leaves around the pig pen. Francis and I found a shady spot under a tree in front of the house and let Rose sleep. Veronica and her husband, Jose, came and sat with us. The couple was proud of their home and thankful to be able to host us. Jose talked about how hard it had been to live with his new wife in his parents' home since there was very little space for so many people. He told about his work, six days a week in the factory. I was happy that I was able to understand so much of the Spanish they spoke. Elizabeth joined us and engaged our visit.

We knew that Juan Pablo would be back to pick us up around 8:00 a.m., but it was only about 6:30, so we had more time to talk. Before long, the sleepy children wandered out and joined us. The morning was mostly quiet. A man on a bicycle rode up and waved as he stopped in front of the house next door. We watched him ring the bell on his handlebars. That seemed to be the signal to see if the household wanted to buy milk. A woman stepped out to speak with him. He dipped a bowl of fresh milk and poured it into a woman's plastic pail, which she then covered with a cloth towel. Veronica watched without moving. I wondered if she wanted to buy milk but didn't have the funds. The man pedaled away, jingling his bell at the next few driveways as he passed out of our sight.

Rose woke and joined us soon. I asked if I could take photos. Veronica agreed with enthusiasm. We began posing, first with the family. Then I took some with just the family in front of their house. I hoped I could arrange to bring her copies of the photos someday. Time passed quickly until we heard the sound of the van heading our way. I felt a potent intimacy with this family we had barely met, who had welcomed us to their home. I hoped I would see them again. It felt strange to see Juan Pablo's van pull in the driveway and to say goodbye as we left Veronica's world to step back toward our own. We packed up our cots and piled on the van once more.

Our experiences with the home stays immersed us more deeply in Nicaraguan farm life. When we focused on agriculture, the model farm, and home stays with rural families we had a taste of the connection to the earth that typifies life in rural Nicaragua. I wanted to acknowledge the beauty and wonder of campesino identity that is central to Nicaraguan pride. However, I also wanted to raise consciousness about a potential tendency to romanticize rural life or to essentialize people by reducing them to some abstract concept or overgeneralization. I wanted to understand more about peasant studies as discourse that has influenced intercultural relationships. One assignment my students engaged prior to travel included examination of the history of the term and consideration of the following reasons for my concern about the Western construction of the term "peasant."

Campesino is a difficult word to translate. I ask students to notice consequences of the English term "peasant" as a common translation of the word. Most students say the term "peasant" evokes a pejorative sense of othering. Nonetheless, it is still widely used in many disciplines and regions of the world. As a global category or conceptual frame, the moniker conflates people from different continents and historical time periods. JustHope partners can enhance our shared work by exploring the concept of campsino identities in Nicaragua in relationship to terms such as peasant, Indigenous, poor, rural, traditional, and communal. We can notice usage of the term in contemporary anthropological and interdisciplinary research in other geopolitical contexts as well as transnational discourses. The complex identity politics of peasant movements have sometimes acted as a lightning rod for conflict surrounding processes of globalization, environmental exploitation, economic oppression, and neocolonialism. The term is reductionistic and unclear. It is an excellent example of the imperious attitude or gaze that distorts understanding and prevents respectful mutuality.

I think the term peasant is no longer ethically appropriate to describe people in the present day because of its neocolonial, historical construction. This does not mean that I think the campesino identity is inherently problematic, although certainly it is elusive. The attempt to capture that identity with the English translation "peasant" is the problem. A quick search yields a broad array of recent, academic literature about peasants in such diverse places as Ireland, India, China, Mexico, and Poland. In other words, the conceptual framework of the concept of peasant identity generalizes across continents, cultures, nations, and ethnicities in ways that both illuminate and distort individuals and communities.

My class remarked on the prevalence of the term in the reading they did prior to travel. Walker and Wade's *Nicaragua: Living in the Shadow of the Eagle* is an excellent introduction to Nicaraguan history and politics. Nonetheless, like literature from many disciplines, this volume includes an uncritical use of the term peasant. For example, they convey an immediate sense of similarity when they conflate "the peasant" with "the poor" in a sentence like this one: "temporarily abandoning guerrilla activity and working instead to organize peasants and the urban poor."[4] I describe this as an example of uncritical use of the term because the authors do not define the term but use it to refer to a category of persons, assuming the reader understands the intended meaning. I began to notice the frequent use of this term and became curious about how the import of that terminology shaped relationships with people. Far from being an exception, Walker and Wade's use of the term is consistent with other publications in recent decades.

For instance, Cynthia Chavez Metoyer, in *Women and the State in Post-Sandinista Nicaragua*, published in 2000, writes: "Ortega warned that if Arnoldo Aleman won the presidency, he would eliminate the Nicaraguan army, take all land from peasants, and continue the current policies that fuel unemployment."[5] Her readers do not have the benefit of any description to clarify this category of persons. We are expected to know what it means to be a "peasant." Likewise, the title of Keith Cox's 2012 article, "Happiness and Unhappiness in the Developing World: Life Satisfaction among Sex Workers, Dump-Dwellers, Urban Poor, and Rural Peasants in Nicaragua," also assumes that peasants are a recognizable category. Cox does not clarify the boundaries of who is included in this group of persons either. Another example of the uncritical use of the term is found in Daniel Chávez's 2015 monograph, *Nicaragua and the Politics of Utopia*. He writes, "Even if the protest of consumers, peasants,

---

4. Wade and Walker, *Nicaragua*, 41.
5. Metoyer, *Women and the State in Post-Sandinista Nicaragua*, 114.

students, and indigenous people did not foster all the changes it strived for."[6] These are all examples of the type of history, political analysis, anthropology, and social science research that shape the way readers preparing to travel to Nicaragua relate to persons they encounter through transnational partnerships.

My concern is that the use of the term with all its historical baggage perpetuates implicit bias and neocolonial harm in intercultural relationships. The use of the term is not limited to history, political science, sociology, or anthropology. In a 2019 publication in the field of theology and ethics, Agnes M. Brazal made similar, uncritical use of the term in her book, *A Theology of Southeast Asia: Liberation-Postcolonial Ethics in the Philippines*. She writes, "An example is *The Gospel in Solentiname* which is the fruit of peasants' reflections on the Bible in the context of the Somoza regime (1936–79) in Nicaragua."[7] My students and other volunteers who engage in attempts at building solidarity with rural communities in Nicaragua read literature like this and come under the influence of the essentializing, othering category in ways that shape our transnational encounters.

I want JustHope partners to explore the history and construction of peasant identities in order to deconstruct the term and seek clarification about academic use of the category. Put another way, analysis of this term provides a window into the way a conceptual frame shapes how we interact with Nicaraguans. We carry unexamined presuppositions that we have absorbed. These frames or perspectives influence what we notice and even how we feel about our experiences. This analysis of terminology offers an example of how the imperious, alienating gaze of western academics influences transnational partnerships. It may help to explore the history of the term.

Within the field of anthropology in the United States, titles including the word peasant, often reference pioneering work by Alfred L. Kroeber (1876–1960). In his 1923 book, *Anthropology*, Kroeber wrote about peasants but did not define the term. For example, he said, "It has been stated that many a peasant goes through life without using more than 300 or 400 words."[8] We gather impressions of peasants from his descriptions: peasants are unsophisticated and uneducated. They are associated with the past, simplicity, and poverty. Kroeber writes:

6. Chavez, *Nicaragua and the Politics of Utopia*, 312.
7. Brazal, *Theology of Southeast Asia*, xxix.
8. Kroeber, *Anthropology*, 115.

> It was a time of villages, small towns, and scattered homes; of sacred groves instead of temples; of boggy roads, of ox carts, and of solid wooden wheels; of a heavy, barbaric warlike population half like European peasants half like pioneers; self-content, yet always dimly conscious that in the southern distance there lay lands of wealth, refinements, and achievements.[9]

According to Kroeber, peasants' lives are contrasted with achievement and civilization. He writes, "It is safe therefore to set 4500 B.C. as the time Egypt emerged from a tribal or rural peasant condition into one that can be called 'civilized' in the original meaning of the word: a period of city states or at least districts organized under recognized rulers."[10] Peasants represent the past, the uncivilized, the opposite of progress.

The term also carries baggage of neoliberalism. For example, in 1938 Raymond William Firth (1901–2020) published *Human Types*, an influential anthropology textbook republished for decades that included this definition of peasants, "The term peasant has primarily an economic referent. By a peasant economy one means a system of small-scale producers, with a simple technology and equipment, often relying primarily for their subsistence on what they themselves produce. The primary means of livelihood of the peasant is cultivation of the soil."[11] Firth and others made explicit the identity of peasants as a group connected by structural political economy. Whether subsistence farming was the only identifier of peasants in Firth's work remains unclear. Readers are left to wonder if there are peasants who are bakers, butchers, homemakers, or carpenters. Are there farmers who are not peasants? Must peasants own land or are landless field laborers also peasants?

The contrast between the depictions of the same community by two anthropologists was examined by George M. Foster (1913–2006), who published his analysis in his 1960 essay, "Interpersonal Relations in Peasant Society." Foster concluded that researchers would find a "rather uniform nature of interpersonal relations" which "characterize peasant societies in many parts of the world."[12] Foster writes that he agreed with "Kroeber's classic definition of peasants," namely that peasants are "rural peoples living in relation to market towns."[13] Note that this definition is

---

9. Kroeber, *Anthropology*, 425.
10. Kroeber, *Anthropology*, 443.
11. Firth, *Human Types*, 87.
12. Foster, "Interpersonal Relations in Peasant Society," 174.
13. Foster, "Interpersonal Relations in Peasant Society," 174.

not limited to those who cultivate the soil or own land. Foster agreed with one scholar who had noted patterns of "violence, disruption, cruelty, disease, suffering and maladjustment."[14] But Foster criticized another anthropologist who had studied the same village and found it cooperative and harmonious. Foster concluded, "A village must be approached with the assumption that most of its people are naturally uncooperative, not that they are cooperative."[15] This conclusion supports the presupposition that peasants are recalcitrant, backward members of communities that are unlikely to successfully cooperate to improve their own lives. The lens of neoliberal economics is obvious as anthropologists defined peasant societies as lacking the dynamics necessary to develop a capitalist economy.

This portrayal of peasant societies as deficient was perpetuated in the literature for decades. Foster quotes Edward C. Banfield's 1958 book, *The Moral Basis of a Backward Society*, saying, "Beyond the nuclear family, concerted action for the common good is impossible."[16] Banfield's book was republished for a decade and widely read. The implicit assumption that progress equates with capitalist development, and some societies lack qualities necessary for advancement is clear from the book's title. Foster does not question Banfield's perspective or theoretical framework. Foster writes, "It is difficult for me to understand why, in the face of visible evidence to the contrary, so much work in community development and related programs is based on the starry-eyed assumption that there is something 'naturally' cooperative about peasants."[17] These scholars characterized peasants as a human type whose folkways help predict behavior in various communities perceived to be similar in geopolitical locations around the globe. Development studies are still haunted with this conceptual framework. As I researched these issues and taught students to think critically about the use of the terms, I realized that much of my formative education reduced people to identity categories structured by capitalism and Western imperialism. The consequences reach far beyond transnational relationships with Latin Americans.

The discourse constructs peasant society as a pattern to be recognized across cultures. Privileged academics, usually from North American

---

14. Foster, "Interpersonal Relations in Peasant Society," 174.

15. Foster, "Interpersonal Relations in Peasant Society," 178. See also Lewis, *Life in a Mexican Village*, and Redfield, *Tepoztlán*. Foster and Lewis both criticized Redfield for romanticizing peasant society.

16. Banfield, *Moral Basis of a Backward Society*, 10.

17. Foster, "Interpersonal Relations in Peasant Society," 178.

or Eurocentric institutions, built careers studying persons they called peasants. However, this type of generalization about peasants is found in Marxism as well as capitalist and neoliberal societies. Peasant studies continue to flourish as a robust focus in various academic disciplines.

From a neoliberal economic perspective, the failure of rural communities like many in Nicaragua to successfully join the global capitalist industrial economy is both a result of and a description of their political economy. What it means to be a peasant is to be peripheral to the urban, developed, capitalist economy. The Marxist analysis that links workers internationally also offers comparisons between subsistence farmers outside the industrial, capitalist economy. Karl Marx (1818–83) published *Capital: A Critique of Political Economy* in 1887, and peasants are foundational to his theory. According to Marx, "capitalist form presupposes from the outset the free wage-labourer who sells his labour-power to capital. Historically, however, this form is developed in opposition to peasant agriculture and independent handicrafts, whether in guilds or not."[18] Marx draws a distinction between farmers who aspire to be capitalists versus those who eschew technology and industrial agricultural methods. I question that distinction.

Marx claims that farmers are different from peasants because they are "distinguished from peasant agriculture mainly by the number of workers simultaneously employed and the mass of means of production."[19] Some writers adhere to this distinction between subsistence level farmers who are peasants versus large scale farmers who are not. It is common for peasants to be associated with the proletariat in Marxist analysis of the revolution and social movements in Nicaragua. However, in the literature there is no consistent, clear definition of who is a peasant and who is not.

For instance, according to many of the academic scholars noted above, Pedro Luís would be considered a peasant because he is a subsistence level farmer using primitive technology. However, it is unclear whether Pedro Luís would expand and modernize his operation through use of a tractor and the purchase of more land if he could do so. In other words, knowing farmers who are struggling to feed their families in Nicaragua, I am not at all convinced that they would not seek more industrial farming methods if they could afford to do that. The distinction between

---

18. Marx, *Capital*, 452.
19. Marx, *Capital*, 453.

farmers who are often considered peasants and those who are more like capitalists is problematic.

Peasant studies continues as a subfield of anthropology represented by *The Journal of Peasant Studies*, founded in 1971 and continuing with wide readership in 2023. In some ways, that school of thought represents a type of objectifying, exoticizing, essentializing approach to the study of societies conceptualized as other. The privileged educational resources and institutional context of that scholarship was never free of the Western gaze rooted in imperialism and capitalism. Despite the flourishing subfield of peasant studies popular with these anthropologists in the United States and Britain, it is intriguing to notice that I was unable to find literature about peoples within the United States who are labeled peasants. With the exception of recent immigrants from other parts of the world, there are no peasants in the U.S. However, there are subsistence farmers and rural workers tangential to urban cities who might be called country folk, hillbillies, rednecks, hicks, or backwoods people. Why was the term "peasant" not invoked? This seems like evidence of a tendency within Eurocentric academia to exoticize or essentialize peasants as others. The ambivalent relationship of the field of peasant studies to Marxist analysis may offer another explanation of the complicated use of the term.

Marxism provided tools for critique of the colonialism that drove global capitalism. Anticolonial theory should acknowledge the contributions of Marx. In fact, the appeal of Marxist ideology is best understood as an alternative and an "adversary of colonialism."[20] Questions for global sustainability and mutuality arise from study of the competing narratives about motives for both Marxists and capitalists. Perhaps, Western imperialism and colonialism were driven by complex motivations that cannot be completely reduced to greed and economic ambition. No doubt, greed and lust for dominance drove Western empires. However, in some cases, benevolent motivations to share assistance may have been a motivation for international exchange. I do not defend imperialism, but we should examine the complexity of motives involved in our history. Sadly, an assumption of cultural superiority accompanied economic incentives for transnational trade. This is illustrated in the 1912 words of a French lawyer, Mérignhac, who wrote:

> To colonize is to establish contact with new countries in order to benefit from their total range of resources, to develop these

20. Grimal, *Decolonization*, 142.

> resources for the benefit of the national interest and at the same time to bring to the native peoples the intellectual, social, scientific, moral, cultural, literary, commercial and industrial benefits of which they are deprived and which are the prerogative of the superior races.[21]

The blatant claim of superiority shocks contemporary readers formed by egalitarian values. Yet, notice how Mérignhac claims that colonialism has some benevolent motivations, providing opportunities and help to those understood as deprived and inferior. This is similar to the claims of missionaries who believed they had good motives. Nonetheless, even if we assume the impulse to assist is charitable and sincere, the framing of less economically developed societies as backward is evident. Colonizers' crass economic interests in extracting resources and labor from subjugated peoples is also explicit. In contrast, the leveling equality of the Marxist revolutionary movements has appealed to those who have been on the receiving end of colonial brutality.

Post-colonial and subaltern studies have developed Marxist critiques more fully and continue to question assumptions of Western cultural superiority. Published in 2020, *Fifty Years of Peasant Wars in Latin America*, by Binford, et al., seeks to update the analysis of Eric Wolf and the political project of advocating for peasants. Careful analysis of the term and its history would improve the book. Binford writes, "Peasants have not disappeared. The proportion they represent of national populations may have declined, but in absolute numbers there are more than at any time in history."[22] The point of this analysis is simply to unmask presuppositions that disable just and healthy transnational partnerships.

Ideological battles related to Marxism versus capitalist economic development models continue to rage in transnational or global economics. However, discourses have been improved by the work of subaltern studies represented by Antonio Gramsci, who often used the terms peasantry and proletariat interchangeably. Gramsci appreciated the problematic construction of the term in academic discourse. He writes, "The peasants are treated as picturesque representatives of curious and bizarre customs and feelings."[23] Gramsci's analysis of the subaltern continues to develop. The unifying concern of subaltern studies is that instead of objectifying

---

21. Grimal, *Decolonization*, 2.
22. Binford et al., *Fifty Years of Peasant Wars in Latin America*, 16.
23. Gramsci, *Selections from Cultural Writings*, 213.

groups like peasants, scholars and activists should make every effort to amplify the voices of the subaltern persons. Gayatri Spivak famously encouraged listening to ways the subaltern would name themselves if scholars listened more to those whose voices had been excluded.[24]

Spivak's articulation of questions about how the subaltern can speak and how scholarship can either amplify or silence subaltern voices demonstrates the need for respecting peasant subjectivities. Postcolonial scholarship offers tools to analyze and dismantle the baggage connected with terms like peasants. Although many JustHope partners may not be interested in this academic research, critical consciousness of these issues can prevent perpetuating harm from the neocolonial gaze. By amplifying Nicaraguan voices from the margins, JustHope partnerships can move toward mutuality and solidarity. It helps to identify scholars working on projects that promote subaltern voices.

For example, ethnomusicologist T. M. Scruggs documents Nicaraguan efforts to forge a national identity toward the end of the twentieth century. He analyzes Indigenous influence in folk music and dance. Scruggs writes:

> Within the Indian-Mestizo-European continuum found throughout much of Latin America, socioeconomic success demanded distancing oneself from the cultural practices of more rural-based, lower class population associated in the national consciousness (sometimes inaccurately) with a higher proportion of Indian blood, not to mention those communities actually identified as "Indio" (Indian).[25]

In Nicaragua, campesino pride and participation in dance and music became emblematic of those movements in the revolution and in anti-imperialist, national consciousness movements. The desire to recover pre-colonial, Indigenous traditions connects people who identify as Indigenous but also Nicaraguans who identify as mestizo. The Sandinista movement for national autonomy included embrace of campesino music and identity. Scruggs writes, "In the 1930s, individual members of Nicaragua's small middle class began unsystematic and often highly personalized investigations into campesino (peasant) culture and what they hoped were vestiges of pre-European Nicaraguan culture on the

---

24. Spivak, "Can the Subaltern Speak?" 282.
25. Scruggs, "Let's Enjoy as Nicaraguans," 301.

Pacific coast."[26] JustHope partners can promote the poetry, lyrics, art, and theology of those Nicaraguans while questioning the construction of the concept of peasants.

One of the most enduring and beloved examples of this reclamation of campesino identity is expressed in the Misa campesina nicaragüense (Nicaraguan Peasant Mass) of 1975.[27] In his 2005 article reflecting on this mass as an expression of re-indigenization, Scruggs uses the term "folk mass" rather than "peasant mass" in his title. This may indicate sensitivity to the problematic nature of the term "peasant." As we listened to stories of leaders in Chacraseca, many of whom would be included within the group called "peasants" by academic scholars, I hope we questioned the label. By studying and appreciating the lyrics written by Carlos Mejia Godoy and others, we honor Nicaraguan voices.

In his reflections on the history and influence of Bartolomé de Las Casas in Nicaragua in the 1500s, Gustavo Gutiérrez analyzes "the arrogance of the modern spirit, which regards itself as the final stage of history and which distorts past reality accordingly."[28] Las Casas objects to the injustices and inhumanity of colonial and imperial domination in Nicaragua and other parts of Latin America. The arrogance and assumption of cultural superiority exemplified in even benevolent motivations of churches illustrates the distorting depiction of traditional cultures, often labeled peasant cultures.

JustHope is committed to work that reduces harm and fosters true, respectful mutuality and collaboration. We become more human as we struggle to unlearn concepts and attitudes we absorbed unconsciously from colonial culture. Citizens of the U.S. and citizens of Nicaragua have a history of international relations fraught with imbalance of power and inequalities of resources. My interest is in removing obstacles to mutuality and solidarity through transnational partnerships like JustHope. I maintain that the use of the term "peasants" to identify certain rural peoples in Nicaragua is antiquated, conceptually unclear, and harmful to respectful relationship. It is not enough to avoid the term. Mutuality requires deconstructing the conceptual lens and actively dismantling the attitudes of superiority undergirding the history of the term. Solidarity work must be enhanced by more critical reflection about identity, especially the unique

---

26. Scruggs, "Let's Enjoy as Nicaraguans," 302.
27. Scruggs, "(Re)Indigenization?," 96.
28. Gutiérrez, *Las Casas*, 8.

construction of the campesino identities in Nicaragua. JustHope partners need this critique of the ways that Western hegemony operates through a conceptual gaze that is often unconscious but nevertheless dominant.

The liberation theologians and activist priests insist on consciousness raising and critical thinking in public pedagogy among both urban and rural communities in Nicaragua. To become human, we must think collaboratively and question how knowledge is constructed. JustHope strives to sustain mutual learning and spiritual discernment. In the quest to become more humane, our words and concepts matter.

For example, Father Uriel Molina unmasked economic and cultural barriers to genuine mutuality in base communities. Priests should not expect to be effective, Uriel explains, if they merely want to "reach down and rescue the poor." Such aloofness is paternalistic and insulting, and hardly indicative to an authentic meeting between persons where they learn from one another and collaborate as equals. Uriel's position is that those who save others do not embrace them as comrades but as debtors.[29] Put another way, efforts to save someone are obstacles to mutuality and solidarity with that person. For these reasons, we must think together about conceptual frames we use to make sense of our experience. Furthermore, we must engage in the political struggle for just agricultural policy. Farmers need partners to stand in solidarity in the work for land rights. We can value the redistribution of land after the Nicaraguan revolution as an effort for equity and dignity.

Those who were landless became landowners through the reform and redistribution when huge plantations were broken up during the revolution. Property disputes continue to unsettle the Nicaraguan economy and disrupt efforts at development. Land rights especially affect farmers and workers in rural areas, those previously thought of as peasants. Liberation thinkers recognize the potent consequences of land reform. One alternative to dependence on the wage economy and jobs created through global capitalism is sustainable agriculture. Ecofeminist thinker Maria Mies writes, "Only societies which are to a large extent self-sufficient in the production of basic necessities can maintain themselves free from political blackmail and hunger."[30] She argues that "Third World and First World women" can build solidarity and mutuality through collaborative, transnational activism. She claims that an alternative economy

---

29. Murphy and Caro, *Uriel Molina*, 185.
30. Mies, *Patriarchy*, 219.

and a "consumer liberation movement" call for sustainable agriculture. "This would be a movement of people to use the land and the human and material resources available in a given region for the production of those things which they need first: food, clothing, shelter, health, and education."[31] The appeal of this thought resonates across borders as we seek new models of sustainable living.

Similarly, theologian John Cobb studied the importance of redistribution of land as a step toward self-sufficiency in food production. He writes, "Such self-sufficiency will make possible truly free trade; namely, a situation in which a country is free either to trade or not."[32] Those interested in agriculture can connect as international partners and share concerns about global trade, environmental issues, and tension with urban centers. JustHope requires intentional commitment to dismantling inequalities and working toward mutual respect for the dignity of each person. Such work is not easy. It demands rigorous honesty, self-examination, and humility. JustHope invites partners to ongoing spiritual transformation to sustain this work.

---

31. Mies, *Patriarchy*, 233.
32. Cobb, *Sustainability*, 47.

8

Locally Led Construction

"When teams come to Nicaragua for the first time all they can see is the poverty," Leslie Penrose had said. Those words echoed in my mind Friday morning, as potent silence settled over our group when our van pulled in the muddy drive of Marta's house. I felt myself struggling to remain fully present given the harsh realities of poverty in front of my eyes.

"This is Marta's home where we have our first visit this morning," Leslie announced.

Our goal for the day was to learn about the construction programs that the community organized with JustHope. We had learned that almost half of the people in Chacraseca live in plastic houses and heard that the community consistently names housing as a priority. Our visit with Marta was an opportunity to learn about this from her. As I walked with the group toward her house, I knew my own formative experiences influenced what I saw. Her house seemed like an inadequate shelter for livestock. The fact that a woman and her young children live in this structure was unimaginable given our North American mindset.

We were determined not to participate in poverty tourism, that objectifying and demeaning phenomenon we had studied before travel. We had been in Nicaragua less than a week, yet we were growing more acutely aware of the formative influence of our economic class position. What could be done to enact mutuality in this encounter? Regardless of the intentions of travelers who want to learn or help, when people interact across economic divides, the dynamics are problematic. We needed to bring awareness of power differentials between economically privileged people with sufficient resources to travel like us and those who are made poor by systemic structures beyond their control like Marta. How can JustHope raise consciousness and bring a balance of mutual respect to a meeting like this? Would it be better if we had never come? Yet, Marta had collaborated with neighbors, organized through local collaborative leadership, and invited JustHope to build a new home for her family.

No more than a frame of poles fashioned from tree trunks and limbs with black, plastic sheeting stretched to construct walls, the small structure was topped with old, corrugated sheets of metal. Limp strings of barbed wire separated the yard from the neighbors' property on either side. The overwhelming first impression was that of the dark, damp earth that seemed to cling to everything. A bright orange, plastic bowl floated atop a rusty barrel of water beside a concrete sink and a worn table fashioned from roughly hewn, heavy boards. The scene was marked by contrasts: the pervasive, dark Nicaraguan soil blanketing the yard and coating everything from the damp house and even the children in sharp contrast to the bright, freshly washed clothes draped on the barbed wire fence to dry. Our group of North Americans with cameras and cell phones stood out as if we had dropped in from outer space. Marta, with a baby on one hip and a barefoot toddler hanging on to her side, smiled at us as we approached. Two other children, naked from the waist up, peered shyly and looked a little nervous. A woebegone dog, also caked with mud, seemed almost too weak to twitch off the flies pestering its boney hips.

Although we had driven past structures like this and seen them from the road during our week in Nicaragua, to stand in the muddy yard where Marta spends most of her daily life scrubbing clothes by hand and caring for her four children seemed surreal at first. I hoped others in the group remembered what Leslie Penrose had taught us: that our North American assumptions and attitudes about poverty were not shared by this community in Nicaragua. Here, there was no shame attached to being poor. The condition of needing resources was not associated with personal failure. We stumbled for awkward seconds, hoping the discomfort we felt was not visible to Marta. We were shocked by the material conditions of her life, but we were there to learn from her, as a person of sacred worth and dignity. Marta wiped her hands, wet from washing clothes, and welcomed us as Julio translated our brief introductions. Although it was early morning, Marta already looked warm from her work; I felt exhausted thinking of her life as a young mother. She introduced her four small children, the oldest being six years old. It took a few minutes for us to introduce ourselves. We shifted awkwardly, glancing around at the home we had come to witness and trying not to stare rudely.

Marta knew that we were visiting her because her family had been designated by the base community's leadership committee, ACOPADES, to receive a new house. I am impressed as she explained the process. Clearly, she understood herself as a valued member of the community who made herself available to teach us about the community organizing project. She looked forward to the fulfillment of this dream over the next year, when JustHope volunteers would come and construct a cinderblock home with a floor as well as a new latrine nearby. Leaders from her sector had identified her need as among the most urgent. Her anticipation was plainly visible as she talked about her hope of having a new home.

Marta welcomed us to step inside and view her plastic home, knowing that as JustHope partners, we represented the potential for relationships of mutual respect, transformation, and collaborative justice-seeking that were led by her own community. Paula, Elizabeth, and George ducked through the doorway and looked in the house. Martin and Rose exchanged smiles and words with the kids. The situation felt awkward still.

Marta had been working at a wash board, scrubbing a soapy garment when we arrived. "Tell us about your laundry business," Leslie asked. Marta showed us her washing system that included several fifty-gallon drums of water and a short length of garden hose connected to a water faucet in the middle of the yard. Marta explained that she depended on the money she earned washing clothes. I worked to keep the tone of conversation light and friendly. Rose asked how long Marta lived here. Marta explained that she had lived here with her husband and children for six years. Before that, she lived in a different sector in the community. Bill asked about her husband's work. Marta explained that he works as a farm laborer, planting and then picking yuca during the five or six months of the year that comprise the growing seasons. The rest of the time, he looks for firewood or searches for wild honey to sell. Martin asked how much money they bring in. Marta said they usually live on about two dollars a day. Marta smiled and seemed relaxed during this exchange. She seemed to enjoy sharing her story.

Rose and Paula bent down smiling and engaging the small children. The oldest girl ran giggling to hide and then peeked playfully back at them from the corner of the house. I observed my students who seemed to be struggling to bridge the gulf between our lives and Marta's daily reality. This visit magnified the challenge of relating across the chasm of rich and poor. During our encounters in Nicaragua earlier in the week, we had felt connected with people we met through music, art, faith, and our shared desire for building a better world. Now, in these moments visiting Marta's plastic house, I felt jolted by the disjuncture of her poverty versus our material privilege. We were tasting the extreme difficulty of solidarity ethics. There was nothing romantic or simple about the stark reality of that morning's encounter.

Marta continued inviting us to come inside and see her house. I felt unsure of how to respond. On the one hand, I did not want to invade the intimacy of her personal family space, especially since the level of poverty was so extreme. On the other hand, I didn't want to offend her by refusing her invitation to enter her home. How could we interpret this reality to others back home unless we took photographs? We were determined to avoid enacting the voyeuristic poverty tourism so destructive of solidarity ethics. Taking photographs of Marta, her children, and her plastic house seemed like a step in that direction toward oppressive objectification. I tried to ask myself why it felt shameful or embarrassing to take a photograph of a family who was inviting me to do that. Marta did not seem at all embarrassed. The discomfort was my issue. Not knowing what to do, I stayed outside while others stepped into the small room that was their house. Later they shared a few photos illustrating the very few possessions inside: a bed that was merely a wooden shelf without a mattress, one curling, faded photograph, a few plastic dishes, a plastic chair, and a shelf with some clothing, a wooden crate that looked more like a feeding trough for livestock than a baby crib.

While our group relaxed into interacting with the kids and looking inside the house, a few of us continued to visit with Marta who had not moved far from her laundry sink during our conversation. I ventured a question, thinking I could learn more about their typical diet and the line between what they usually ate versus what they longed for: "When you are able to earn a little extra money during good weeks, what do you buy that is different from a usual week?" I asked. I expected that she would name some food item that was not regularly available in their diet. I thought this would be a clever way to get an idea of the types of food they usually eat versus the items they consider rare treats or luxuries.

"When I earn extra money, I save it for the times when we don't have income," she replied matter-of-factly. It occurred to me that my question struck her as something only an idiot would ask. She clearly knew some things about which I was truly ignorant.

I was stunned; her response totally took my breath away. My face warmed with shame that I had never learned that severe food insecurity meant saving every extra cent for times when there was no work and no income at all. Despite years of visiting Nicaragua and hearing from people struggling to survive, still the distance between my privilege and Marta's reality shook me deeply. It was as if we were from different worlds. I felt my ignorance like a naked vulnerability that exposed some guilt related to my lifestyle. My economic position disfigured my awareness in a way that was a barrier to my relationship with Marta. In that encounter, Marta offered a rich opportunity to learn and grow. This was an invitation to a spiritual exercise of humility and activism motivated by the discomfort I felt discovering the chasm between us.

Our visit to Marta's home was brief. We were not there more than twenty minutes before it was time to load the van and leave. After wrapping up our conversation, we thanked Marta and said our goodbye.

"Does Marta have a husband?" Rose asked Leslie once the van was moving.

"I heard her mention him, but I don't think he is around much. I have never met him," Leslie explained. "That is typical of families around here. Men come and go. Maybe he is working in some other area. Women seem to take care of things on their own."

We were mostly silent as we rode to our next stop. Each of us needed time to reflect and process our thoughts and feelings from the day. I thought we would have plenty to discuss at our evening reflection meeting that night.

We had one more visit that morning. Leslie took us to see the home of a family in another sector who had been selected to receive a new home a year earlier. Juan Enrique, the elected leader of ACOPADES, met us at a corner of the road on his motorcycle to guide us through the winding dirt roads to find the location. An older woman stepped from the shade of the porch, waving a dish cloth and smiling to greet us as we stepped from the van. She gave Leslie a sideways embrace, smiling and talking warmly.

"This is Maria Elize," Leslie said. "A year ago, she and her family were living here in a plastic house."

We enjoyed hearing Maria Elize tell her story. She and her family had lived on this land all her life. Hurricane Mitch had destroyed their old home, and they had been living in a plastic house since that time. She and her children worked picking crops when they could, but the drought had reduced the amount of work they could get. They were thankful to be selected because of their great need. She proudly showed us her simple one-room house and new latrine. The new house is a single room structure made of concrete blocks.

"Before we lived in this house, we lived in mud when it rained. We could not keep the rain out. The walls and roof leaked. Our dirt floor was like a river," Maria Elize said. "Now, we thank God for this new house."

"Please tell us about your green stove," George asked. He was interested in getting a good look at the new stove construction some of us had been hearing about.

Maria Elize led the group to the side of her house where a compact stove emitted wisps of smoke. She proudly explained that this stove was a big improvement because it used much less wood to cook.

After seeing her home and hearing her story, we thanked Maria Elize and departed. On the return van ride, I asked Leslie to explain more about the green stoves. She explained that deforestation is escalating as one environmental impact of using wood for cooking fuel. Too many people are gathering fallen branches, so cutting down trees is the only way to meet the demand for firewood. In addition to the ecological problems of deforestation and air pollution from millions of wood fires, communities suffer from the economic cost of cooking with wood. Even the poorest families often spend almost as much on firewood as they do for food. Clearly, there is an urgent need for alternative methods of cooking and fueling stoves.

JustHope learned about a local leader named Alonzo who was working to combat the problems through a new method of building stoves. Alonzo has built several hundred green stoves after being trained by Elmer Zeleya, another local leader. Now, Alonzo works with JustHope to install green stoves for new homes. The construction of a green stove costs approximately four hundred dollars in U.S. currency. Only locally manufactured materials are used. Clay blocks, concrete, sand, and welded metal are all available for low costs in Nicaragua, so the construction of green stoves is not dependent on imported supplies. Empty glass bottles turned upside down and surrounded by layers of dry sand create the insulation and direct concentrated heat toward the cooking burners.

A green stove uses approximately 80 percent less wood than a traditional Nicaraguan stove. This substantial saving of wood benefits families in three ways: by saving money, improving safety and health outcomes, and reducing ecological impact. Households that decrease firewood needs to ten or twenty percent of previous usage enjoy noticeable savings when purchasing firewood. Because the green stoves are strategically insulated and have side walls that do not get hot, they are less dangerous than traditional stoves. The chance of a child getting burned is much less. Smoke is carefully ventilated outside, so the green stoves dramatically reduce the respiratory problems for families, especially the women who do most of the cooking and the small children whom they keep near. The traditional stoves emit high temperatures in areas where women feed firewood to the flames. Doctors urge pregnant women to avoid close proximity to the high levels of heat that the traditional stoves generate. However, in most homes pregnant women have few or no ways to follow this medical advice. Both air quality and tree growth improve by switching to green stoves.

George said, "The green stoves are an inspiring innovation. I was glad to get the opportunity to see one in use."

We shared lunch. Our group was mostly silent and seemed thoughtful. At one point during our meal, Paula said, "This morning was hard. I am glad we have some down time this afternoon to think and process it all. Our visit to Marta's house was intense."

We were all thankful to have free time that afternoon. As an introvert, I am aware that the group process of living in close quarters, eating all meals together, and spending long days in group activities is difficult for me. I reflected on the challenge of wanting to include as many experiences as possible while we are in Nicaragua, yet also wanting to honor the need for time to reflect and process. That afternoon, some of us napped; others began organizing and repacking. Bill, George, Rose, and Elizabeth started up a lively card game. The afternoon heat was sweltering, and the sun was brutal. It was our last full day in Chacraseca.

Reflection Time

That evening, I knew our reflection time was crucial. We needed to sort out our questions, thoughts, and feelings about the morning. I asked about images or memories that stood out from the day.

"The heat really got to me today," Rose said.

"Yes, for a while today, I was comfortable if I could stay in the shade, but now I can't seem to cool down," Laura said.

"A few hours in the mid-afternoon seem to be the worst time, like today when the sun was blazing and there was not even a slight breeze," Rose said. "The cold shower doesn't even seem cold in the afternoon. It feels good."

"I have been thinking about my environmental footprint at home," George said. "My wife and I live in a two thousand square foot house. We are the only ones who live there, and we never really think about whether we leave the lights on in spaces we are not using. We couldn't even consider going without central heat or air conditioning. I keep thinking about our sprinkler system for the lawn. Last month it was broken, and water was running down the paved street several days. That was potable water, too. When I think about the water system here, it makes me sick."

Martin said, "Our visit to Marta's house was the most painful part of the day. It was as if a chasm opened up between us and her family. I felt bewildered and almost paralyzed by the contrast between the physical wealth we take for granted and the lack of property available to her and her children."

Paula quickly agreed, further articulating the frustration, "It was so awkward seeing how hard her life is. I wondered how we could connect at all across these differences that separate us from her? I wasn't sure whether it was more respectful to go look inside her home or not. I didn't want to be like an ugly, gawking American tourist, but I wasn't sure how to convey respect. It was almost like an emotional minefield, as if dangers that we would hurt her or insult her seem treacherously embedded all around us as we tried to relate. We need to see what poverty is like here, but we don't want to embarrass anyone."

After allowing the group time to acknowledge the strong feelings, Leslie quietly said, "This is part of the difference between Nicaraguans and North Americans. Here, there is no shame associated with being poor. She does need a better house, and she hopes we will find partners to make that happen."

Elizabeth said, "I was surprised to see how dirty her children were at first. I mean, my family didn't have much money, but we always did our best to be clean. That is how we were raised. But then I realized the kids were playing like they were making mud pies, just like my brothers and I did when we were kids."

Bill said, "The people here seem happy with their lives. They talk about how God has blessed them. I don't understand why so many try to immigrate to the U.S. Why would they want to come?"

Leslie responded, "The people here have a faith that allows them to be happy in their lives. That doesn't mean they are happy with the conditions of their lives. They are putting their best foot forward when they meet us."

George said, "All week, I have compared my own material wealth with the resources of people we have met in Chacraseca. I realize that back home I am often obsessed with some new thing I want to buy like a new phone, new computer, new car—my economic situation looks starkly different from this location. I have never been food insecure."

Laura said, "What was so hard for me today was admitting to myself how terrifying it was for me to try to imagine myself living like that. Then I realized that the physical comforts I enjoy of having so much stuff make me put my trust in money. The first thing I kept thinking of was how to get Marta and her family money. As if money was always the answer to every problem."

Leslie nodded. "We North Americans always think of fixing difficult situations with solutions based in money."

"We need to be vigilant to avoid the exploitation of just thinking about poverty," I said. "Kwok Pui-lan is a theologian who warns against what she calls being 'fascinated by the suffering of the poor' without engaging in action for change.[1] I believe our spirituality is rotten unless it is fused with justice-seeking action."

"Maybe that is a kind of poverty of the spirit that we have ourselves," Laura replied. "These questions are going to work on me for a long time."

"We have not had an opportunity to talk about the homestays yet," I said. "I have been pondering a question that Veronica, our hostess asked us. She asked how many rooms I have in my house. I had not thought of that before. I started adding up the rooms: two bathrooms, four bedrooms, a kitchen, utility room, den, living room. Her eyes got wide when I said I have ten rooms in my house. My house has about fifteen hundred square feet. It is not large, new, or expensive compared to many in my city. But for a moment I caught a glimpse of her perspective as a person who is thrilled to have one tiny room for herself, her husband and two children." I shook my head at the incongruity of it all.

---

1. Kwok, *Postcolonial Imagination*, 74.

"Veronica was amazing!" Rose said. "I was touched that she was so intrigued with us and our lives. When she asked if I had ever driven a car, I suddenly had an inkling of the chasm between her experience and mine. The homestay with her was the best part of our trip for me. It was hard, but I won't forget it."

"This evening, I have asked Leslie to share her JustHope story more fully," I said. "You have heard bits and pieces of her history here, but we are blessed by this opportunity to travel with her leadership." The group listened eagerly as Leslie reflected on her experience. A transcript of her narrative is included in a later chapter. The experience of hearing her observations and wisdom felt like a rare gift.

"Tonight is our final night in Chacraseca," I said. "Tomorrow night we stay in Managua close to the airport. What insights or questions will you take with you from this time here?"

Slowly students began to articulate some of their learnings.

"I am thinking that maybe private property is an impediment to happiness in many cases," said George. "People need access to material resources to live with capability, but my own life and community back home are enslaved to possessions. That is not a new awareness, but now I have new motivation to change some things in my life."

"Art, thought, and dignity flourish in a balance of freedom and community," Rose said.

Bill contributed, "Simplicity and connection to the land are both important for health and community. And I need to keep pondering what I think about prayer."

"Imperialism is evil," Martin said. "I believed that before, but now I know it in my bones. And I need to keep wondering what I think about prayer," he added grinning.

Paula added, "Our military spending is about protecting the inequitable distribution of wealth—especially the wealthy elites. There is no way that faith or spirituality should pacify our responsibility to change that."

Elizabeth said, "I have new insight about the resource of diversity. In other words, I needed to awaken to the limits of my own worldview. It is easy to get encapsulated by the dominant stories regarding what matters in life. I have been thinking all week about what spirituality means to me. The quest for meaning is individual but also communal. To say something is true amounts to saying it is real beyond just my subjectivity, right? So maybe we have been practicing collaborative meaning-making.

It seems right that intercultural efforts at that are better than isolated, local attempts."

Rose offered, "Wow. I love that idea. I am drawn to the type of liberation theology faith I have learned about here, but I don't know how to find anything like that back in the U.S. Any suggestions?" she asked.

"I suggest checking out the work of Mary Hunt and her ideas about 'Cosmic Catholicism,'" I responded. "She thinks that new forms of expressing faith are emerging that move beyond old forms of Roman Catholicism in the U.S. She is part of a liberation theology network in the U.S."[2] My own spiritual practices feel frustrating unless I can connect them with action beyond my personal serenity and joy. Connections like those help me deepen my journey.

"And there are some great ways to stay involved through organizations like Witness for Peace." Leslie said, "Their website is a strong source for good information about sustainable economics, just trade policies, and international programs," she added. "Some of the best spiritual resources are written in secular lingo."

"I want you to read an essay written by a Nicaraguan feminist liberationist theologian, Luz Beatriz Arellano," I said. "She wrote about working to replace what she called the 'Eurocentric, male, and clerical culture' with new forms of spirituality she saw emerging that focus on practice that is liberating. She talked about how rereading the Bible in connection with the revolutionary struggle has been important to transforming consciousness."[3] I turned to a page in my journal where I had copied a quotation from Arellano. I asked the group to listen as I shared from her work. "She writes, 'The incarnation of this new spirituality transcends what is individual and commits us to struggle for the life of the whole body of the people and for all of life.'[4] That line captures the connection between the work of learning to collaborate for justice and the spiritual journey required to sustain the work," I said.

"That is the kind of spirituality that draws me to this work," Rose said. "I want to stay involved with JustHope in the future." Others nodded in agreement.

---

2. Stoltzfus, "Across Generations," 187.
3. Arellano, "Women's Experience of God," 335–36.
4. Arellano, "Women's Experience of God," 333.

— 9 —

Gringo Day

JUSTHOPE REFERS TO THE final day of the trip as "Gringo Day." The schedule for this day is designed to begin the transition back from Chacraseca toward León, then to the urban pace in Managua, and finally to prepare for the journey home. Travelers need intentional care and awareness about the culture shock of re-entry to the U.S. to best integrate learning. So the final day in Nicaragua includes activities and reflection about moving from Chacraseca back toward the border. Shopping and exploring León can be educational in itself as participants increase cultural awareness of the local political history. We would begin with a simulation experience of buying food in the local market. On Saturday, our group would say goodbye to Chacraseca, get a taste of life in León, visit a live volcano, and learn about the art of making pottery from the Lopez family in a traditional artists' community. To avoid stress and problems with transportation to the airport, we would spend our final night in Nicaragua near the airport. We needed to be in line when the airport opened at 5:30 Sunday morning, so we would sleep across the road from the airport at the Best Western that had once been an army barracks.

Saturday morning after a quick breakfast, we shared warm farewells with Nimia and Estella in the kitchen. We gathered the last of our belongings and passed our luggage up to Juan Pablo who secured our bags atop his van. Juan Enrique, Janeth, Maria Jenia, and others were there to say goodbye and see us off. Although we had only spent a week together, the intensity of the experience forged strong relationships. Saying goodbye felt tender. How could we have bonded so deeply in these few days we shared? George and Rose both told our local hosts they planned to return someday. Everyone posed for a few last pictures sharing hugs and smiles. We had agreed to be ready to drive away no later than 7:30 a.m., and we were only a few minutes short of meeting that goal. Our team was silent as we absorbed the last glimpses of Chacraseca: Casa de Paz, the church, the clinic, the cultural center, neighbors' houses, the hardware store, the dusty, washed-out roads where children were already walking to school. A man on a bicycle was herding a dozen cattle on the road, and our van had to stop and wait for them to move to one side. The smells and images of the countryside offered rich witness to life all around us that we now saw with new eyes.

After a few more minutes, we passed the sweat shop factory, Yasaki, that was a main employer in the area. Hundreds of bicycles hung on racks in the parking lot, while laborers worked day and night in long shifts. The factory sprawled on the edge of León, and traffic there slowed to a crawl on the narrow, crowded road lined with people walking, carrying bundles or children. Leslie explained that workers at Yasaki are required to have a high school diploma. Since less than forty percent of people in Chacraseca have that, not all are eligible for that employment. Those who work at Yasaki earn approximately three dollars a day. I shared with the group about my experience of a Witness of Peace trip focused on union organizing attempts with sweat shop workers in Nicaragua. Most workers appreciated having the jobs but wanted the Nicaraguan government to enforce the labor protections. Workers wanted stockholders of the corporations to feel pressure for more just wages and working conditions. As consumers who benefit from inexpensive products made in factories like this, and as people whose pension funds are often invested in transnational corporations, U.S. citizens are implicated in the working conditions in places like Yasaki. Our group discussed these complicated ethical issues as we rode into the town.

León was founded in 1524 by Spanish colonists, but the first location was near Lake Managua, miles from the current site. The city still has some stone streets and cathedrals from the structures built in 1610, when León was moved to its current location. Our group marveled as we drove by colonial cathedrals, historic and political murals, and universities that attract students from all over the world.

"I am amazed to think of the history," Bill said, looking at old buildings beside the narrow streets. "Most of my life I have lived in communities where a building was considered old if it had been there one hundred years. Just think of that cathedral being here since the 1600s!"

"I am trying to imagine what life was like in the 1700s or 1800s," Paula said. "Imagine all the history and change people have witnessed in these streets."

"Yes, and this town was the site of a number of important historical events in recent decades," Leslie said. "There are still bullet holes in the walls of some houses and buildings from the revolution."

Market Simulation Experience

Juan Pablo dropped us off near the main cathedral and town square at a busy market that looked like a warren of simple stalls for vendors. We circled up in a busy parking lot, crowded with vehicles and people on foot; we saw Julio, Francis, and a third translator, Roberto, who would all help us in the market. Our visit in León would begin with a simulation market experience before we enjoyed free time to explore the central square near the largest cathedral. Leslie reminded us of the instructions for the simulation game and told us to be back at the van within thirty minutes. Each of us would be part of a family group. The families represented real ones from Chacraseca with actual income and needs depicted in the simulation. Each family would receive an envelope with a description of their family and Nicaraguan money to buy groceries. The family would then have thirty minutes to explore the market and make purchases, using only the money in the envelope. A translator would accompany each group and explain to the vendors that we requested their help to teach us about the local economy and asked for their patience as we decided what to buy.

George, Rose, Laura, and Bill volunteered to be in the roles of the first family. Leslie gave them an envelope, and George read the description aloud.

"Our family includes a mom, dad, and three children. Two of the kids are elementary school age, one is high school age. We live on the far north edge of Chacraseca, in Las Lomas sector, about five miles from the high school. We own our own farm, about four acres in size. We use our land to raise corn for our family; but this year, crops failed due to lack of rain. Both mom and dad work in the peanut fields as day laborers when that work is available. Mom has a micro-credit loan with which she raises pigs to butcher and sell. Our average total income is sixty cordobas (two U.S. dollars) per day."

George pulled a few worn paper bills and coins from the envelope and showed his group their money, looking grim. "It won't take us long to spend this. How about gallo pinto for supper?" He smiled wanly.

Rose replied, "I hope the peanut crop is good this year. How long do we have in the market?

"Before you go, let me give you some ideas about questions to consider," Leslie said. "Your family has to make decisions about whether the kids go to school. It costs about seven cordobas per day to ride the bus to high school, plus kids have to pay for photocopies of all tests and handouts in high school or elementary school. Safe water costs about one cordoba, and electricity costs about two cordobas per day for most families." We made notes as Leslie answered questions about the cost of daily life.

Leslie reminded everyone to meet back at the van in thirty minutes. "Stay with your translator, it is easy to get lost in the market," Leslie said. Julio went with the first group and Leslie passed out the remaining envelopes.

I joined a group with Martin, Paula, and Elizabeth. Francis was our translator. Elizabeth was holding the envelope, and we asked her to read the description of our family.

"Our family includes a mother, father, and three children." Elizabeth read. "One child is elementary school age; two are preschool age. Mom is six months pregnant. We live in the Pedro Arauz sector, about eight miles from León. We own five acres of farmland. We could grow corn and beans on our land if we had the starting capital to plow the fields and buy fertilizer and seed. However, we don't have that money, so we have agreed to rent our land to an agri-business peanut farming company for about one hundred and twenty-five cordobas a day (four dollars). Mom raises chickens and cares for the children; dad works as a day laborer on near-by farms when work is available. Our total average income is two hundred cordobas (five dollars) per day."

"I'm tired of gallo pinto, let's see if we can find some chicken!" Martin exclaimed.

"We need to decide if our oldest child is going to school," Paula replied. "I think we need to save some money for that. What did Leslie say it costs for school supplies and fees?"

Elizabeth spoke up, "We also need to save money for water and electricity, so we can't spend all our money on food. I wonder if we have a cell phone. What does that cost?" She turned to Francis.

"Most people just pay for minutes on their phone when they are able. The plans are all different," Francis explained.

"We probably need to save some money for transportation, like the bus. If mom is pregnant, she needs to go see the doctor sometimes," Paula said. "Do you think we should limit our spending to about seventy-five cords for food? We could save the rest for school, transportation, water, electricity and some minutes for our cell phone."

The group agreed. "Let's go see how much rice and beans we can get to start with," Elizabeth said. As the friends walked through the aisles of merchandise, they enjoyed the riot of colors, textures, and smells on display.

"We need some fresh fruit and vegetables," Paula replied, as our group moved into the busy marketplace with rows of vendors selling from rough tables.

The first area we entered had piles of colorful produce. We found stacks of onions, carrots, yuca, mangoes, cucumbers, tomatoes, and plantains. Most vendors were women, and many were tending small children as they worked.

"Let's see how much things cost before we decide what to buy," Elizabeth suggested.

Our group agreed to check prices before we bought anything. Francis, our translator, guided us through the market. On one aisle we found barrel-sized burlap sacks of dried beans of various types. The quality of the beans varied, but the average cost seemed to be about fifteen cordobas for a pound of dried beans. A pound of dried corn cost about five cordobas, and Francis said that would make about ten tortillas. We would also need some oil, she said, and that would cost about ten more cordobas for a small bottle. We began to see that our funds would not go far toward purchasing enough food for our family. One onion cost three cordobas. A small parcel of salt cost two cordobas.

We started to get discouraged when we looked at the quantity of rice and beans our money would buy. Even though we knew our ability to eat the next few days did not depend on this simulation exercise, we felt deflated as it dawned on us how little we could buy. Even though we knew our new friends in Chacraseca struggled with food insecurity, this concrete experience made the harsh economic problems seem more real.

We were undergoing a kind of learning and gaining a kind of wisdom that we could not garner from reading books.

"We need to get a better variety of food since our kids are little and mom is pregnant," Paula said. "Let's go look at the cheese and meat." The look on Frances's face led me to suspect this was futile given our funds. Nevertheless, I was interested to see the prices of those items.

Francis directed us to another section of the market where the smell of blood, meat, and fish made me try to hold my breath and breathe through my mouth. Carcasses of beef and pigs hung from rafters, attracting swarms of flies. Dusty crates with live chickens were stacked beneath tables piled with glassy-eyed fish. One table had a live iguana chained with an ankle cuff. We didn't want to spend much time in this area. Martin and Francis asked about the price of one pound of pork and learned that would cost eighty cords.

"Well then, that answers that. No meat for us. No wonder the microcredit women like to raise pigs," Elizabeth said. "What about eggs?"

Francis led us away from the meat aisle, and it was a relief to step away from the stench. Soon we found a table with eggs in cardboard crates. Francis and Elizabeth inquired about the prices. We learned that each egg cost four cords, so a dozen would be more than half of our daily food allowance.

As we were considering our options, we saw another group of our friends approaching. Bill, Rose, Laura, and George walked up holding a small plastic sack.

"How is it going?" Martin asked.

Rose rolled her eyes. George said, "It didn't take us long. All we could buy was this small bag of rice and beans. We wanted a tomato, but we settled for an onion when we saw how expensive everything is."

Laura laughed and said, "I'm not sure Bill is speaking to us anymore." Bill grinned ruefully. "I never did like shopping for groceries."

"Did you find the meat section?" Elizabeth asked.

"No," Rose said.

"You ought to check it out. Very memorable," Elizabeth suggested.

"We only have a few more minutes, what are we going to buy?" Paula prompted.

"We will see you back at the parking lot soon," George said.

Our group worked through some decisions and opted for buying one pound of rice, one pound of beans, four eggs, one pound of corn for tortillas, one small bottle of oil, a little salt, an onion, and one tomato.

The total cost was seventy-seven cords. It didn't look like much food for a family of five with a baby on the way. We moved through the market looking wistfully at the cheese we could not afford to buy. As we passed back through the produce area, the watermelons looked wonderful, but out of our price range.

"I know I am only getting a hint of a glimmer of what it feels like to live on a few dollars a day," Elizabeth said. "But, holding the small packages of rice and beans and seeing all the things we can't buy is an experience I will remember." The rest of us nodded as we circled up near the entryway waiting for the rest of our team.

One by one, the groups returned, showing their purchases, and talking about their discoveries.

"Laura wanted to buy cheese, but it was sixty cords for a small bag of crema and eighty cords for a small package of crumbles," Roberto said.

"How do people manage?" Laura asked.

"You can see why most families only eat twice a day and have little besides rice, beans, and tortillas," Leslie responded. "Even if they are able to grow a few vegetables or fruit, they may have to sell that rather than eat it themselves. What do you think your family spends on food for a day?" she asked.

George groaned and others also rolled their eyes and grimaced. "I go out to eat or get take out almost every day," George said. "I know I could get by spending a lot less on food."

Paula said, "Even when we try hard to eat at home, we still spend at least fifteen dollars a day on food for the two of us, and that is when we economize. It is not cheap to eat fresh, healthy food." Others nodded in agreement.

"And food costs are still a much smaller percentage of my income than they are for these families we imagined for this exercise," Elizabeth said. "What will we do with this food we bought?"

"Julio will take this food back to Nimia for the next group. It will not be wasted. Each of the families you shopped for represents an actual family in Chacraseca. These are representative of average family situations and incomes," I said.

"I hate doing simulation games, but I have to admit I will remember this," Laura said.

"We have free time for an hour," Leslie said. "We can walk from the market to the main town square. I will show you our meeting place there.

It is a favorite restaurant called El Sesteo that is a good place to have a cold drink."

We followed Leslie through the crowded streets, trying to walk in the shade of buildings to avoid the harsh sun. One block from the market, we identified the spot we would meet later. Paula and Martin were happy to have time to visit a world class art museum a few blocks away. They had read about the museum in a guidebook, and I told them about my previous visits. The museum is housed in what was once a monastery with rich, walled garden courtyards and centuries of art dating back to colonial culture. The buildings themselves portray the history of European influence and Spanish cultural elitism. The art collection includes Nicaraguan contemporary paintings providing critique and alternatives to the colonial paintings. I was glad that Martin and Paula were motivated to visit the museum. I encouraged other students who appreciate art history to go. Elizabeth, Nick, Paula, and Martin set off, knowing they would want more time at the museum but thankful to have the opportunity to visit.

Bill, Rose, and Laura were excited to go inside the main cathedral that stands as the focal point of the square and the city. I recommended that they pay two dollars to walk up to the roof of the cathedral if they could manage the steep stairs.

"It is a bit of a climb, but the view of the city from the roof of the cathedral is magnificent. You can see the span of the town and surrounding countryside from that vantage point in a way that provides great scope for imagination," I said. "Seeing that view fills me with wonder thinking about the history of the city."

George wanted to buy some of the renowned Nicaraguan leather items for sale in local shops. Leslie agreed to help him navigate the blocks nearby. I was happy to have a little time alone for my own visit to the cathedral. We all agreed to meet back soon.

I approached the old cathedral with a sense of awe trying to imagine the construction process centuries ago. I thought of all the scenes of drama, public, personal, and private, that played out here on the square. I thought of the heart aches and joys that people carried to the church here over hundreds of years. That day, dozens of people sat in the benches on the square in front of the cathedral. One old man seemed to stare off into space as if he was unaware of the busyness around him. A young mother fanned her nursing infant with a rag to shoo away a fly. A man with a cart jingled the bell to announce his shaved ice fruit drinks. Several school children in dazzling white shirts huddled together, sharing candy. I saw all this as I walked up the cathedral steps and into the shadowy, cavernous stillness of the sanctuary.

Inside, the scent of beeswax candles and incense pervaded the warm space. Sound echoed in the live, acoustic setting, so every sound was magnified: a bench scraping the floor, footsteps, murmuring prayers, and whispers. I thought about the balance of hushed, profound quiet and the penetrating sounds of life that broke the silence. I saw Rose and Laura near an icon along the left wall. Bill was seated alone on a wooden pew. A few old women were kneeling in prayer in pews near the front. Incandescent light added to the ethereal feeling in the place. The cathedral walls were lined with shrines and altars featuring various icons of saints. The plaster statues were freshly painted in bright colors, mostly depicting white-skinned people. I dropped a few coins in a box, which emitted a noisy clatter before I lighted a candle or two. I thought of a line from a favorite poem by Mary Oliver, "I don't know exactly what a prayer is."[1] I remembered the stimulating conversation with the class about prayer earlier in the week. I still didn't know what I thought about prayer either. Somehow, I continued to practice it nevertheless. I thought of William James's letter to Helen Keller when he wrote, "act as if what you do makes a difference."[2] My prayer was an inexorable longing for transformation of both myself and the world.

Thankful that I had opportunities to study the cathedral before and hoped to return many times in the future, I wanted to spend time reflecting near the tomb of poet Rubén Darío. I found the tomb near the front right of the sanctuary and sat down on a nearby pew. No one else was seated in that area, and I was glad for some time and space to think. The tomb is marked by a virile lion, león, who looks agile and powerful. The respect, veneration, and love for the poet is manifest in the statue. The most remarkable aspect of the lion is a tear running down its face. This captures something of the passion and beauty of the poignant, Nicaraguan determination to rise above injustice and oppression, to aspire for a better future. I sat reflecting on centuries that have unfolded since this cathedral first stood on this square. Perhaps Reubén Dario sat in this pew once. I thought about grimy coins dropped in collection boxes, faces etched with deep grooves of worry lines, resigned silence, furtive

---

1. Oliver, *House of Light*, 60.
2. James, *Correspondence*, 135.

petitions for help, burdens and losses born to these pews, the oily smells of candles, and the compassionate power we sought. I wrote in my journal and prayed before returning to find my group. When I stepped from the protection of the cathedral into the brilliant sunlight, it took some moments for my eyes to adjust.

Leslie and George were enjoying frosty drinks at a patio table in front of El Sesteo just across from the cathedral. I joined them. Several minutes later, Martin, Paula, and Elizabeth returned. George regaled us with his enthusiastic reports of a visit to the Museum of Myths and Legends. He and Leslie had time for a short visit to that center after some successful shopping. George described the museum that illustrates Nicaraguan folk tales.

"The displays were both funny and creepy," George said, "made with quirky, spooky mannequins. They had cheap wigs and weird paint. To add to the grotesque atmosphere, the building was previously a prison used by Somoza's brutal dictatorship and national guard to incarcerate and torture those who spoke out against his dictatorship. It was bizarre to see the historical photographs of prisoners and guards in each room but also fantastical storybook characters from legends. If you ever have a chance to come back, make time to go there," George suggested.

Paula and Martin raved about the art museum. Each of us shared about our adventures, and soon, all members of our group had returned. Leslie invited us to study a mural across the street that offered artistic interpretation of historical highlights. She pointed out depictions of William Walker, Uncle Sam, Sandino, and symbols of the changing history. She reminded us that as a university town, this was a place of innovative and idealistic thinking. We walked to the next block to see another important memorial. Leslie guided us to one of the university campus buildings a block off the central town square. Some basketball courts and benches served as a gathering place where large, colorful murals adorned walls of the buildings. Leslie shared the history of the uprising that sparked waves of the revolution here when four college students were shot and killed by Samoza's national guard on this spot.

As we walked, I was beside Elizabeth, Nick, and George when a young woman approached us and asked for money. Her clothes were tattered and her shoes frowzy. Despite the limits of our Spanish language skills, we understood her story about her sick child and need for money for rent and medicine. George reached in his pocket and pulled out a bill—two hundred cordobas. He passed it to her, and she nodded her thanks.

"How much money did you give her?" Elizabeth asked. "I keep getting confused about the exchange rate."

"Two hundred cords are worth about seven U.S. dollars," George said. "Do you think I was wrong to give her the money?" he asked.

Elizabeth shrugged her shoulders. "Who can say? You never know," she said.

"In the U.S. I don't give money to beggars," George said. "I have seen them head straight to the liquor store too many times when I used to give it to them."

"We were asked for money by some beggars earlier," Nick said. "I never know what to do."

"Our appearance declares our economic privilege. We are tourists. We can afford to travel," I said. "I have asked our Nicaraguan partners what they think we should do when we encounter these requests. They don't have easy answers either. Some have said it encourages dependency and begging in ways that are not helpful. Others think it is the only compassionate response to give money. The only thing I know for sure is that regular, intentional giving through locally controlled and led organizations like JustHope is part of my ethical obligation. When I face a request like that, I feel better knowing that my monthly expenditures include routine giving to mutual and collaborative development efforts."

Our group walked on in thoughtful silence and soon boarded the van to leave León. After a hot, sweaty ride through the countryside, we enjoyed our stop at a national park to see an active volcano. The Masaya volcano is one of many that attracts tourists.

Nick said, "I have always wanted to see a live volcano. I was hoping we would get to do this."

"It is important for partners from the U.S. to see some of the wonders and culture of Nicaragua," Leslie said. "Gringo day gives us an opportunity to experience more of the diversity in this country."

"I have to say, it has been a little weird for me to be labeled as a gringa," Rose said. "As a Black woman, I have to think about being lumped in the category of the dominant oppressor."

"Yes, all of us from the U.S. are in an awkward position in relationship with Nicaraguans. Our access to economic resources and national citizenship have formed our positions and worldviews in ways we see with new eyes as we listen to our Nicaraguan partners," Leslie said.

"One of the extra translators who came to translate for a team last month on Gringo day grew up in León. She had never been to the museum near the volcano before or seen several other places tourists from the U.S. often visit," Julio said.

The conversation continued as the van passed farms and houses. The hot air blowing through the open windows carried scents of diesel fuel, manure from farm animals, and smoke from cooking fires. Before long, we turned in the drive to the volcano. At the entrance, we stopped and paid the visitor fee.

We were intrigued by the lava rocks and fields of blackened earth as the road wound up to the top of the mountain. When we reached the top, there were fewer than a dozen cars in the parking lot. George and Bill remarked about the way all vehicles at the summit were parked facing the exit. Juan Pablo grinned, admitting that the potential danger motivated this arrangement that would facilitate a quick evacuation. We appreciated the cooler air at this elevation as we disembarked from the van. We walked to the rails, awed by the massive crater. From the rim we could see smoky steam and even a glimpse of orange lava far below. All week, we were intrigued with the volcanoes we saw from a distance. Having visited this site before on numerous trips, I was ready to go before the others.

I noticed how hospitable and enthusiastic Leslie was as she answered questions. I envied her grace and generosity as she entered fully into the exuberance of those seeing a volcano for the first time. Her spiritual depths allow her to be with people exactly as they are. I had time to reflect on my own fear in the face of the staggering, immense mystery of the volcano. When I forced myself to lean over the rail enough to see the lurid, orange lava roiling far below, the sensation was eerie and potent. Later, back on the van, our group tried to find words to describe the uncanny encounter with the volcano. We rested during the ride back toward Managua. I told the group about a previous trip with a JustHope partner group that took time to visit a nature preserve nearby. We had seen several monkeys in trees on that trip. Unfortunately, our schedule did not include time for all the places we wanted to see.

Lopez Pottery

Our final stop that day was a visit to the home of the Lopez family who demonstrated their traditional process of making pottery. Leandro and Isaias Lopez were learning the art and craft of pottery making from their parents. These two brothers demonstrated techniques for producing the complex, geometric designs of their art. Their mother's pottery was my favorite, featuring dragonflies, birds, turtles, and flowers. Every step of the process is done by hand the way their ancestors did it for centuries in that same area of Nicaragua.

We learned that they dug up the clay nearby, worked the clay with their feet, and shaped pottery on a wheel turned by foot. Paula and Rose both volunteered to try shaping the clay while using one foot to spin the wheel. We were all impressed with the complicated procedure of shaping the wet clay and then baking it in the kiln heated with firewood. The family members explained how they drew intricate designs and patterns on the pottery using a stylus made from the sharpened spokes of a bicycle wheel. I was intrigued when the artist showed us a paintbrush he used made of his wife's hair. Thoroughly impressed by the skill and ingenuity of the traditional art of making pottery, we were delighted to visit the shop where items for sale were on display. Each of us bought items to take home, thankful to have met the artisans whose hands crafted the pottery.

As the day drew to a close, we arrived at the hotel across the street from the airport. It was a sad, intense moment when we said goodbye to Juan Pablo, who had traveled with us all week. He would return to his home and family in Managua, so we would not see him in the morning. The stark difference between the upscale hotel and our lodging at the Peace House was jarring. For the first time in a week, we would sleep in rooms with air-conditioning and shower with hot water. My feelings about this were mixed. I appreciated the comforts; I wished everyone had access to such amenities. We settled in hotel rooms before meeting at some patio tables near a swimming pool for our final conversation as a group.

By the time we gathered, Paula and Martin had already been for a rejuvenating dip in the pool. Laura and George were sipping frosty, tall drinks from the bar. They looked revived, too. Our group members pulled up chairs and began reflecting about our overall impressions and memories from the week. When everyone had arrived, I asked students to spend some moments in silence, writing about their reflections on the trip. After a time, several volunteered to read from their journals. Each gave me permission to share their statements.

Rose read, "Preparing for this trip deeply challenged my sense of what it means to be an 'American.' I developed an intense awareness of being a privileged gringa from the U.S. and felt deep grief for all people who are forced to endure the consequences of centuries-old imperialism and colonialism. This course deeply challenged my understanding of God's dream for creation and what it means to come alongside God in making that dream our communal reality."

George shared, "This course exposed the legacy of U.S. imperialism in Latin America, particularly because it provided the opportunity to witness firsthand the devastating impact of U.S. policies in Nicaragua that privileged U.S. interests above all others. When historical facts and figures become real people with unforgettable faces and desperate lives, my faith cries out for me to raise my voice and move my feet for justice. I can never be okay with the injustice of having more than I need, when my global sisters and brothers struggle to create a life that meets even the most basic of human needs."

Paula had written, "When enrolling in the Immersion course I had the intention of learning what and how theology could help the first-order issues of hunger, water, and education in the third-world contexts. I couldn't anticipate how apt the lessons would be in my work and understanding of community organizing. Nevertheless, the trip was restorative, healing, and encouraging. From the short week in Nicaragua among the people of Chacraseca I learned how community can work together in unison and what gets accomplished with vision, resilience, and open hearts. Now I reflect on Nicaragua anew and see a whole new narrative of my power now as a community member in mid-western America and the story of persistence and dedication to the hope of change. I was intrigued by the strong rapport among our group and the insights I gained from living in such close community."

Martin said, "The ways of Jesus require reducing inequalities in power and economic privilege. Maybe the campesinos who live off the land outside the global economy offer possibilities for solving environmental problems in ways that attend to the human rights of future generations. This experience makes me think more about what kind of work I want to do to make a difference that matters."

Laura reflected, "I am thankful that we discussed terms like poverty tourism and the voyeuristic tendencies related to the paternalistic motivations of so many mission groups. I had not thought about that before. My own faith and spirituality are richer because of this week."

"Part of my learning has just been the result of living so closely with you people," Bill said, smiling. "I realized I am not used to collaborating with a group. I'm used to doing things my way on my time. I don't like feeling as if my big sister is bossing me around again." We all laughed and nodded in sympathy. "Really, though, there were moments when I felt resentment at a couple of you who were playing with kids or sitting in the shade. I was out there sweating, and you were doing something I wasn't giving myself permission to do. At first, I felt as if some of you weren't doing your share when we were working on that latrine. Later, I realized maybe I needed to take more breaks myself. I can tell you one thing, I am going to buy a Spanish Bible and try to learn at least a few phrases after I get home. Maybe some of the Hispanics in our county will come visit our church."

I also shared what I had written: "All week I reflected on the question of my motives for coming to Nicaragua. One thought that continues to surface is that I feel called to solidarity with those made poor. I am not sure exactly what that means for my life. I have been reading Jon Sobrino's writing about "the world of the poor" and solidarity with the revelation of the divine in those who are hungry or suffering economic deprivation.[3] Once Elba asked me why I kept coming back to Nicaragua. I found myself saying that I came because my thirst for God demands it."

We listened deeply to one another. We felt a bond forged from our meaningful shared encounter. The mood was congenial. We reminisced about highlights from the week, laughing at ourselves and laughing together with rueful, new insight.

Leslie encouraged each of us to prepare to communicate about our experiences.

"People are going to ask you how it was," Leslie said. "But most people don't really want to know much about your experience. I have learned to simply say, 'It was wonderful and terrible.' Some people will want to hear more and be ready to listen. You have had experiences that many people can't comprehend. It can feel alienating, especially with those people who are closest to you. Maybe the best thing is to invite people to hear a presentation about your experience. Those who are interested in hearing more will appreciate learning from you."

"Crafting a presentation about your experience can help you sort out your own thoughts and feelings about how this experience will inform your own future," I said. "The first time I came here, I was furious when I went home. I remember going in a shopping mall back home and glaring with rage at all the opulent, superfluous material goods. It was the start of a long, slow process of being less materialistic myself. I am still working on that," I said. "I also began learning more about various types

---

3. Sobrino, *True Church and the Poor*, 335.

of transnational activism and different concepts of internationalism.[4] I hope each of you will consider how you will stay connected."

"Inviting others to come on a JustHope trip is one way to respond to what you have experienced," Leslie said. "I hope you will consider coming again in the future. You will have a different experience each time you come," she said.

"I want to close our conversation tonight with these lines from the book *To Repair the World*, written by Gustavo Gutiérrez and Paul Farmer. They write, 'Unless we link our spirituality to justice and to the good works we know to be necessary in a world in which a billion people go without adequate food, clean water, health care, and a modicum of justice, we will have, as was noted two thousand years ago, nothing but dead faith.'[5]

The meeting ended, but most of us hung around and talked informally. We discussed ways to stay involved for those who wanted to continue connecting with JustHope. We talked about what we looked forward to about going home. We ate pizza and swam in the hotel pool. Finally, we said good night, returned to our airconditioned hotel rooms, repacked our suitcases, and went to bed early with alarms set for 4:30 a.m. to make the early flight.

4. Besley, *Interculturalism*.
5. Farmer and Gutiérrez, *To Repair the World*, 212.

10

Three Priests and a Woman Pastor
Chacraseca and JustHope

When I give food to the poor, they call me a saint. When I ask why the poor have no food, they call me a communist.

—Dom Helder Camara[1]

On our final night in Chacraseca, we were fortunate to hear Leslie Penrose reflect on her own journey with JustHope. We sat in a circle of rocking chairs on the porch of the Peace House listening to her story, surrounded by the natural beauty of insect music, occasional night breezes, moonlit trees, shrubs, flowers, and evening sounds of the neighborhood. We had heard a few parts of this history earlier, but there was so much new information to absorb that it helped to hear her reflections again and clarify details of the story.

Leslie Penrose:

In the early 1980s, I was working with the sanctuary movement, taking undocumented Central American refugees from the U.S./Mexico border to the Canadian border. I would get a call asking me to drive a family from one location to another, knowing that this could result in being arrested. I only did this about four times, but it got me interested

---

1. Camara, *Essential Writings*, 11.

in the whole refugee justice movement. That led me to begin traveling to Central America with the Center for Global Education. I wanted to understand the situations that refugees were fleeing. I started in Honduras, then I went to El Salvador, and then Guatemala. We saw soldiers with machine guns everywhere. I learned more about how my country was supporting Honduras, El Salvador, and Guatemala with huge amounts of foreign aid. Those three nations had repressive, brutal governments operating death squads, killing their own people. Why was the U.S. supporting these violent dictatorships? We visited body dumps; I saw the issues with my own eyes. It was horrible. Anyone who questioned those U.S. backed dictatorships disappeared or ended up dead. Often their family members were killed, too. No wonder refugees were fleeing to seek sanctuary!

But then we went to Nicaragua. We got off the plane, and there was nobody with machine guns meeting us, like there had been in those other countries. In fact, the Nicaraguan army was all out picking coffee because there were not enough people to pick coffee. Although my government portrayed the new, revolutionary Nicaraguan government as scary communists, I saw the contrast between that depiction versus what I experienced. Nicaragua felt like the safest country I've been in ever. All over Nicaragua, people were painting murals with all this incredible hope around their revolution. I got to spend some time in a base community. I got to worship in Father Uriel Molina's church. I didn't go up for communion because it was Catholic. But this lovely little woman brought the host back to me, and said "Jesus is for everyone" as she gave me the host.

That was during the time of the Contra War. We traveled up to the area of Jinotega, where we met with a group of farmers who had been given land a year earlier in the agrarian reform. As part of the revolution, the new, Sandinista government confiscated land from the wealthy and redistributed it to the poor. This group of farmers we met had been given land to own cooperatively. We were standing in a circle, and the Nicaraguan farmers were guarding us from the Contras. We were in the mountains, where there were Contras shooting people. The irony was that Nicaraguan farmers were trying to protect me from Contras that my government was paying to try to kill people.

The farmers were bursting with pride because they had just completed their first harvest as landowners. They had gigantic tomatoes and carrots as long as your arm. They were showing us all this amazing *produce they had grown. Before the revolution, the land had been owned as huge plantations by Somoza or his cronies. These farmers I met had lived there for generations and had worked the land like sharecroppers their entire lives. Now, they owned the land.*

I said, "Tell me, what's different? Why are these vegetables so fabulous? You have been farming this land forever; what's different now?" They hemmed and hawed a minute. Then this one farmer, who looked as if he was older than God, said, "We have always had hope, always, but now our hope has the strong legs of justice." I wrote in my journal that night that at that moment I heard the Holy Spirit say, "That's your life's work, to give hope the strong legs of justice." So, I've been going back to Nicaragua ever since to learn what that means. And how do we do it? How do we give hope the strong legs of justice? I still don't know, but sometimes we stumble into it and glimpse it. Mostly, I've just witnessed it, over and over again.

I continue to marvel and wonder about how to do this work well. Nicaraguans are still facing all these horrible issues. Situations look as if there is no hope. But then all of a sudden, a Nicaraguan friend will say, "But yes, we are continuing forward; we are in the struggle permanently!" I still don't know how they do it, over and over and over again in the face of things that are unspeakable. I can't even imagine. But they say, "Oh well, we are not giving up; la lucha sigue!"

After those trips in the 1980s, I went home and decided to go to seminary. Before that, I had given up on church completely. We weren't going to church at all. But I found a church in Nicaragua that was alive and meant something. It was the liberation base community church that helped me reimagine what church could be. It motivated me to go to seminary. A couple years later, while continuing seminary studies, I began working as part of the pastoral staff of a church in Tulsa. One day, a nurse called me and said, "Will you come visit this young guy that doesn't have any visitors?" I did, and that was my first introduction to HIV.

I was working at Memorial Drive United Methodist Church in Tulsa then. Soon a group of LGBT folks and people living with AIDS started coming to that church. At first, the congregation was tolerant. When it was just a small token group, the church accepted them. But when these newcomers filled up three pews, older church members started freaking out. During the HIV/AIDS crisis, society's fear of the disease was coupled with homophobia. The pastor wrote a letter to two new leaders, Brad and Mark. That letter said, "Okay, here's where we are. The congregation doesn't like having so many people with HIV/AIDS. So, you are welcome to come to church here, but you are not allowed to teach Sunday school. You are not allowed to drink out of the water fountains. You are not allowed to go in the kitchen, and you're not allowed to read Scripture in worship." I was Mark and Brad's pastor and companion through that terrible time. The public controversy was ugly for years.

Out of experiences like that then, in 1993, the United Methodist bishop invited me to start a new congregation to reach out to the HIV+ and LGBT communities. But the cabinet, the group of district superintendents of each area, did not support the bishop and voted "no." We were not allowed to start a church that was going to be open and affirming. However, the bishop had just gotten back from England where he had been spending an entire summer studying liberation theologians from Latin America. So, the bishop said, "You know what a base community is? How about starting a base community? I'll give you $12,000 and a Bible. That's it; go start your community." I don't really believe in divine intervention, but Holy Moly! And so, we did. Mark and Brad were among the leaders who started the new base community. The Latin American base community model made it possible to start a base community in Oklahoma.

Our new base community in Tulsa was called Community of Hope. The title came out of my journal writing from Central America. During my travels, I had written, "How do they do it, how do these communities of hope and faith continue to survive?" The question fit the context in Tulsa during that time for our new base community, too. There we were with a whole community of people who were living and dying with HIV/AIDS. We struggled to know what hope could mean. In the early 1990s, members of our community were dying every week. Later, new medications were developed, and HIV began more treatable, but at that time death and dying were a continuous reality. For those with HIV/AIDS, hope could not mean "I'm going to live." In the early 1990s, that type of hope could not have been real. Our community members in Tulsa started going to Central America to learn about hope. The Community of Hope in Tulsa had our first meeting June 21, 1993. A team of members from that community went to Nicaragua the first time in August 1993. From the beginning, the link between

Nicaragua and our community in Oklahoma was essential to our work and life together.

During the first week of the Community of Hope, Brad said to me, "I want to start a ministry feeding the homeless." I said, "Brad, we don't have a chair. We don't have a building. We don't have any money." And he said, "Get out of my way, I can do this." And he did. He did it with food stamps from people who were too sick with AIDS to eat, so they gave away their food stamps. They fed the homeless once a month for ten years, at the Day Center for the Homeless. That was just one more time that people who thought they were in the worst situation ever would find themselves serving people who were in worse shape than they were. It was very powerful. Actually what Brad said was, "I don't want to just go to church, I want to be the church."

The base community model from Nicaragua led us to make some highly intentional decisions. For example, the only time I ever wore my clergy robe was when there was a funeral. We needed to dissolve the idea that one person has authority. So, in our weekly worship, we would sit in a circle. I was just one more person in the circle; everything would happen in the circle. But when there was a funeral of somebody who had died of AIDS, I wore my robe. At a time like that, my role as pastor and the symbols of the church needed to be clearly, officially present. Since the United Methodist hierarchy would not allow our group to be recognized as a church, it was especially important to claim the presence of the church at those times. I was ordained by the United Methodist Church and appointed by the bishop to serve this base community. We chose very carefully when I would wear my robe. The circle of companions that was the community did all that work together making decisions about these issues and about what it was going to mean in our life as a community.

Teams from the Community of Hope continued going down to Nicaragua every year. Not only that, but we made the decision after we got back from Nicaragua, that 50 percent of all money donated to the Community of Hope would go to missions. Every dollar that we took in, 50 percent of it went to missions. We continued that practice for the next fourteen years, until I left. We spent all those years in the life of the church trying to figure out "what does it mean to be a base community?" This is a phenomenal question for people in the church to be asking, because when you are going to church, you think you know what church is. You don't have to ask those questions such as: "What are we *supposed to be doing?" and "What does that mean?" You are just going to church. You know, you dress up pretty, and you go and say certain words. You assume you know what church is. But we didn't know what a base community was, so we were constantly saying, "So what does it mean to be a base community? Do we have to have this creed thing? Do we have to do this? Can we say the words, "gay and lesbian" out loud? What does it mean to be a base community? Seriously!*

From 1993 to 1996 the Community of Hope took teams to different areas and regions of Nicaragua. We went to Managua two years and worked in barrio Memorial Sandino. We also organized short-term medical brigades. Then we discerned that we wanted to forge a long-term partnership with people in one community, so we could deepen our mutuality. We went to Matagalpa first to explore that possibility. We hoped Matagalpa might be a place we could settle in partnership because we heard that it had a strong base community. In Matagalpa, at the time, we did not find the fit we needed.

We were actively looking for a community that had enough social groundwork and strength, so that we could come alongside without dominating. We had lots of questions about how to do that with integrity. We were looking for a community that was strong enough that it could tell us "No." I remember talking about that as one of our particular criteria. Our Nicaraguan partners would need to be able to say "No" if we proposed a project or did something that they didn't want. Other than that, we needed acceptance of our LGBT folks. We were looking for a base community that was still functioning with its leadership and its worship style. Because that's what we were there to learn: how does that kind of community life together nurture and empower people? There was a lot more dialogue about the challenges of trying to do partnership with integrity. We did not move quickly. We were determined to avoid North American dominance and paternalism.

I heard about the community in Chacraseca. 1997 was our first time to visit there. Sister Joan was still strong and healthy then. My first memory of Sister Joan is her coming out of the door of the only building, which was kind of an office/storage room. She wasn't living there then; she was living in León. She came out to meet us with this incredibly hospitable vibe from who she was. She spent hours talking to us, meeting with us almost every night to help us do reflections. She talked with us about who these people in Chacraseca were and what they had been through. She focused not so much on the needs of the people in

Chacraseca, but on how much we needed them. We continued to explore our hope that we might form a long-term partnership between our base community in Tulsa and the base community in Chacraseca.

We met Doña Clarissa who was the head of the Pastoral Leadership Committee in Chacraseca. As we got acquainted with her, she also evaluated our potential to be good partners. She said, "So let me ask you a question. Are you going tell us who we can serve and who we can't?" We assured her we would not. That week, we sat for hours talking with Clarissa, and Antonio, and Armando, people who were the leaders then. We talked about who we are, and who they were. We explored the possibility of long-term partnership. It was crucial to talk about LGBT identity and whether that was going to be acceptable here. Were leaders in Chacraseca going to be able to live with openly gay folks working in solidarity with them?

Doña Clarissa was the one who worked most closely with Sister Joan to start the Leadership Committee. Father Donald had been working there for years and had gotten the community organizing piece barely started. They had organized the area into sectors. But it became Doña Clarissa's job to fully form the Pastoral Committee and get people involved. She and Sister Joan went door-to-door in sector after sector, knocking on doors and saying, "You have got to get engaged, you need to come and be part of the leadership. We have got to serve ourselves." They shared all that liberation theology: "We have to be the church when the church isn't here for us."

Doña Clarissa did all of that. She also fought in the war. She took up arms. She never felt good about it. She hated the fact that she had taken up arms. But she would say, "There are some things more sinful than shooting." The reason that she took up arms and felt it was justified was because she had watched Juan Enrique's father be tortured by the National Guard. She didn't ever say any more about that.

When we first came to Chacraseca in 1997 or 1998, the only building near the church was a little storage building where we rolled out our sleeping bags to sleep and stored supplies. That building survived Hurricane Mitch. There weren't many plastic houses before Mitch, but a gazillion of them were constructed after Mitch. The main focus of the leaders in Chacraseca then was building houses for people who had been left homeless by Mitch. Before Mitch, there were old houses that had been standing when the people inherited the land through agrarian reform in the 1980s. Most of those houses were in poor condition because the folks couldn't afford upkeep. Over the years, the leaders in Chacraseca put us to work building schools, houses, and latrines.

We were using our learning in Nicaragua to build our community in Tulsa, to nurture and empower people who were living and dying with AIDS. They felt completely disempowered. We needed our partners in Nicaragua who taught us about healing. Our partners in Chacraseca were healing us; they were absolutely healing us. Our focus was not on the resources we were bringing, as much as what an incredible spiritual experience there was for us in Nicaragua. There was a really big shift from when we started "mission trips" until we started JustHope. The focus of our community in Tulsa changed to building partnerships and relationships beyond just the circle that was Community of Hope. Over the years, our understanding of solidarity and mutuality deepened through the work.

So, in 2007, when it was time for me to leave Community of Hope, that just seemed like a natural kind of thing. I knew that I couldn't go start another congregation because I would just be trying to recreate what I had just come from. It just seemed like Nicaragua was the place where I could invest, continue to learn, and have community. Leaders from both Oklahoma and Nicaragua helped envision the new organization, JustHope. I had the privilege at that time of serving on two national boards for the UCC, so I had lots of networking possibilities that made some of our first partnerships happen and are still good partnerships today. I learned from Sister Joan and her dreams with the people here. At first, they did not have skills to lead; they weren't organized. I think Sister Joan saw it as her calling to get them to the point where they could lead. She worked to recruit leaders, to train them, to make them come sit on this porch week after week for reflection about leadership. When Sister Joan retired, she entrusted JustHope with continuing her commitment to genuine mutuality in partnership.

Over the years, when groups from the U.S. came, Sister Joan had always insisted that every team go walk the labyrinth first thing. She would direct a spiritual process for walking the labyrinth, and when you came back, she led a reflection time to talk about why you were here. She was part of reflection circle most nights, especially if we had beer or chocolate. Also, she made anybody who was not brave enough to challenge her participate in the daily order of prayer with her in front of the cross every morning. When I say, "made," I mean she extended the invitation in a way that you were not going to say no, especially if you were clergy. She was a tremendously formative person. As partners from the Community of Hope, we worked with her for years before we founded JustHope. One of the most challenging goals the leaders in Chacraseca faced during those years was building a water system.

The sisters recruited an NGO from Austria that did the first pilot project for the community's water. It started where the red water tower is in the Pedro Arauz sector in 2002 or 2003. The Austrian government is very involved in León and Nicaraguan charity, but they never finished the water project for all the sectors. JustHope was asked to help extend the water system in 2007. JustHope also started the medical clinic and hired the first doctor. Before that, they didn't have a doctor at all in Chacraseca on a regular basis. The Students for 60,000 group, another NGO, built the first little clinic building. JustHope expanded that and later included a pharmacy and lab. JustHope and our groups have been supporting medicine and a doctor in Chacraseca, at least part time, since around 1999.

The goals and priorities were always initiated by the people in Chacraseca. I remember early on, around 1999, we were using FUNDECI's big yellow school bus for our team. We had been in Nicaragua about a week. We were getting ready to leave. We climbed on the bus, and a little crowd of kids came running out to the bus in their school uniforms. A couple of teachers were with them, and they handed us a letter. The letter said we need to start a school lunch feeding program for our schools. They asked if we would help with that. It was like sliding the request in under the door as we were leaving the community. That was their request, for us to go home and start a school lunch program. We did.

Now we only work through the ACOPADES committee doing community projects the elected community leaders have prioritized. If we get a request now, we tell people you can submit your idea to the committee. That avoids putting us in the position of choosing projects or deciding which projects we will do. JustHope tries to match goals that ACOPADES identifies with the skills and enthusiasm of a partner team planning a trip.

For example, a church group that is coming in July wrote to me about six months ago when they knew they were coming. They said, "You know we have two teams coming. What are the community's priorities this year?" I told them what the leaders had decided at the summit we have every January. That year the community prioritized housing and construction repairing a school. That church had people who wanted to do a group construction project. The ACOPADES leader committee discussed which project was best for that group based on the gifts the team could bring, their interests, and timing of other groups coming in the summer. The community leaders collaborated with JustHope to assign those teams to work on a house construction project. One team started the house the first week. The second team finished the house the second week.

The collaboration is not always easy. As I look back over the years, I think, for me, the saddest moments have been the moments in which I've realized or discovered in some way that I've just completely failed the community. I've been fortunate enough to have had really good, honest, open relationships with the leaders here. Every now and then, we meet to talk about what's working and what's not. There have been times when they've had to share with me ways I've done something or said something that deeply wounded them. I expressed something that I had no idea hurt them. It broke my heart. I would cry through ninety percent of the meeting. Those are my most painful memories because I was not the only one weeping. For instance, Lesbia, whom you met, comes across as a really strong, confident woman. But like many of us who can wear that facade, it's not true in all aspects of our being. There are lots of places where it doesn't take anything to crumble us.

A couple of years ago, she was in charge of the kitchen, and they were asking us to transition to a new arrangement. They did not want us to just assume Doña Nimia was always going to cook for us. So, they asked us to use new cooks. Lesbia was in charge of that. Like all things in transition, it didn't go very well the first time or two we tried it. The food was not prepared as we agreed it should be. People got sick. There were several things we had to meet about.

And then one day, right after a leaders' meeting, I said to her, "Lesbia, Doña Nimia always gives me the receipts at the end of the week, so I can keep records." She just burst into tears. She was devastated. First of all, I had compared her to Doña Nimia. She thought I was trying to return to the old system, as if I was implying, "Doña Nimia does it better than you do." That is how she heard it. She also heard me scolding her, which I don't think I was. But you all know I can come across as kind of intense. She felt scolded in public. She didn't say anything to me for about three days. Then at the end of the week, we had our reflection meeting to evaluate the week. The whole ACOPADES leadership *committee was there to support her, so she would be able to talk to me about how I hurt her. She said she was devastated that I didn't trust that she was going to give me the receipts. She was hurt that I challenged her in front of people. I realized I had done all those kind of North American things, and she was really hurt. The community leaders were trying to protect her. It makes me cry again, even now, to think about it. So, those kinds of things have been the most heartbreaking.*

We said from the very beginning, we are going to screw up, but we are not just going to walk away. We will not be like little kids taking our ball and going home. We are not going to resort to our privilege. We are not doing it. I think if we hadn't made that rule, I might not have kept coming back. We could have said, "Oh, I'm never going back in there again. It's too embarrassing; it's too painful; it's too hard." But we'd already agreed, we were not going to do that. I'm quite sure they would have held me accountable.

David Hoot, one of the leaders at the Community of Hope, liked to talk about the ritual we shared when people became companions at Community of Hope. A part of that ritual roughly paraphrased was, "When things get messy, I'm not going to walk away." I had already made that commitment to myself at Community of Hope, and this was an extension of that, absolutely. There have been many painful times over the years. We have hurt each other and disappointed each other at times. True mutuality means that we are vulnerable. David has been coming to Nicaragua every year for over twenty years.

People often ask about times when I had injuries or illnesses while I was here. I have been asked to share the story about when I broke my leg. You know that JustHope's founding story is of me being on a mountaintop in Jinotega with a group of farmers, and hearing one of them say, "We always had hope, but now our hope has the strong legs of justice." That is important background for this story about broken legs.

In 2013, we were up in La Flor, a little community where people have to walk across a suspension bridge and then hike up a mountain. At that time, there was no other access. Elba and I were leading a team of college students. It was raining, and the roads were slippery. I slid down the mountain and broke my leg in three places. I had compound fractures, so bone was sticking out of my leg. Juan Pablo was there with us, Thank God. The college kids and Juan Pablo found a hammock and a leveling tool. The kids used their bandanas and the level to create a splint for my leg. Then they put me in the hammock and hiked me down one side of the mountain and back up the other side. The rain continued pouring down.

They took me to the little hospital at Matagalpa. The doctors there said I needed surgery. I said, "I'm not thinking so. I need to go to Managua and fly home." Elba was with me, so Elba said, "I'll stay with the team, just get yourself to Managua and fly home tomorrow." So, I did that. I took a taxi, spent the night in Managua and went home the next day. Then, I had one of the very best surgeons in Tulsa and excellent care.

I had left Elba around 5:00 p.m. at night in the town of Matagalpa, and there were no buses back to La Flor. The team had already gone back up with Juan Pablo rather than waiting with me at the hospital. So, Elba wanted to get back to La Flor and our group. Well, the only ride she could find at that time of night was a motorcycle. She is great riding a motorcycle.

She took a motorcycle and started for La Flor. It was still raining. About three-quarters of the way to Santa Emilia, which is in the cloud forest on a curvy mountain road where it is difficult to see, Elba got hit by a drunk driver. It slammed her into a barbed wire fence, sliced open her head, sliced open her knee from one side of her leg to the other, and broke her leg in two places. She broke the same leg I just broke four or five hours earlier.

She laid on the side of the road for almost three hours waiting for an ambulance to come from Matagalpa. No ambulance ever came, but finally, some nice Samaritan stopped and put her in the back of his pickup truck. He took her to the hospital in Matagalpa, where she had just been with me. The doctors told her the only option was to amputate her leg. Elba said, "You are not cutting off my leg." So, the doctors said, "Well, okay, then we will just have to wait a few days to see if it gets better."

She waited about twenty-four hours, and then, we sent a private ambulance to get her and bring her to León, because she wanted to come home. We really wanted her to go to Managua, but she wanted to be home. They brought her to León to the hospital. The doctors in León said, "The only option we have is to cut off your leg." She said, "You are not cutting off my leg." They said, "Okay, well, then we are going to sew up your knee and wait a week or so and see how your bones do."

Three or four weeks later, still nothing had been done. The doctors were still saying the only option is to cut off her leg. So, we put her in an ambulance and sent her to Vivian Pellas, the best private hospital in

Managua to see the best orthopedic surgeon in Nicaragua. The wreck happened March 21st; and it was April when she saw the specialist in Managua. He said there was nothing that could be done for her knee. It was terribly infected, gushing pus and everything else. He kept her in the hospital, put her on intensive antibiotics for two weeks, and finally got rid of the infection.

Then he was ready to tackle the broken bone. He put her leg in one of those fixators. It looked like a towel rack that we used to use in the 50s. That was the only option that they had in the best hospital with the best doctor in Nicaragua.

In the meantime, I was in Oklahoma with one of the best surgeons in Tulsa, best pain medication in the world then, and my cast. I was already home with my little knee support, healing just fine, with all the pain meds I needed, clean and sanitary, with regular doctor's appointments to monitor my healing. All this for me, but Elba was rotting in the hospital in Managua. I couldn't stop weeping, bawling "Elba, Elba." Every time I went to my doctor, I cried and told him about her. Finally, my surgeon said, "If you can get her here, I'll do surgery."

By then it was June. We told Elba about the option to come to Tulsa for surgery. She said, "Well, let's just try this first. I really don't want to leave my family. Let's just give this doctor a chance." In July, she went back to the doctor. The fixator bracing her leg had gotten infected. The doctor said, "You have to leave the fixator on, because your bones aren't healed. We will treat the infection, but you have to leave it on."

Two weeks later, she went back. It was more infected than ever. The doctor said, "Your bones are healed. They're fine." By then it was mid-August. "You're fine," the doctor said, "I'm taking off the fixator and giving you these antibiotics. You can go home now and just learn how to walk again."

We asked for some x-rays that he took. She sent them to Tulsa. The pieces of her bone that had broken were not even lined up. They were overlapping side by side, not even touching. Of course, she could not put an ounce of pressure on it. The pain was killing her. In Nicaragua, they rarely have narcotics, so the only pain medication she had the whole time was extra-strength Tylenol. Except, when my surgeon prescribed pain medication for me, I took them down to Elba, so she had that a few times. Finally, Elba agreed to come to Tulsa. She came for surgery on September 10th. By that time, I was walking again. I was fine. She had been suffering since March 21st. It was hard for her *to leave her family, but the surgery was successful. The doctors in Nicaragua could have amputated her leg, but you saw her working all week with the micro-credit women and social enterprise program. You saw her riding that motorcycle all week.*

There have been times like that when we provided support that was not sustainable for the whole community in Chacraseca. As a JustHope staff member, Elba received help that others in her community and even her own family would not have received. We struggle and reflect on times when our solidarity demands actions that are in tension with other core values like mutuality. There are no easy answers. Being in the struggle means we do this work imperfectly, but we keep trying to change toward our values.[2]

When Leslie concluded her story, a vibrant, rich energy hung over the group.

"What happened to Sister Joan?" Rose asked. "Everyone here talks about her as if she was a saint. I wish we could meet her."

"Sister Joan developed health problems and serious memory issues," Leslie said. "She lives in a retirement community for Maryknoll sisters in New York. Sadly, she does not even remember Chacraseca anymore at all due to her dementia."

"That really is sad," Rose said. "But what a difference her ministry made in this community! We are truly fortunate to learn from you, Leslie."

My students cherish the opportunity to learn from Leslie Penrose. She is quick to attribute her own learning to wise Nicaraguan mentors and liberation theologians. In order to understand the history of JustHope and the base community in Chacraseca, one needs to view the development of liberation theology in the context of Nicaragua's relationship with the United States. Encounters with three Nicaraguan priests who embraced and taught liberation theology shaped my insight: Father Miguel d'Escoto, Father Uriel Molina, and Father Donald Mendoza. Leslie Penrose was mentored by a network of activists and religious leaders including these and others influenced by them, especially Sister Joan Uhlen. Throughout our week in Nicaragua, I shared information with our class about what I had learned in my interviews and correspondence with these three priests: Father Miguel, Father Uriel, and Father Donald. Through in-depth interviews and correspondence with these pastoral theologians in Nicaragua, I deepened my own understanding

2. Interview with Leslie Penrose, June 2019. Transcribed by Donna Greene.

of liberation theology. Each made important contributions to the events and movements that resulted in Maryknoll sisters and lay volunteers building long-term, sustainable partnerships in Chacraseca. JustHope volunteers continue to hear about the work of the sisters and priests who organized leadership development for rural communities. Those Nicaraguan leaders found in Leslie Penrose a kindred spirit whom they trusted to continue the ministry in the base community they had begun.

My interviews and correspondence with these priests continued after the trip in 2016. Future JustHope partners and students can benefit from the following stories and wisdom that documents the history of these three priests who were friends and mentors.

Father Miguel d'Escoto Brockmann

In 2015, Leslie Penrose and I visited Father Miguel d'Escoto Brockmann at his home in Managua. In previous years, we had taken groups to learn from him about liberation theology many times. I had conducted in-depth interviews with him about the intersection of politics and theology. On that visit, Leslie asked him what it was like to be able to do the mass after being forbidden for so many years. In 1985, the Vatican suspended his priesthood because he held a position in the new, revolutionary, Sandinista government. He was reinstated as a priest recognized by Rome in 2014. He said,

> *Look, I always believed that the mass is to be lived, not to be said. To live the mass is to live those words: "This is my body; this is my blood." In other words, this is my life, my earthly life. I put it at risk for the cause of the kingdom of God. You have to understand it in the sense of a sacrifice. That is a word we use, but sacrifice means to make sacred. It means to give it to God. Sacred is everything that belongs to God. No trespassing. It is an honor. That is what we do in the Eucharist. We say this is my body and my blood which I would risk for the sake of proclaiming the kingdom.*
>
> *What is the kingdom? We don't understand the message of our Lord. Kingdom is a political concept. But, you know, he came to preach the kingdom of God. It is 100 percent political, but it is 100 percent religious. This is the way God wanted you to relate to one another and to creation: the kingdom of equality. There are no second or third-class human beings. You can have a second-class ticket on the airplane, or*

the third-class ticket on the train. But the people are all first class. You cannot have an empire. The empire will justify itself by saying they were meant to rule it over the others because the others are God-forsaken people. They said the people had to be civilized. One of the Spanish colonial authors, writing his chronicles back to the crown, said: "These people must be civilized. They don't like war. So, they must be civilized, so that they like to kill one another."

I like to think that I think the way Martin Luther King Jr. thought. He was a great inspiration to me. Being in the U.S. at the time when MLK was doing his proclamation was very important. But even in the U.S. some very respectable priests in my own society, they were telling me, don't be so taken up with MLK. I was buying his books, especially one book, The Strength to Love. *I would give it to all the priests to read. Priests would tell me, "Be careful. MLK is a communist." But then I say: more power to the communists!*

Yes, I wanted to celebrate mass, but what I wanted most is to live the mass. If in your whole life you had only one mass, you have to consider everything prior to that as a preparation for that mass, and everything after that as a living out of that mass. I am still considered dangerous or something. Don't blame the bishops. They are not people who have read very much. They are following that orientation of John Paul II. Never be bitter. Our Lord said you have to love even those who behave against us like our enemies. There are so many problems in the world, that we should not over emphasize my problem. The thing is to keep going.[3]

The last time I saw Father Miguel was on July 10, 2016, only about sixteen months before his death. He was pleased to hear that I was on my way to volunteer with JustHope in Chacraseca. In our conversation at his home in Managua, he shared a story I had heard him tell before. He said,

This is the thing I most remember from childhood. One day we were being driven to church, and I saw people looking in the garbage pails. So, I asked my mother, "Mother, what are they doing there?" She said, "They are hungry. They are looking for food." I didn't understand how they could be that hungry. I asked, "Why are they hungry? Why are they looking for food in the garbage?" My mother was the daughter of a wealthy family. She said, "They are hungry because it isn't true

---

3. Interview with D'Escoto Brockman, 2015. Transcribed by Kathleen McCallie.

that we are Christians." So I learned that to be Christian means to be revolutionary, to change things. But the dice are loaded on the side of the rich.[4]

As he spoke, his facial expression conveyed the vehement sense of outrage and confusion over this injustice he felt when he had seen through the eyes of a child. The bewilderment he had felt then still troubled him as an old man retelling the story. The perplexing conundrum that shocked him as a young child in that moment continued to baffle him through his life. Still puzzling over the way privileged people can harden their hearts toward those made poor, Father Miguel expressed dismay and anguish over systems that perpetuate poverty and suffering in a world where others enjoy abundant wealth. This problem framed the spirituality and work of Miguel d'Escoto; likewise, it is a central issue for JustHope partners.

Questions of justice and fairness are embedded in spiritual, ethical, and theological issues related to circumstances of our birth in either conditions of relative prosperity or poverty. Father Miguel's influence in the Sandinista movement of the 1980s and 1990s is difficult to overstate. He served as foreign minister and a close adviser of Daniel Ortega from 1979–90. He strategized and led the lawsuit in the international court against the United States for the mining of the Nicaraguan harbor. He served as President of the United Nations General Assembly from September 2008 to September 2009, presiding over the 63rd Session. His influence in international and Nicaraguan politics continued until his death. The fact that I first learned about Father Miguel and Maryknoll ministries through the ministry of Rev. Leslie Penrose, knowing she was a pastor in the controversial United Church of Christ,[5] illustrates Father Miguel's commitment to ecumenism and interfaith partnerships. As a young priest, Father Miguel was trained by the Maryknolls. He shared the conviction that congregations must attend to the material, social, political, and relational needs of the community.

Father Miguel was adamant that sectarian divisions between Christian faith groups were serious problems. He said, "We talk about ecumenism, but we either don't understand it, or we don't really believe in it. This sectarianism is not Christian." Conflicts between Protestants and Catholics continue to rage with leaders on both sides, demonizing or refuting

4. Interview with D'Escoto Brockman.
5. Penrose was a pastor in the United Methodist Church until 1998, when she joined the United Church of Christ.

the faith of their opponents. Yet, Father Miguel always treated visitors as brothers and sisters. As I told our group, he often said to groups of volunteers, "You people are crazy! You left your comfortable beds, air conditioning, and nice neighborhoods to come work in the dusty, hot, Nicaraguan communities. You are insane! And I believe the world needs more divine insanity like this."

The prophetic ministry of Father Miguel d'Escoto was part of a movement for ethical spirituality and religious practice that took matters of wealth distribution seriously. His work included organizing and leading community development throughout Nicaragua. For example, he founded a Nicaraguan organization, FUNDECI, that invited volunteers from other countries to come work in solidarity to learn and serve in the poorest communities. Leslie Penrose was one who responded to that call.

Father Uriel Molina

Our class had a meeting scheduled with Father Uriel Molina, who agreed to share his story with the seminary students. However, this meeting was cancelled due to Father Uriel's illness. Of these three priests who each had a significant influence in the base community model in Chacraseca, Father Uriel's ideas are most accessible to students because scholars have published writing about his work. Our class read *Uriel Molina and the Sandinista Popular Movement in Nicaragua*, a history by John Murphy and Manuel Caro before travel.[6] Father Miguel d'Escoto wrote the forward to that 2006 volume. The two had been friends since they were young men; I met Father Uriel through Father Miguel's work with Leslie Penrose. I was fortunate to interview Father Uriel several times and shared insights from his reflections with the group.

Uriel Molina's signature contribution may be his leadership in developing the concept and practice of base communities. As a young priest working from the mid-1960s in a barrio of Managua called El Riguero, he gained a reputation with the conservative church hierarchy as a troublemaker for criticizing the Somoza regime. His church, renamed Santa María de Los Ángeles after the rebuilding needed after the 1972 earthquake, was known as a center of resistance to the U.S. backed Somoza dictatorship. Father Uriel estimated that approximately two hundred youth from his parish were killed by Somoza's guards during the revolution of

6. Murphy and Caro, *Uriel Molina*.

the 1970s.[7] He credited the students who became community organizers under his leadership for developing needs assessments and distinctly local forms of collective action. The role of the base community in consciousness raising, economic development critical of neoliberalism, and sustainable systems of egalitarian decision-making served as a model used by Father Donald and Sister Joan in Chacraseca, as in other places throughout Nicaragua.

Father Uriel was not afraid to draw on tools within Marxism while still maintaining his Christian faith. Like Father Miguel d'Escoto, Uriel Molina saw common ground between the teaching of Jesus and Marx, who "wanted to end misery, eliminate poverty, reduce social conflict, and create a more humane and commodious world."[8] Marx's critique of liberal capitalism and global economic structures promoting unfettered markets provided tools needed for social transformation and consciousness raising. Both priests thought that the institutional leadership of the church was complicit in forging and maintaining the widening gap between rich and poor. Father Uriel insisted that neoliberalism has resulted in an idolatry of the market, as if the market is God. Murphy and Caro write,

> As a result, societies are referred to as markets, institutions are corporations, persons are resources, and values that clash with this perspective are considered to be unproductive . . . And persons have become "enslaved," adds Uriel, "by the resulting egoism, consumerism, and materialism."[9]

Uriel Molina taught that solutions that dismantle neoliberalism and question loyalty to the dominance of the market will come from the margins.[10] Therefore, communities like the one in Chacraseca that manifest the creative resistance of the people's imagination and hope offer alternative models the world needs.

Father Donald Mendoza

Father Donald Mendoza was born in 1947 and was seventy years old when I first met with him to hear about his ministry in Chacraseca. That day, June 2017, was only two days after the funeral for Father Miguel

7. Murphy and Caro, *Uriel Molina*, 87.
8. Murphy and Caro, *Uriel Molina*, 67.
9. Murphy and Caro, *Uriel Molina*, 123.
10. Murphy and Caro, *Uriel Molina*, 129.

d'Escoto, who had been one of his closest friends. Father Donald was grieving over the death of his colleague and reflecting on his own fifty-two years of serving congregations. He had gone to seminary in Columbia when he was about eighteen years old, in 1965. He had joined the Piarist order, dedicated to education. That order, also known as The Order of Poor Clerics Regular of the Mother of God of the Pious Schools, had been working in Nicaragua for sixty-nine years. When Father Donald returned to Nicaragua after completing seminary, the order sent him to work at their school in León. He was ordained as a priest in 1973. In his own words:

> *In the early years of the revolution, I had a very close relationship with Father Miguel and Father Uriel Molina because there was a viacrusis for peace, since it was a time of war. We were very good friends. We walked alongside for a long time. My relationship with the fathers dates to about forty years ago.*
>
> *When the revolution came, the victory in 1979, we saw the struggle in the war against Somoza. Some of our students who were Agriculture students were already adults. They got involved in the fight against Somoza. And we saw how Somoza's guards killed them. Others died during the military service during the time of the revolution. So, all of that would get your heart, and you would ask how could you abandon them now when they have really put their lives at risk. One thing led to another, and people started changing their mindset.*[11]

While working at the school in León, Father Donald heard about the rural community of Chacraseca only about ten miles away. Some of his friends who were priests invited him to go along when they went to Chacraseca to say mass. Soon he began teaching and serving in Chacraseca as well.

> *I said mass every weekend. But the problem was I had my own way to understand the ritual . . . not only the ritual of it, but also an opportunity to encourage the Christian community. When I came to Chacraseca, there was not a sense of community. When I got there, the community had a bad reputation. They would kill each other. There was a lot of group vengeance. I don't know how we started to dissipate that behavior, but God helped us a lot. Because back then, when*

---

11. Interview with Donald Mendoza, 2017. Translated by Julio Delgado, transcribed by Donna Green.

I would be asked, "Do you work in Chacraseca?" people said, "Life is worth nothing in that community." People were surprised I could work there. And I would say, "No, no, no. These are human beings; our brothers and sisters are there." When I would go to Chacraseca I would ride a horse or just walk from León.

Elderly men and women in Chacraseca still talk about how Father Donald walked out to be with them even through dangerous years when helicopters and airplanes engaged in the military conflicts flew low overhead. Roads might be blocked or unsafe, but Father Donald found a way through the countryside.

In many of the rural communities, they didn't have a building to meet. Early on, I would have mass in this building, but later I started going to different communities and having mass in people's houses. The other thing was I was not supposed to just concentrate on the religious aspect of it but also the human aspect like health and education. Then I started to know them, and my love for them started to grow. I would organize what they would call "encounters." They would have youth from Chacraseca come to the school in León for training purposes and for spiritual retreats. Little by little, that sense of community started to grow.

Through the relationship that Father Donald had with Father Miguel d'Escoto and the organization FUNDECI, he connected with Sister Joan and Sister Liz, two Maryknoll religious women from the United States who were living and working in Nicaragua. The sisters made the decision to focus their ministry in Chacraseca after having worked in various Nicaraguan communities for many years. Working closely with Father Donald, the sisters organized the base community there. They started building new schools and holding regular community leadership training opportunities. Over the years, the community developed numerous programs for health care, education, agriculture, business, and construction. When the Sandinista party lost power in 1990, the community and the leaders of the Piarist order decided that it would no longer be safe for Father Donald to continue his work in that community, so they moved him to another ministry in Costa Rica. Years later, he was able to return to visit in Chacraseca. The sisters were still working with community leaders there. Children who had been on baseball and soccer teams Father Donald had started or had been students in school were now effective leaders continuing the work of improving their community.

> *So one of the greatest satisfactions I had was when I came back was to see that the work that I had started in Chacraseca had experienced continuity precisely because of the work of Sister Juanita and other sisters. The community had improved their way of living. For a person who knew the community in the 1970s and now goes to visit, they will say there has been a tremendous change. And the majority of the change has been because of the work of the sisters. When I was there, I worked with them for about thirteen or fourteen years in Chacraseca.*

The base community in Chacraseca always invited international partners to collaborate with them in achieving their goals. Sister Joan, whom Father Donald called "Sister Juanita," and Sister Liz had strong connections with communities in the United States. They facilitated transnational delegations who came to volunteer, and organized opportunities to contribute resources to meaningful work. Father Donald was quick to give credit to the sisters for the work in the community over the years.

> *At first, we didn't achieve a lot of material improvements. However, over time, along with the sisters, a partnership with the U.S. started developing. There were brothers from Wisconsin, too. They would come and look at a little bit of our reality, and then go back and do fundraising in the U.S. They would help. That was how the women's co-ops came to be—the bakery. It was because of this that the way of living for people started to improve. Then, Sister Juanita saw the need to establish herself right there in the center of the community. Early on, I was working in the priest house; it was a very old house. We changed some walls, and we did some fixing. There, the sisters lived in a space that was smaller than this. They had their beds and little tables. And over time with the help from outside, then we built the Peace House.*
>
> *Back in the 1980s, we started to have partnerships with people in the United States. Later on our sisters continued that relationship. Besides those relationships, we also started having a relationship with friends from Austria. So that also opened opportunities for people from Chacraseca to go to the U.S. and to Austria as well. And so, for many that has opened their eyes to the world.*

Father Donald repeatedly emphasized the value of international travel and education, as well as the value of international friendships and organizations. He spoke of ways the support of friends and colleagues from other parts of the world was often better support than some of the other priests in Nicaragua. He celebrates the progress made in the material and spiritual condition of the people in Chacraseca, but at the same time, he longs for more equal opportunities for all people.

> *I am a man of hope, and I always think the future is going to be better. And the truth is that Nicaragua has improved, slowly, but unfortunately there is not equal opportunity for everyone. We have a lot of college students that finish as professionals, but they have no jobs. I am eternally grateful to the sisters and the people of Chacraseca. If I have been able to persevere in the priest work, that has been because they have been there for the friendship and faith and commitment.*

In the final moments we shared that day, Father Donald reflected again on the loss of Father Miguel. Then he gave thanks once again for the power of international friendships and partnerships.

> *And now, Father d' Escoto is in the presence of God. So, people of my age, when somebody dies from my generation, we say that he went ahead of us (chuckling). So, we will see when they call my ticket. Every time somebody passes away, it really shakes us up inside of us. Last year was the last time that I saw Father Miguel, when we were celebrating his 40th anniversary as a priest.*
>
> *I have an indelible memory of friendship with different Americans. Do you know Father Gregorio Esmoto, who was an anthropologist in the Caribbean? I remember how these different ones had love for people from Nicaragua, how they shared our difficulties along the Atlantic coast, which has been a very difficult area. Many of them have passed away already. The fact that you are religious, and part of an international congregation, allows us to have a relationship that sometimes the national clergy does not have. I have lived outside of Nicaragua for only a few years. For work of the congregation, I have visited other places. I have never lived in Spain or in America. Our center of operations has been in León and Managua. And I bless God to have another mindset, to have seen other cultures.*[12]

Father Donald's health and age prevent him from active participation in the community-led work in Chacraseca now. I appreciate the opportunity

---

12. Interview with Donald Mendoza.

to consult with him and hear about his work. At the time of this writing in 2020, he lives in an assisted living facility in León, Nicaragua.

JustHope continues the work begun by these courageous leaders like Sister Joan and Father Miguel, Father Uriel, and Father Donald. Many characteristics of JustHope illustrate the influence of the Maryknoll Sisters and these priests. The willingness for Roman Catholics to invite others to serve as equal ecumenical partners, the emphasis on solidarity, and the commitment to social and political justice are all evidence of the shared values that connect JustHope with the liberation theology movements in Nicaragua. Father Miguel organized and supported these partnerships through FUNDECI. Father Uriel started the first base community and led a movement sharing that model. Father Donald's patient work in Chacraseca connected Sister Joan and other partners in the work. Leslie Penrose established an access point for North Americans to form transformational partnership, raising consciousness of injustice, analysis of political systems, and alternative visions of church. This pastoral leadership bridged the intercultural divide that allowed us, as U.S. citizens, to partner with Nicaraguans despite the bitter relationships between our governments.

— 11 —

Liberation Theologies, Spirituality, and Social Epistemology

In her book, *Church of the Wild*, Victoria Loorz argued that the most pressing work of our time relates to spirituality. She writes,

> The Great Work is spiritual at the core. Gus Speth, an environmental attorney, ecologist, and climate advocate, has summarized the problem brilliantly: "I used to think that top global environmental problems were biodiversity loss, ecosystem collapse, and climate change . . . But I was wrong. The top environmental problems are selfishness, greed, and apathy, and to deal with these we need a spiritual and cultural transformation. And we scientists don't know how do to that." Do we spiritual people know how to do that?[1]

People who speak of spirituality should have something helpful to offer during this precarious age of global vulnerability when human life and planetary biodiversity are at risk. If spirituality is more than a tranquilizer for individual palliative care, it must have transformational power. My claim is that JustHope is one model of the work that is needed at this time in history. What partners in Nicaragua as well as liberation and feminist theologians call becoming human is spiritual transformation. Thus, spiritual formation is interwoven with ethics, liberative theology,

---

1. Loorz, *Church of the Wild*, 9.

and political action. Toward the end of her long and productive life, Rosemary Radford Ruether wrote, "The new relationships we are entering to survive on our tough new planet need to generate a new sense of responsibility to other humans, other animals, and the ecosystems around us."[2] Hope depends on relational movements toward justice. JustHope is one such avenue for transformation. In community we discern future steps toward justice. We practice reducing greed and apathy in hope of more humane relationships and systems.

Some children are born into debilitating poverty while others are born to conditions of excessive privilege. Yet each of us seeks answers to the questions of how to live well. The students who traveled with JustHope in this class engaged a type of solidarity that explores issues of ethics, theology, and social justice praxis. Global problems can no longer be solved by great individuals. Urgent problems demand transnational, intercultural collaboration. Jon Sobrino writes, "To serve the Third World is to give, but it is also to receive, and to receive something of a different order from what is given and normally superior to what is given. It is to receive humanity and, for believers, to receive faith."[3] The colonial model of missions acted as if the rich had something the poor needed, but that paternalistic attitude was inhumane. Partnerships establish possibility for collaboration by recognizing and acting as if need is mutual. That type of collaboration can generate new learning and knowledge production for solving critical global problems.

However, societies often entrust seeking knowledge and wisdom to academic disciplines with sharply demarcated boundaries. As a person attempting to learn skillful collaboration across borders, sometimes I have been impeded by academic culture. Polemical discourse, pressure to make a mark by staking a new claim, and defining knowledge in terms of master-y, all perpetuate approaches to learning that are competitive rather than collaborative. The very term mastery illustrates the subjugating, problematic posture of learning that is typical of much academic knowledge production. The social relevance of faith in a rapidly globalizing world depends on work to overcome inequities based on race, economic class, gender, sexuality, or nationality. JustHope requires learning beyond the limits of academic disciplines and their ethos of exclusion, dominance, and efforts to master subject matter.

2. Ruether, *My Quest for Hope and Meaning*, 157.
3. Sobrino, *Spirituality of Liberation*, 172.

Both liberation theology and studies in social justice require intercultural dialogue and relational knowledge production. Before we ask how to do more good than harm, we must explore what we mean by the term "good." To identify overlapping consensus about social goods is no easy task. By emphasizing solidarity, mutuality, sustainability and, collaborative work in community, efforts like JustHope can have transformational power that elitist tendencies of academic discourse often lack.

In this book, I have used an interdisciplinary approach, transgressing boundaries of academic disciplines. Readers may be troubled trying to locate this study within the borders of any one discipline. I have written in ways that are un-disciplined and unruly, avoiding a focus on a single, linear argument. I understand the work of JustHope to defy reduction to a theory or argument. My hope is that this book is more like an invitation to join the struggle or to come and see than it is like a rational argument. To follow the ways of Jesus requires facing old questions about God, meaning, and responsibility as lifelong learners. Nicaraguan partners like Pedro Luis, Elba, Julio, Nimia, and others have taught me that coming to work in solidarity with them is potent. They insist that sending money would not be as valuable to them as coming to share encounter. Spiritual formation is not purely theoretical or individual.

Liberation theologians insist that religious practice and theory must connect with economic problems. We need to study academic analysis and research about systemic wealth distribution. Ethicists who study systemic poverty often care deeply about distributive justice issues.[4] However, JustHope asks us to learn to act, not only as individuals but in community. This collaborative learning requires open-mindedness and expanding the circle to include those who have been excluded from knowledge production and dialogue. Often those who benefit from the current economic system are not the best seekers of new insights or new directions. The prevailing distribution of wealth and political power must be dismantled or overturned in pursuit of collaboration and justice as fairness. Pope Francis says,

> In this context, some people continue to defend trickle-down theories which assume that economic growth, encouraged by a free market, will inevitably succeed in bringing about greater justice and inclusiveness in the world. This opinion, which has never been confirmed by the facts, expresses a crude and naïve trust in the goodness of those wielding economic power and

---

4. Singer, *Life You Can Save*.

in the sacralized working of the prevailing economic system. Meanwhile, the excluded are still waiting.[5]

He advocates for a peaceful, sustainable future that will require both personal and systemic transformation from greed and materialism to collaboration and justice. That type of transformation happens best in communities of practice that cross borders.

JustHope offers a type of grass roots international diplomacy, contextual religious education, and spiritual formation. The essential focus on economic development and redistribution of resources through projects attracts many partners. The process and praxis of building and maintaining community is equally valuable. Through mutual work and solidarity, partners engage in interchange that collaboratively generates wisdom and knowledge. The work is messy and requires perpetual self-examination and dialogue. Mindfulness and vigilant scrutiny about the dynamics of the collaboration are necessary to avoid doing more harm than good.[6] As a theological educator, I view JustHope as an opportunity for students to gain global perspectives on systemic issues of oppression, liberation, and justice. Theological education is not simply about intellectual, academic book learning. It requires skillful practice of critical thinking and action in community.

Critics of intercultural, transnational collaboration are quick to point out the potential for perpetuating neocolonial imposition of Eurocentric values that disrespect local autonomy and diversity. The insight of this critique is well taken. Skepticism about the work of JustHope and similar organizations is appropriate and helpful to guard against unexamined assumptions. Skepticism can enhance knowing because it acts as a corrective against unskillful practices and unjustified beliefs. Collaboration requires common ground for acting together in a process of sharing power. Thus, collaborating is a political and sociological skill that requires thinking together with an interest in knowing. Learning to collaborate better is a process of thinking, communicating, and consensus building. At the very least, it involves knowing that some practices undermine the intended outcomes of the collaborative process. Of course, agreement about what constitutes better praxis requires discerning common ground or collaborative evaluation of the goals or inherent value of the collaboration to begin with. Those who desire to collaborate toward

5. Francis, *Evangelii Gaudium*, no. 54.
6. Probasco, "Prayer, Patronage, and Personal Agency."

justice and human flourishing need the help of skillful epistemology. Put another way, theories of knowledge can enhance responsible, collaborative thinking and learning, especially across borders. Active skepticism and critical thinking are necessary and beneficial to the process.

Recognizing Obstacles to Collaboration

It can be painful to discover that a person from Chacraseca views me as inhumane or unethical. The vulnerability of true mutuality in dialogue requires that I allow myself to be mirrored, seen, and re-cognized by my Nicaraguan colleagues in the quest for skillful collaboration and new understanding. One step toward better shared praxis is identification of obstacles to partnership. Obstacles to mutuality and true solidarity include systemic racism, U.S. hegemony, and economic class differences, as constructed and maintained by colonialism in the past, and neocolonialism in the present time. The problem is that persons often do not know how to collaborate well because radical individualism has been formative for knowledge in Western culture. Knowing about good collaborative process requires increased understanding about possibilities for shared knowledge.

By viewing transnational relationships with insufficiently critical thinking, Westerners often operate with a problematic, alienating gaze that undermines respectful collaboration and knowledge production. Some theories of knowledge have perpetuated this form of cultural hegemony. My deconstruction of the term peasant is an example of dismantling that type of elitist knowledge claim. Another example is the analysis of thinkers who critically examine claims of solidarity. Through attempts at caring and collaboration JustHope partners can discover deleterious effects of unexamined assumptions.

Secular education and sacred quests call for liberating methods. The teachings of Jesus can come alive when those born to economic privilege walk with those who were made poor by systemic economic patterns. JustHope illustrates liberation theology and methodology that transforms older models of mission by first listening and learning from the poor, then sharing praxis led by the poor that moves us all to conscientization and more mindful, mutual action for justice. Therefore, I agree with thinkers who claim that not only is liberation theology not dead, but it is invigorating newer movements like feminist, anti-racist, and anticolonial theory.

In 2018, Michelle Gonzalez Maldonado wrote, "Critiques from within the church and in the academy have led to the premature proclamations of the death of liberation theology."[7] Some theological educators dismiss liberation theology as bygone fad. However, Maldonado demonstrates that spiritual seekers, scholars, and activists continue to find inspiration in liberation theology. My research supports her claim. Scholars recognize agreements between postcolonial, process, postmodern, Womanist/Latino/a/feminist liberation, and Black liberation theology and liberation theology movements in Latin America, Asia, and African communities.[8] Liberation theology intersects with postcolonial theology as both critique colonial systems and continue to generate fresh, significant scholarship.[9]

My companions and friends in Nicaragua remind me that academic scholarship and systematic theology are most fruitful when grounded in praxis that maintains awareness of class and economic oppression. Interdisciplinary work of political theorists, ethicists, and liberation theologians illustrates the fluidity of geopolitics and critical analysis to transcend national borders. Liberation theology generated seeds that grew out of critical reflection on imperialism, colonialism, and domination. I first learned about liberation theology in the 1980s through studying feminist, liberationist theology. For example, in the mid-1980s I began reading Ruether's keen critique of colonialism. In her 1972 publication *Liberation Theology: Human Hope Confronts Christian History and American Power*, she analyzes the attraction that communism had for revolutionary movements in Central America. To explain the pull of communism, she writes, "First, because communist states prove to be the states most sympathetic to this national and social struggle in practice, while Western nations are both the present and former colonialists and the counter-revolutionaries."[10] The ties between postcolonial and liberation theory were strong. Ruether called for colonial legacies to give way to new systems.

Feminist liberation theologians and liberation theologians in Latin America generated fruitful renewal. As Gulio Girardi writes,

7. Maldonado, "Liberation Ecclesiologies," 22.
8. Collins, *Black Feminist Thought*.
9. Rajan, *Ethics of Transnational Feminist Research and Activism*.
10. Ruether, *Liberation Theology*, 161.

"Revolutionary Christians feel that they are discovering what is most essential about what is human and what is Christian. For them what is essential is no longer found in abstract worship of God, but in love for human being."[11] I began waking up to U.S. hegemony and oppressive international relations through liberation theology praxis. I saw how developed nations were widening the gap between rich and poor through trade and military policies that worsened inequities in wealth distribution. By naming economic exploitation as sin and grace as liberation from imperialism, Latin American theologians interpreted the gospels in ways that came alive. Thus, liberation theologians led the way in methods of critical inquiry as a pathway to deeper faith and spiritual practice. By asking the hard questions about political power, wealth, and poverty, these thinkers insisted that spiritual and religious practice requires analysis of the economic implications of Scripture. For example, Gustavo Gutiérrez writes:

> When we speak about the preferential option for the poor, we must be very conscious about the practical dimensions, too. Here I refer to the causes of poverty. For a long time, poverty was understood as a fate: some people are born poor, other people are born rich, and both must accept this fate . . . The assumption was that, for some, poverty is the will of God. We cannot accept this. Indeed, to be for the poor is not to accept their poverty.[12]

Although some North American Christians argue that such theology is too political and not adequately grounded in Scripture, the basis of liberation method begins with reading Scripture. An attitude that approaches Scripture with a view toward mastery of one right way to interpret, teach, and view Scripture is based in knowledge as dominance. A liberating approach to Scripture does not seek to vanquish curiosity or answer every question. Rather it encourages imaginative interaction with the text. The life experience and social location of the readers can be a critical part of the study of biblical texts in liberation practice. Juan Segundo writes:

> When we view religion under the lens of ideological suspicion, it shows up two things: (a) as a specific interpretation of Scripture imposed by the ruling classes in order to maintain their exploitation—though this intention may never be made explicit; and (b) as an opportunity for the proletariat to convert religion

---

11. Girardi, *Faith and Revolution in Nicaragua*, 101.
12. Farmer and Gutiérrez, *In the Company of the Poor*, 29.

into their own weapon in the class struggle through a new and more faithful interpretation of Scriptures.[13]

Put another way, those who engage in spiritual or religious practice must liberate their thought from systems that exploit and appropriate Scripture as a means to defend economic inequality. Liberation theologians think that readers who are most like the earlier followers of Jesus in their economic class position can best understand his teachings. In Nicaragua, when those who are poor and oppressed read Scripture together, they generated power to act from liberated imaginaries for a different world. They view Jesus as one who taught that God is on the side of the poor. This has consequences for the economic decisions and social structures Christians make. Leonardo Boff writes:

> The group may meet under a huge tree and every week they are found there, reading the sacred texts, sharing their commentaries, praying, talking of life, and making decisions about common projects... The principal characteristic of this way of being Church is community. Everyone is a true brother and sister; all share in common tasks.[14]

The collaborative, dialogical approach to this type of discernment and knowledge production is typical of the process of ethics and learning that JustHope advocates. As a revolutionary pedagogy that identifies and resists any alienating gaze, JustHope fosters learning and praxis for social justice. The liberation approach insists that "context needs to be the starting point for theological articulation and the text needs to respond to questions raised by the context."[15]

Liberation theology is grounded in critical education and ideas about spirituality. Rather than thinking of salvation as an individual matter that is achieved through healing a person from the sin of pride or disobedience while saving them for heaven, liberation theology rejects abstract, idealized answers. Instead, communities of persons wonder and question together, viewing sin as greed and materialism, grace as struggle in the work of liberation, and redemption as new creation. Liberation theology poses essential questions about suffering, joy, and blessing in this life. The focus of faith is no longer another heavenly world beyond

---

13. Segundo, *Liberation of Theology*, 16.
14. Boff, *Church*, 128.
15. Chhungi, *Building Theologies of Solidarity*, 140.

death. The relational method of liberation praxis is a type of social knowledge production about living well in community.

Relational Knowledge Construction

Thinking, analyzing, and reflecting collaboratively yields shared wisdom. The process of liberation praxis is not unlike the best academic thought. In fact, the reflection part of praxis should draw on the vast array of theory that the community finds helpful in the struggle for justice. I surmise that what Martha Nussbaum meant by Aristotelian Construction of knowledge is close to social epistemology, knowledge that is produced through dialogue and action.[16] Knowledge workers like philosophers interested in what it means to know and learn can enrich JustHope and liberation spirituality by examining terms like care or solidarity. For example, Lorraine Code warns that the rhetoric of care sometimes masks uncaring motives. We know that paternalism is an obstacle to collaboration. She reminds us that proffered caring can be insulting, invasive, and destructive. Code says that part of the problem is "inadequately informed development practices."[17] Drawing on the research and analysis of Vandana Shiva on neocolonialism, Code notes problems of failing to recognize the interdependence of caring and knowing.[18] She writes:

> The assumption and/or assignment of caring positions in a society operates from a presumed—if usually implicit, and often unsubstantiated—knowledge that the situations in question are appropriate sites for the practice of care; that their participants/occupants need or want this kind of care; and that the presumptive carer(s) know(s) them well enough to provide the care they require.[19]

Diligent safeguards against paternalism are conditions that must be in place to avoid more harm than good in these transnational encounters. Ongoing dialogue about partnership dynamics is necessary to dismantle barriers to mutual understanding between Nicaraguans and North Americans. Care ethics, transnational feminist theory, and development theory intersect in efforts to eschew paternalism and work toward

16. Nussbaum, "Human Functioning and Social Justice," 202–46.
17. Code, "Who Cares?," 104.
18. Shiva, *Earth Democracy*, 184.
19. Code, "Who Cares?," 106.

justice. JustHope partners need to study Martha Nussbaum's human development work on the capabilities approach as well as the dialogical approach of Yuval-Davis and others.[20] Across various sites of knowledge production and activism, knowing and caring intersect with the work of collaborating for justice.

Human development models have often been infected with a colonial gaze and a paternalism stemming from mission mentality. In contrast, Martha Nussbaum analyzed and espoused a human development model called the capabilities model. Because she is a U.S. feminist, her work has been critiqued as being insufficiently responsive to anticolonial theory. That criticism that her work is tainted with the western gaze is ironic, since Nussbaum credits the approach as the creation of Indian economist, Amartya Sen.[21] Yet, the universalist claims about human flourishing based on necessary capabilities represent a liberal stance. Nevertheless, I agree with Nussbaum who takes access to education as a universal value that expands capabilities. Therefore, the promotion of education in Nussbuam's development work is similar to the transnational literacy and efforts of Spivak and other subaltern thinkers working for equitable distribution of epistemic agency.

Nussbaum's capabilities approach promotes solidarity and respectful mutuality in transnational collaborative partnerships for social justice like JustHope. The framework of attending to capabilities, while allowing agency for specific development goals, allows the production of social goods to be controlled through the most collaborative process possible. How capabilities are to be developed in specific situations remains messy and complicated. Within the organization of JustHope, partners from the U.S. and Nicaragua work out annual goals for shared activities. Sometimes, JustHope partners in the rural Nicaraguan community of Chacraseca all reach consensus on the goals for the year. For example, goals might include building six houses, twelve latrines, and repairing two schools, as well as providing teacher training and school supplies. Yet, partners from the U.S. who travel to work toward fulfilling these goals could discover that not all residents in Chacraseca were included in the goal-setting process. The imperfect systems of representation and communication in the community may fail to include every individual. Learning to develop agency and access to collaboration is an ongoing

---

20. Yuval-Davis, "Dialogical Epistemology."
21. Nussbaum, *Creating Capabilities*.

process of expanding capacity and access to shared decision-making. In other words, the means to engage in community collaboration may need to be expanded.

To illustrate the challenge with trying to equalize epistemic agency, consider this example studied by Martha Nussbaum. She analyzed a case of a women's literacy campaign in rural Bangladesh described by Marty Chen in the monograph *A Quiet Revolution: Women in Transition in Rural Bangladesh*.[22] The least invasive approach would have simply been to post information about the opportunity for literacy training and do no more unless requested to do so. However, one intervention by the development agency went further. As Nussbaum noted, local polls did not indicate that women in the village desired "a higher rate of literacy." However, in the village, women were "less well-nourished than males, less educated, less free, and less respected."[23] Recognizing the barriers to epistemic agency and imaginative capacity, the development workers sought to undo the uneven capabilities for self-determination. In ways that could be accused of being paternalistic, the development workers in that village "set up women's cooperatives in which members of the development agency joined with the local women in a searching participatory dialogue concerning the whole form of life in the village."[24] The key to the process was dialogue based on the goal of collaboration. The cosmopolitan, liberal assumption of a common intrinsic worth as subjects and knowers was the basis for the dialogue. Nussbaum writes,

> Had the women not been seen as human beings who shared with the other women a common humanity, the local women could not have told their story in the way they did, nor could the development workers have brought their own experiences of feminism to the participatory dialogue as if they had some relevance for the local women.[25]

This case illustrates the complex challenge of rejecting paternalism, yet simultaneously redistributing resources and power. Every effort should be made to increase capacity and respect agency of Nicaraguan partners through the work of JustHope. There are times when working toward undoing inequality requires redistributing material resources in order to

---

22. Nussbaum, "Human Functioning and Social Justice," 235.
23. Nussbaum, "Human Functioning and Social Justice," 236.
24. Nussbaum, "Human Functioning and Social Justice," 236.
25. Nussbaum, "Human Functioning and Social Justice," 236.

facilitate equalizing epistemic agency. The imperfect processes of attempting mutuality in collaboration require our best thinking and knowing. Theoretical analysis supports this view; incorporating all available viewpoints enhances our ability to see new possibilities. Rather than maintaining a dominating gaze, inclusion improves vision. Investing financial resources in a community that was made poor by colonialism is necessary to equalize power to speak, act, and collaborate in decision-making.

Lorraine Code advances theories of knowledge by insisting on attending to the social relational nature of epistemology. She claims that seeking knowledge should be "recognized as a cooperative-collaborative, textured human practice."[26] How we understand ourselves and others is a contextual framework that affects each aspect of our understanding. JustHope is committed to education and development that work toward mutual knowledge production through collaborative, transnational partnership. Nevertheless, the inequalities in access to education and access to resources and meaningful options can thwart genuine collaboration and result in perpetuating injustice. Sometimes Nicaraguan leaders suffer from a credibility deficit or excessive humility that undermines strong collaboration in decision-making. Furthermore, different cultural styles of dealing with conflict function in ways that can make mutual dialogue difficult. Mitchell Hammer's work on intercultural conflict styles is another helpful tool for transnational partnerships.[27] Until the voices of Nicaraguan campesinos have mutual power in collaborative decisions, more learning and spiritual development is necessary.

To go a step further in understanding collaborative knowledge, consider the insight of another social epistemologist. In her work on testimonial injustice, Miranda Fricker analyzes the discursive impact of what she calls credibility excess and deficit.[28] I agree with Fricker that there are times when too much humility is the result of uneven epistemic power. What Fricker calls credibility deficit leads to diminished capacity for knowing. One can have too little confidence in one's insight and miss opportunities to contribute to knowledge production or wise collaboration. I return to the case study that Martha Nussbaum considered in relation to the development workers in Bangladesh who persisted in setting up the women's cooperative. If the development workers had too much epistemic humility they might not have set up the cooperatives for dialogue

26. Code, "Epistemic Responsibility," 90.
27. Hammer, "Intercultural Conflict Style Inventory," 675–95.
28. Fricker, *Epistemic Injustice*, 17.

at all. Complex material and political realities make dialogue difficult. Yet, many insights from social epistemology point to dialogue as a strong methodology for knowledge production. There are times for listening and times for sharing convictions or insights. When groups want or need to act in ways informed by their best knowing, too much open-mindedness is no longer a virtue. In other words, sometimes action requires stepping away from a posture of too much humility or open-mindedness.

Miranda Fricker's attention to epistemic injustice is based in something like a Kantian metaphysics of personhood that seems similar to Nussbaum's belief in "a common humanity."[29] Fricker writes, "A culture in which some groups are separated off from that aspect of personhood by the experience of repeated exclusions from the spread of knowledge is seriously defective both epistemically and ethically."[30] Belief in injustice implies belief in something like universal personhood. Fricker claims that testimonial injustice results from inequalities in "agential vs. structural power, but also imaginative power."[31] She writes, "Rather, the unequal disadvantage derives from the fact that members of the group that is most disadvantaged by the gap are in some degree, hermeneutically marginalized—that is, they participate unequally in the practices through which social meanings are generated.[32] Nussbaum and Fricker agree that the ethical and political dimensions cannot be totally separated from the epistemic issues.

For JustHope partners from the U.S., the ability to honor and approach Nicaraguan farmers as equals can be thwarted by academic frameworks like peasant studies. At the same time, for JustHope partners from Nicaragua, the ability to engage U.S. visitors as equals can be thwarted by excessive humility or lack of confidence. However painful it may be for North Americans, openness to receive information about how Nicaraguans view us can motivate ethical and spiritual growth. The vulnerability to be curious and receptive rather than defensive about critiques of capitalism, materialism, and inhumanity of unjust U.S. hegemony allows us to be seen in ways that expand our understanding. More importantly, the honest mutuality of seeing and being seen as equal partners makes collaboration possible. Solidarity requires seeing another person as a

29. Nussbaum, "Human Functioning and Social Justice," 239.
30. Fricker, *Epistemic Injustice*, 58–59.
31. Fricker, *Epistemic Injustice*, 14.
32. Fricker, *Epistemic Injustice*, 6.

valuable collaborator and respecting their subjectivity. However, the injustices of unequal epistemic agency are obstacles to collaboration.

Fricker writes, "Eradicating these injustices would ultimately take not just more virtuous hearers, but collective social political change—in matters of epistemic injustice, the ethical is political."[33] But as a social epistemologist, Fricker is not only attentive to the social processes of knowing. She recognizes that all knowing happens in community, so analysis of how individuals relate to each other is a necessary part of seeking to know. Constructing and reconstructing community is an epistemic prerequisite and practice. Fricker writes, "Somebody subject to this sort of injustice may not have the sort of community in which to find resources for resistance, since the formation of such a community is itself a social achievement and not a social given."[34] To be shut out of the process of knowledge production is to be denied personhood. To live in a circle of strong community is to experience solidarity.

This is similar to the claim of Sonia Kruks that recognition of others' subjectivity is necessary for the feminist project of seeking justice. Kruks claims that the type of solidarity she espouses is not based in sharing a common oppression. She writes, "My concern is with solidarity in situations where an injury to others does not directly injure oneself or one's own group . . . Such solidarity requires an act of generosity—a gratuitous giving of attention, time, effort, resources to others."[35] That giving of attention is the type of recognition of the other as a knower, a subject. Kruks writes, "Feelings of concern for others must develop, and forms of intersubjective embodied experience that are not discursively thematized may be important in the development of such feelings."[36] This claim of intersubjective, embodied experience is a type of caring and knowing, perhaps the type of knowing that matters most. JustHope's value of reciprocity can be elusive given the gross inequalities between U.S. and Nicaraguan partners; nevertheless, the hospitality and friendship exchanged can build community.

Universalism is a controversial concept. It has been invoked in service of domination, silencing local diversity and crushing minoritized voices. The imperious gaze claims access to global jurisdiction regardless of borders. At the same time, activists and scholars seeking to defend

33. Fricker, *Epistemic Injustice*, 8.
34. Fricker, *Epistemic Injustice*, 54.
35. Kruks, *Retrieving Experience*, 154.
36. Kruks, *Retrieving Experience*, 155.

local knowledge construction can find the concept of universals serviceable and necessary. For example, Shuddhabrata Sengupta recommends "a nonspecific, tentative universalism" to disrupt binaries in identity categorization.[37] Serene J. Khader argues for a transnational feminist ethic that enhances justice while acknowledging different strategies are required in each context.[38] Put another way, transnational partnerships are possible because some values are shared regardless of borders, but non-ideal practical concessions are necessary. I agree with Parker J. Palmer that community can emerge despite inequality. He writes, "If community is to emerge, it will have to be in the midst of inequalities that appear whenever two or three are gathered."[39] Perhaps moments of solidarity are miraculous mysteries. Spiritual growth and development lean in toward such encounters. JustHope invites partners to undergo a journey of transformation that is not easy or painless. In order to improve the work of JustHope, partners, staff, board members, and supporters accept life-long learning, practice, and curiosity about what it means to know partnership or to collaborate well.

My conclusions suggest three directions for skillful collaboration and knowledge production in international partnerships. First, an emphasis on embodiment and tacit knowing is fruitful for building wisdom in community. Second, attention to the advantages and disadvantages of conceptual frames or perspectives can be helpful. Finally, skillful dialogue as a process of knowledge production is a smart direction for better collaborative partnerships. JustHope and other transnational partnership models would do well to heed these insights from social epistemology.

First, consider the benefits of forms of knowing that are often dismissed or devalued, like contextual, embodied knowing. Recognizing interdependency with others as experts of locality enhances collaborative partnerships. Nicaraguans have much to teach U.S. partners. When we travel to Nicaragua and work with farmers there, we observe a kind of tacit knowing they have about how to survive off the land. That knowhow involves layers of tacit information and wisdom that even they might not be able to completely explain. Tacit wisdom is acknowledged by some scholars despite being overlooked frequently as a resource for legitimate knowledge. For instance, Alan Musgrave claims, "There are obviously cases where a person knows how to do something but cannot

37. Sengupta, "I/Me/Mine," 637.
38. Khader, *Decolonizing Universalism*, 136.
39. Palmer, *Courage to Teach*, 137–38.

articulate the propositional knowledge which may be involved and may never have been explicitly aware of those propositions at all.[40] It may not be an overstatement to claim that human survival could depend on ways of knowing that are commonly demeaned by developed cultures. Those who live outside the wage economy have attitudes and approaches that are valuable. Finding the spirit of joy and meaning despite material wealth is an impressive accomplishment.

One example of this earthy wisdom is represented in an encounter our group had while visiting the farm of Pedro Luis. With delight, he told about a time when lack of rain led to crop failure. His garden dried up; his income was gone. He and his wife had eaten the last of their food. Not knowing where their next meals might come from, he prayed as he walked his small plot of land. Suddenly, he heard faint cooing from some brush. When he searched there, he discovered a nest of twenty guinea eggs. This would provide nourishment they needed. He understood this experience as an example of God's unfailing love. Although that view of prayer or theology challenges my beliefs, Pedro Luis has an unshakeable confidence and joy that comes from being satisfied with what he has. I do not suggest that prayer is an answer to poverty. However, I respect his wise embodiment of a spirituality that affirms in life or death, famine or abundance, God is love. Feminist epistemology's attention to the phenomenon of embodiment as an epistemological tool makes tacit knowing a significant resource for enhancing partnership. Perhaps spirituality involves tacit knowledge about intuitively perceived values. Normative claims about justice or compassion may relate to aesthetic judgements that rely on what we call spirituality. Is spirituality a skill of discovering the sacred and affirming it fully?

Secondly, drawing attention to conceptual frameworks raises consciousness and adept collaboration. Lorraine Code acknowledged the work of Maria Lugones, who coined the notion of "playful world-traveling" to describe a process of trying to shake free of the confines of one's own frameworks to understand the experience of another person.[41] In a move that sounds like trying to correct the imperious gaze, Code appreciated the way Lugones drew on Marilyn Frye's distinction between the "arrogant eye" which in perceiving "arrogates" another as an object, and the "loving eye." To approach another person in a non-objectifying

---

40. Musgrave, *Common Sense, Science, and Scepticism*, 7.
41. Code, "Care, Concern, and Advocacy."

manner, Lugones suggests an attitude of "loving playfulness" for those who would attempt world-traveling.[42] Moving between frames, perspectives, and worldviews requires a detachment from one's own insight, an open-mindedness, a stance of humility, or a playfulness. This is not wisdom about international travel as such. Rather, it is a form of consciousness raising through self-examination and openness to discovery of truth. JustHope's transnational partnerships invite participants to see their own world with new eyes as they travel between dramatically different contexts.

The third direction for best collaborative praxis is dialogue. Fricker notes the importance of dialogue in "psychological formation" to develop healthy epistemic credibility and self-confidence.[43] Dialogue requires and fosters open-mindedness and epistemic humility. Patricia Hill Collins claims, "Partiality and not universality is the condition of being heard . . . Dialogue is critical to the success of this epistemological approach."[44] The motivation to dialogue includes new knowledge production and collaborative action. Hamsa Rajan argues for the work of "discovering common viewpoints"[45] Dialogical praxis is an attempt toward exploring shared values and commitments. It illustrates what Catherine Elgin recommends in seeking "reflective equilibrium" and her claim that when it comes to epistemic agency, "We are people who need people.[46] Dialogue with others is a means to correcting excessive individualism and the tendency to attempt domination.

I agree with Lorraine Code that we need to strive for "dialogical culture." In fact, what we mean by solidarity must include something like dialogical knowledge construction. Hence, I applaud the work of Nira Yuval-Davis who called for "dialogical epistemology" as a form of resistance. She argues for seeking what she calls a "transversal dialogical politics of solidarity." Specifically, she claims this as a type of epistemological praxis. She writes,

> While politics of solidarity can be directed by care and compassion to defend any victim of racialization, discrimination, inferiorization, and exclusion, transversal solidarity is an alliance of

---

42. Code, "Care, Concern, and Advocacy."
43. Fricker, *Epistemic Injustice*, 53.
44. Collins, *Black Feminist Thought*, 236–37.
45. Rajan, "Ethics of Transnational Feminist Research and Activism," 270.
46. Elgin, "Epistemic Agency," 11.

mutual trust and respect, recognizing but transcending decentered differential positionings of power.[47]

Solidarity is a value that JustHope aspires to embody. The cost of solidarity is spiritual transformation. I agree with her conclusion: "Thus, the only way to approach 'the truth' is by a dialogue between people of differential positionings, and the wider the better."[48] JustHope curates dialogue between citizens of the U.S. and citizens of Nicaragua. Sometimes that dialogue reveals unintended harm and wisdom for future direction.

Social justice activists are learning to recognize the unintended consequences of international aid and human development work. Despite intentions to build toward anti-racist, anti-colonial systems and respect and protect diversity, transnational activists sometimes perpetuate the imposition of values and coercive influence of Western, colonial cultural imperialism. Within the organizational life of JustHope, partners strive to avoid operating as if North Americans know what is best for Nicaraguans. Every effort is made to avoid imposing values or assuming knowledge about what is needed. In planning partner trips and activities, leaders often claim that we should ask people in Chacraseca what they want the goals for the year to be. However, like the workers in the case reviewed by Nussbaum, JustHope partners sometimes go beyond simply polling Nicaraguan partners and attempt deeper dialogue as a step toward more equalized collaboration.

I take seriously the reflections of Nikita Dhawan, and her claim, "The biggest challenge to a postimperial philosophy is how to facilitate a nonviolent relation to the Other." She cautions against problems with transnational ethics that oppose local loyalties in favor of "normative espousal of an expansive global consciousness." Following Spivak, Dhawan argues that equalizing the epistemological work of intellectual labor should be prioritized even over providing access to material resources in some cases.[49] As Sonia Kruks writes:

> Moreover, it is not necessarily condescending or appropriating to act on behalf of others. We should not automatically assume that oppressed groups are always able to speak or act for themselves better than others can do it for them . . . As Linda Alcoff has argued, to retreat from speaking for others (or, I would add,

47. Yuval-Davis, *Dialogical Epistemology*, 52.
48. Yuval-Davis, *Dialogical Epistemology*, 51.
49. Dhawan, "Can Non-Europeans Philosophize?," 489.

acting on their behalf) for fear of "appropriating" their voices is sometimes, de facto, a form of irresponsible complicity with the status quo . . . (Alcoff, 1995, 242).[50]

Thus, working to equalize agency through dialogue and other redistributive efforts furthers both caring and solidarity. At times, advocacy may require actively collaborating for equity. Skepticism about knowledge production limited and distorted by an alienating gaze or universalizing abstractions clears the way for more just, compassionate knowing. Whether they are from the United States or Nicaragua, those who hunger and thirst for wisdom find in JustHope a model for reflective education. JustHope does not have all the answers. As an organization, it is committed to a posture of listening, learning, and openness. The praxis of seeking justice happens relationally in embodied circles of friends.

In many ways, JustHope echoes values and methods of the Highlander school founded in the 1940s by Myles Horton, Septima Clark and others as an intercultural, experiential learning praxis seeking faithful steps toward a more just, hopeful world. Horton described a flash of insight that advanced his learning about community organizing and casting the vision for the school. He writes, "Here I've been trying to be a loner, trying to do this all by myself and never thinking about asking anybody else."[51] But the secret to Highlander was bringing people together in "islands of decency." Interracial community where people from different backgrounds work together for a better world offers hope and justice. JustHope contributes to efforts to transform the U.S., Nicaragua, and the world. Our struggles are interconnected. As visionary theorist bell hooks teaches, "liberation struggles led by oppressed peoples globally who resist formidable powers" inform revolutionary movements for a radically changed world.[52]

As we reimagine liberative spirituality and new concepts of the sacred, we need new ways of learning—new pedagogies of crossing borders.[53] Adults seeking community and meaning value the type of spiritual formation encounter that JustHope offers. I need JustHope myself, to pursue the burning questions of our time, to break my own heart of stone, and reach for greater integrity between my values and actions. Christine

---

50. Kruks, *Retrieving Experience*, 174.
51. Horton, *Long Haul*, 20.
52. hooks, *Feminist Theory*, 166.
53. Alexander, *Pedagogies of Crossing*.

Smith, UCC pastor, activist, and spiritual teacher asks, "Who among us chooses to travel into every painful transformation that we actually can avoid?"[54] That is a good question for self-examination and reflection. In some ways, JustHope asks North Americans to go on a journey without an ending. The invitation is not unlike Jesus's call to become learners. Becoming human, rather than persisting in inhumanity, requires transformation. As a mechanism for survival of the fittest, materialistic greed is understandable. Humans often hoard and protect privilege in the face of another human's suffering. Yet, a planetary perspective reveals the necessity of resisting radical individualism. The kind of partnership JustHope offers allows the ability to catch glimpses of our culture from an outside perspective to spur transformation. This type of encounter can further our ability to resist the "me-first mechanisms" that Karen Armstrong describes so aptly in her book *Twelve Steps to a Compassionate Life*.[55] She writes, "We want instant transformation and instant enlightenment . . . But it takes longer to reorient our minds and hearts; this type of transformation is slow, undramatic, and incremental."[56]

The impulse for self-advancement can be replaced with the ethic of unconditional love that honors the equal, sacred worth and value of each person. An imperious gaze stunts the development of both the privileged and the oppressed affected by that system. Year after year, as I have traveled back to Nicaragua with JustHope, I have watched partners from the U.S. become more aware of interconnectedness despite national borders. Through JustHope, people practice mutuality through collaborative learning and cooperative wisdom. In contrast to the inhumane impulse to hoard and dominate regardless of the suffering of others, the willingness to become human in the best sense is based in solidarity. Statements from two North American partners, Ted Campbell and David Hoot, illustrate spiritual transformation.

Ted Campbell is another leader from the Community of Hope who has been a key part of the JustHope story. He said coming to Nicaragua gave him a new understanding of what faith is really about, especially faith in action. He said:

> Nobody demonstrates faith in action more than the people of Central America. They are incredibly, powerfully spiritual. They

---

54. Smith, *Risking the Terror*, 115.
55. Armstrong, *Twelve Steps*, 21.
56. Armstrong, *Twelve Steps*, 24.

teach us, or they teach me, over and over again, about putting one foot in front of the other when the odds are just insurmountable. You just keep putting one foot in front of the other. That really helped us in a lot of ways through so many losses of friends and patients during the HIV crisis. I think that gave us a lot of fortitude to keep pushing through, pushing through, when what we wanted to do was just stop the whole thing. It was that opportunity, that reaching out that was transformational. How do you ever even say thank you for that?[57]

David Hoot, a U.S. citizen who has been part of JustHope from its beginning, reflected on his experience, saying:

> My trips to Nicaragua have taught me so much about hospitality, faith, and how we are all One Human Family. The warm welcome I receive each year is heartfelt and genuine. Their faith is deep, inspiring, and soothing to my soul. We are all interconnected on this planet. This is reaffirmed with each visit. My actions at home can have a direct impact on my companions in Nicaragua, both positively and negatively. I also return to Nicaragua each year to be re-centered. The visits help me realize what is important in life. I'm reminded to live a simple, modest life and be happy with the many blessings I have. Leslie and JustHope introduced me to the term Solidarity, and it is a commitment to follow each and every day.[58]

Receiving and giving mutual respect generates reciprocal honoring of human need and capability. David emphasizes oneness of all creation and one human family, but he does not minimize the inequalities, injustices, and differences that can divide people. His is the type of spiritual practice toward solidarity that builds JustHope partnerships. As Father Miguel d'Escoto often said, "You get to the point where you need to love even more than you need to breathe." Yet after the murder of Eric Garner in 2014, that saying no longer lands well. Breathing is a prerequisite for loving. I suspect that Father Miguel would have noted this and changed his saying to something like, "You get to the point where you need to love even more than you need to continue living."

A reader might wonder what new knowledge has been generated by the partnerships described in this book. The answer is partial and imperfect; it is mostly an arrow pointing in the direction of action and

---

57. Interview with Ted Campbell, May 2019.
58. Interview with David Hoot, May 2019.

reflection. Embodied collaborative consciousness-raising is the work that points toward hope and justice. As Leonardo Boff writes, "Theology's task is not primarily to chart courses, but to let courses chart themselves as they are carried forward in the hushed love of God and reveal the meaning of their own direction."[59]

In the final pages of this book, I analyze future challenges for JustHope given the tragic situation in Nicaragua in 2018.

---

59. Boff, *Ecclesiogenesis*, 90.

— 12

Updates
Political Uprising and Then COVID

> Nonetheless, the seeds of a different world were always present in Nicaragua, as they also are in any place where people, receptive to the Spirit, allow themselves to dream.
>
> —Miguel d'Escoto[1]

REASONS TO HOPE ARE needed now more than ever before. Recent political conflict in both the U.S. and Nicaragua has been discouraging. In 2023 leaders in Chacraseca, JustHope volunteers, and families described in the pages of this book are divided over political issues polarizing Nicaragua. One young woman from Chacraseca said her elderly grandparents who had been married more than sixty years disagree with each other about Daniel Ortega. What is indisputable is that in April 2018 a political conflict erupted that continues to unfold. Friends in Chacraseca refer to this as "the crisis." The Nicaraguan government responded with violence to student protests. In 2018 more than three hundred people died, approximately two thousand were injured, more than seven hundred were arrested, and since then more than one hundred thousand have fled the country due to the political unrest, according to data from the UN Human

---

1. D'Escoto, foreword, in Murphy and Caro, *Uriel Molina*, 4.

Rights. The Organization of American States (OAS) has an autonomous, Inter-American Commission on Human Rights (IACHR) that reported,

> Two years into this human rights crisis, the IACHR observes a persistent violation of the separation of powers and efforts to weaken Nicaragua's democratic institutions . . . The evidence further shows concerted efforts by the National Police and groups of government supporters to constantly attack, watch, threaten, and harass anyone who is identified as an opponent of the government.[2]

Latin American countries united in concern for Nicaraguans and documented human rights abuses. In 2021, continued conflict over presidential elections increased cause for scrutiny. In 2022, the Organization for American States (OAS) continues to criticize Nicaragua for repressive human rights abuses. According to a 2022 Reuters news report, "Nicaraguan Foreign Minister Denis Moncada said on November 19 that his government had initiated the process of withdrawing from the OAS after it denounced Nicaragua's elections as illegitimate."[3]

Political unrest is not new to Nicaragua. Since colonial powers determined current national borders in Latin America, local communities have been dominated by foreign influence and interests. The newest drama in Nicaragua seems like an echo from bygone centuries. As political historian Stimson writes,

> The most striking characteristic of Nicaragua's political development is the pervasive role played by external powers in the definition of its political agenda and in the resolution of the disputes among domestic power contenders. Foreign interventions have drastically reduced the possibilities for Nicaraguans to achieve political stability and democratic consensus.[4]

That is as accurate now as it was in the 1980s and 1990s; outside interests dominate Nicaraguan economy and politics. Chomsky and others have observed that U.S. pressure results in Nicaragua's inclination to rely on Russia.[5] This relationship with the former Soviets is taken as a justification for hostile actions of the U.S. toward Nicaragua. The stakes remain high.

---

2. OAS, "Two Years," para. 1.
3. Reuters, "Nicaragua," para. 6.
4. Stimons, *American Policy in Nicaragua*, 73–74.
5. Chomsky, *On Power and Ideology*, 33.

Because of the violence and political unrest, the U.S. State Department advised against travel. JustHope suspended partner trips beginning in April 2018. Since the funding of the organization was reliant on fees partners paid for travel, JustHope was forced to lay off staff. Since the crisis began, JustHope partners continue to donate funds and to connect through online communication. I traveled to Nicaragua in May of 2019 with a group of JustHope leaders. We heard accounts of the violence and conflict. Everyone hoped to resume partner trips soon. The political tension and unstable conditions in Nicaragua made it difficult to plan. We visited a coffee farm in La Flor. There we met a coffee farmer who said sometimes people are forced to feed babies coffee when there is no milk or formula.

I stayed in Chacraseca for four weeks in July of 2019, glad to offer support and document the continuing programs of the microcredit banks, scholarship program, music lessons at the cultural center, health care programs, model farm, and construction of new houses and latrines. I witnessed the deepening poverty, hunger, and job loss due to the political crisis. The overarching memory from that trip is an image of young men and older teen boys gaunt with insufficient food, milling around unable to find work. Just when we anticipated partner groups traveling again, COVID-19 hit.

Some of the students who were part of the trip described in this book have continued to engage as JustHope partners. Two have organized and led groups from their own churches and established ongoing commitments to JustHope. Other students have expressed desire to return to Chacraseca when travel is safer. Many have made financial donations and shared information about their experiences on the trip. Students have continued to educate others, support fund-raising, and advocate for justice. Even years after the trip, students refer to our experience in Nicaragua as "life-changing." They express appreciation for deepening spirituality, expanding theology, and growing community with others who have engaged as JustHope partners.

The power of the trips is evident in the high level of financial commitment that U.S. partners continue to enact. Fund-raising has been a challenge for JustHope during these past years of difficulties with no possibility of travel. In February 2022, there were still no direct flights to Nicaragua on major airlines. David Hoot managed to travel to Chacraseca and reported on continuing JustHope programs. At times the struggle was so difficult that we wondered if the organization could continue at all. Hard work, prayerful stubbornness, and persistence keep dreams alive. The board worked to reimagine solidarity without regular travel. The jobs of Nicaraguan staff continued until the end of that year, but the position of executive director, and all other U.S. staff, except one part-time administrative assistant position, were terminated. Eventually, JustHope cut paid staff positions in Nicaragua and relies on contract labor arrangements and volunteer workers.

ACOPADES held elections, and a new leader, Osmin, is now the president. Osmin shared that his mother had been a leader working with Sister Joan and Father Donald. Osmin remembers them coming to his house when he was a teenager many times. Now, he is trying to continue the work they started. He said the community needs a soup kitchen now because the problem with hunger is worse. The water system in Chacraseca continues to break down resulting in dire consequences for the community. The political crisis eroded trust and community. Combined with the isolation due to COVID, ACOPADES no longer meets regularly or has robust representation from each sector. This adds another layer of hardship to the collaboration.

The political crisis in Nicaragua has made getting information about the response to COVID-19 there more difficult. Many Nicaraguans lack confidence in their Vice-President, Rosario Murillo, who is also the wife of President Daniel Ortega. Murillo was appointed to head the Nicaraguan vaccination program and COVID response strategy. In May 2019, a public letter signed by more than seven hundred Nicaraguan health workers from both the private and public sector urged the government to require measures recommended by the World Health Organization to prevent the spread of COVID. Reports that doctors have been fired and harassed for criticizing the government's response continue.[6] Daniel Ortega won re-election in November 2021. Many supporters of Nicaragua anticipate the potential for more violence and political unrest because of tensions and polarization in the country. Nicaraguan activists continue to report and document egregious human rights violations.

JustHope does not take political positions, but my research and observations force me to agree with Stephan Haggard and Robert Kaufman that Nicaragua is an example of a pattern of democratic regress. Ortega is restricting free speech, undermining free elections, and increasing his

---

6. Human Rights Watch, "Nicaragua."

autocratic control in alarming ways.[7] It is difficult to imagine a peaceful transition of power to a new administration and equally difficult to imagine many more years of maintaining peace with the current government leadership. Fear of more violence is not irrational. A new law in Nicaragua scrutinizes "foreign agents" in new ways, making international development more difficult. JustHope is committed to solidarity, come what may. The organization's decades of sustained partnership and strong network of relationships is a valuable resource for weathering this difficult time.

Between the political crisis and the pandemic, economic conditions have become more grim with increasing hunger and poverty. *The Economist* briefing sheet on Nicaragua confirms that conditions are worse in Nicaragua now than compared with those described from the trip in 2016. In April 2021, they wrote,

> The economy will stage a modest recovery from a recession that began in 2018 and deepened as a result of the coronavirus (Covid-19) outbreak and a difficult hurricane season in 2020. Real GDP will not return to its 2017 peak until 2025. As a result, Nicaragua will remain one of the poorest countries in the entire western hemisphere.[8]

JustHope's microcredit lending circles are essential to promote dignified work and prevent hunger. The model farm switched to growing emergency food supplies for the poorest members of the community. In 2022, the cost of building a latrine in Chacraseca through JustHope is four hundred dollars; construction costs and materials are rising. Although no one can predict exactly when JustHope trips will resume, the network of donors and supporters of this collaborative, transnational partnership continue to dream together of a more just, equitable future. The JustHope board continues to discern how to pursue steps toward solidarity through these uncertain times. In July 2023, the U.S. travel advisory for Nicaragua is set at Level Three, "Reconsider travel to Nicaragua due to limited healthcare availability and arbitrary enforcement of laws. Exercise increased caution in Nicaragua due to crime, and wrongful detentions."[9]

Interchange between local leaders in Nicaragua, JustHope volunteers, and partners in the U.S. continues despite the challenges. We

---

7. Norris, "Voters against Democracy."
8. EIU Views Wire, "Nicaragua," para. 1.
9. U.S. Embassy in Nicaragua, "Travel Advisory," para. 2.

encourage one another during *Zoom* conversations and meetings. We often recall how, over the years, Leslie frequently asked all of us to be mindful of the question: what would happen if partners stopped coming to Nicaragua? With bittersweet awareness, we recognize how prescient those insights have been. During an online meeting in October 2020, one staff member said,

> I've got faith we are going to overcome. If countries are united, we can overcome adversity. Pretty soon we will be able to shake hands like we used to, not just wave at the screen. I will be able to see faces of friends. But we have to go slow. In the U.S. everything goes fast. We need to take this time for encounter. Right now, we are caring about our own people, discovering new things we can do together. This is making our partnership stronger.

JustHope has adopted a new mission statement: "JustHope fosters cultural understanding by creating mutually beneficial partnerships between communities in the US and Nicaragua." This shift reflects the organization's determination to avoid older models of charity and mission trips. It highlights the value of mutuality that has always been central to the JustHope ethos, vision, and practice. The loyalty of partners in both countries is calling forth agility and resistance to despair. Hope with the strong legs of justice endures as an expansive, transformative power in the struggle for a more humane future.

Sister Joan Uhlen, Sister Juanita, died on August 12, 2019, at the Maryknoll center in New York. A mass was said in her honor in Chacraseca. Her photo still hangs in Casa de Paz, and her name is still spoken frequently with paramount love and reverence.

Appendix

THIS MATERIAL WAS WRITTEN by Leslie Penrose for the JustHope website. The mission statement has been updated, but these words reflect the guidance groups received until 2021.[1]

JustHope's mission:
To create global partnerships that facilitate long-term partnerships grounded in solidarity, mutuality, and collaboration between Nicaraguan and U.S. communities, combat extreme poverty through engaging one another in cultural exchanges, cooperative learning, mutual dialogue, and sharing resources, with the focus on increasing global understanding and empowering self-determination, and nurture sustainable community by focusing on leadership development and sustainability.

Working collaboratively with communities in Nicaragua, JustHope's partner groups build relationships, learn about themselves, and develop skills while supporting projects that grow out of the Nicaraguan communities we work with.

JustHope works with university service-learning groups, faith communities, and community groups to establish the kind of partnership that best fits.

Values and Principles of Global Interdependence

As JustHope works to move beyond the colonial and paternalistic "missionary" paradigm and practice in global relationships toward a more

1. http://www.justhope.org.

mutual practice and paradigm of "partnership", we are committed to what we believe are fundamental values and principles of global interdependence: Solidarity, sustainability, mutuality, and collaboration.

Solidarity

Solidarity is a mutual commitment to one another's wellbeing as dreamed and defined by the other. Solidarity is about more than investing a week in one another's lives; more than knowing one another's names and caring about one another's lives. Solidarity is about knowing what the real struggles and joys are in a partner's life, and making those struggles and joys your own in a way that has real, concrete effects on the priorities you set, the options you explore, and the decisions you make in your own day to day living. Solidarity means not only asking how something will affect me and my neighborhood, but how it will affect Maria and her neighborhood. It means considering not only how the way you budget your money or your time will affect your family, but how it will affect Juan's family as well. Unlike charity, which is dependent only on the giver's will at any particular moment, solidarity requires an intentional, long-term commitment.

Therefore: JustHope Partners are asked to think about their partnerships as longer-term (five years or more) everyday commitments, rather than one or more annual visits.

JustHope Partner Trips are focused more on growing relationships than on accomplishing projects. Projects are understood and incorporated into Partner Trips as a means of engaging with partners in their context, but the trips are structured to facilitate encounter, dialogue, and cultural immersion as the primary objectives.

JustHope negotiates the terms and parameters of partnership projects, in dialogue with partners, and monitors their development. JustHope also requests that Partners channel all requests for and all donations of partnership funds through JustHope. This is an intentional effort to reduce the temptation toward old patron/client ways of thinking and relating as the partnership is birthed and grows.

Sustainability

The ability for partnerships between communities to be viable over time, is an essential element of JustHope Partnerships, and is integrally related to the capacity of the communities involved to nurture and maintain their own community life. Sustainability, both of the partner communities and of the partnerships, is strengthened when there is an intentional commitment to capacity building and infrastructure support from both partners. The term "infrastructure" is used here to designate those structures and practices within a community that undergird and support vital, generative community life, such as leadership development, community organizing, and community administration: structures and practices that facilitate broad communal participation and empower communal self-determination. Infrastructure, then, may look different from one partner context to another depending on what each particular community's goals are, what its resources are, and where it is in its growth and development. The development of adequate infrastructure to support a strong and vibrant community life requires resources that poor communities often do not have. For instance, leadership training requires supplies and resources; community organizing often incurs transportation and supply costs; project management may include communication and record keeping costs. Simply having a meeting in a poor rural community often means leaders must travel long distances to attend, so meals need to be provided, and a place for the meeting has to be maintained. Financial support for infrastructure development and improvement affirms the critical importance of community development in the journey toward self-reliance and sustainability.

Therefore: JustHope Partnerships include a commitment to financial support of the infrastructure of the Nicaraguan Partner. Whereas partners often respond generously to working on and funding specific projects, the developing-country partner often doesn't have resources for the basic infrastructure support that is critical to a community's ability to engage in self-determination. The covenant contribution to infrastructure is separate from and prior to any project support in which the partners engage.

JustHope Partners are encouraged to offer regular, internal communication within their own group/community about the partnership in order to nurture whole community involvement in the partnership and avoid it being compartmentalized to a committee or small group.

Mutuality

Mutuality is a critical commitment as JustHope's network of partners work together to inspire hope, increase justice, and nurture the common well-being of the world. James Nelson has written: "Justice becomes real when partners have mutuality, . . . when each partner has the power, the self-confidence, and the encouragement to decide freely about their participation or non-participation in every aspect of the relationship." Mutuality in a relationship means there is no coercion, no manipulation, no attempt to bind the other or control the other's decisions, but a genuine and passionate willing for the full integrity and well-being of the other. In a mutual relationship, "each partner is liberated and empowered by the shared energies of mutual respect, mutual care, and mutual delight." Mutuality between global partners can't be imposed. It must grow as the partners practice listening fully to one another's stories, ideas, and concerns; and resist temptations to translate one another's contexts. Engaging with one another in this type of critical thinking requires clarity, flexibility, humility, transparency, mutual respect, trust, patience, steadfastness, self-examination, vigilance, good communication, and grace—above all grace.

Therefore: JustHope Partners are encouraged to engage in regular reflection on their Partnerships, including an intentional examination of motives and evaluation of decisions and actions, as well as consideration of ways to deepen and strengthen the partnership.

JustHope Partners are asked to practice mutuality and empowerment of self-determination by working with and through leadership structures to identify community needs and priorities for projects and avoid privileging individual or personal requests for assistance.

Collaboration

Collaboration can be an effective tool of resistance to a history and climate of colonization, when it is used to empower and give agency to those who, like the poor in Nicaragua, have been disempowered by that history and climate. JustHope encourages collaboration between partners to every extent possible—between U.S. and Nicaraguan partners; between U.S. partner communities; between Nicaraguan partner communities; between partner communities and other agencies; on projects, Partner Trips, grant requests, research and resourcing, fundraising, education, or any aspect of partnership development and nurture. We can accomplish far more together than any of us can accomplish alone.

Therefore: JustHope Partners are encouraged to work collaboratively, not only with their particular Global Partner, but also with the whole network of JustHope Partners.

This includes:

- A commitment by Covenant Partners to engage in face-to-face visits in the global partners' context at least annually.
- A commitment to intentionally learn about their partner's context.
- A commitment to work collaboratively with JustHope to facilitate visits to the US from members of Nicaraguan partner communities.
- A commitment to share information and work collaboratively with other JustHope Partners, where possible and appropriate, on Projects and Partner Trips.

Our primary strategies for accomplishing our mission include:

- Providing resources and leadership support for the creation and nurture of global partnerships.
- Organizing and leading educational and partner development trips for U.S. groups to other countries.
- Providing resources and leadership support to U.S. groups for theological reflection and social analysis before, during, and after exploratory trips, and as the partnerships grow and develop.
- Offering seminars, presentations, and group studies to educate U.S. groups and individuals about the theory and practice of non-colonial global partnerships.
- Organizing and coordinating a viable networking structure for partnership groups.
- Sponsoring projects in global communities that support capacity-building toward self-sufficiency and sustainable community life.
- Supporting and encouraging leadership in Central American Communities that is representative of the whole community; that is not politically, religiously, or corporation based; and that is gender equal (at least 50 percent women).

Chacraseca Cultural Center

- Cultural traditions and art are often the first things lost when a community struggles with persistent poverty, depriving young people of a sense of identity and belonging. This, in turn, puts youth at higher risk of gang involvement, drug use, and dropping out of high school.
- In Chacraseca, teachers, youth, and community leaders are joining together to resist the slow erosion of their culture that puts their young people at risk by reclaiming the traditional music, dance and art that have shaped and defined Nicaragua's history.
- Ricardo is from Chacraseca and is currently studying to become a doctor at the University of León. He serves as a tutor and folkdance instructor for Chacraseca's at-risk youth. "Since I was a child, I have wanted to be an example for the youth in my community. I feel proud to be from where I am, and I feel that my roots will help me to be a great person."
- JustHope is proud to partner with the Chacraseca community in realizing their dream of establishing a Cultural Center. The Center will be an enabling environment, which supports meaningful training and performance in culture, arts, leadership, entrepreneurial and social skills to drive development within the community of Chacraseca. This environment is created by delivering awareness- and training-based workshops to increase skills within youth groups and create a community of acceptance.
- The Center will cultivate and strengthen the traditions of Nicaragua's cultural expression, while also contributing to a brighter future for the people of this region.

JustHope's founder and Executive Director, Leslie Penrose began working to address systemic poverty in Nicaragua in 1986. After Hurricane Mitch hit Central America in 1998, Leslie and a small group established a partnership with leaders in Chacraseca, Nicaragua—a small farming community outside León with 1,500 households (eight thousand people) and an average income of $1 per person per day—to engage together in long-term community development.

Over the next several years, this small but committed group worked side by side with the leadership of Chacraseca on projects to build schools and houses, initiate a school-lunch program, create a microlending program for farmers, and begin what would become a ten-year long project to bring clean water to the whole community. In 2007, Leslie established JustHope as a social-profit organization to strengthen and broaden the solidarity work being done in Chacraseca and expand it to other communities in Nicaragua. In 2008 a partnership was created with the small coffee-dependent community of Santa Emilia in the department of Matagalpa; and in 2009 the mountain top community of La Flor was added as a third partner community.

By the beginning of 2016, JustHope has grown to include over 50 partnerships including colleges and universities, businesses, service groups, faith-based groups, other non-profits, and two Nicaraguan governmental agencies. We have expanded the styles of partnership to include Faith-based Covenant Partnerships, Service-Learning Partnerships, and Corporate Partnerships. We are leading an average of twenty U.S. partner trips per year to Nicaragua and managing integrated development programs in our Nicaraguan partner communities focused on Health, Education, Social Enterprise, Agriculture, and Leadership Development. We currently have twelve full-time and part-time program and operations staff—three in the U.S. and nine in Nicaragua.

Discovery

As part of her first trip to Nicaragua in 1986, founder and executive director Leslie Penrose visited a farming cooperative in the mountains near Jinotega. The coop was just two years old—part of the Agrarian Reform project that the new government had undertaken. And the six or so farmers who had gathered to meet with the visitors were bursting with pride as they displayed some of their recent harvest. Most had been squatters or sharecroppers before the revolution-with little or no hope of escaping the desperate poverty that defined their lives. "We always hoped for land of our own," one of the "campesinos" (peasant farmers) told us. "But it was hope with no legs . . . The Revolution has given our hope legs," he continued. "Now, our hope has the strong legs of justice."

Leslie wrote in her journal that night, "That's what I want my work to be about—giving hope the strong legs of justice."

Sharing in Hope

Leslie returned home, completed seminary, and for twenty years served as a community activist and pastor to those who had "hope without legs" within her home community. But her love for Central America drew her back, and year after year she took people and groups with her-groups from both inside and outside the church body, drawn for their own diverse reasons.

Over and over again, Leslie found that other's lives, like hers, were transformed in deep and profound ways through experiences and connections with people living in a radically different context-often coming home with a greater sense of purpose for their own lives, and a passionate desire to act on this purpose. Ted, an openly gay therapist, came home and poured himself into co-founding and growing a church that embraced all people, and committed itself to equal giving beyond its walls in recognition of the international disparity he saw in Nicaragua. At the young age of seventy, Betty returned from Nicaragua and began to form microbanks. Using her own funds and those she works tirelessly to raise, she has created over twenty independent microbanks in both Nicaragua and Guatemala. A few years after returning from Guatemala, Dr. Jeff sold his private practice and now works with HIV-infected migrant farm workers, while volunteering as a medical consultant in Nicaragua. Shannon's work within her church's Nicaraguan partnership drove her to reside in Nicaragua permanently and begin a non-profit organization working to ensure fair wages for Nicaraguan artists.

For the U.S. participants, global partnerships resulted in making a big world smaller, and wounded people whole. Participants found their values and perspectives changed and their priorities rearranged. As people reflected on their experiences in Central America and engaged in ongoing partnerships with those they had met, they found themselves rethinking earlier assumptions about others, about themselves, about the world.

Changing the Paradigm

Along the way, those who went to Nicaragua discovered that single visits from groups perpetuated the historical colonial relationship between North and Central America, rather than transforming it. This "come, work, and leave" approach actually reinforced the giver/receiver, patron/

client interpersonal roles instead of nurturing and empowering the self-determination and self-sufficiency of the Central American community.

The real transformation was happening not among those people and groups briefly traveling to Nicaragua, Guatemala or El Salvador, but those who were staying: staying connected, staying involved. Those who went and then returned-some physically, but all with their hearts, passion, and checkbooks-are those whose paradigms changed. And, conversely, it was the communities those "returnees" remained with whose hope had a fighting chance of "growing legs."

In 1996, after years of brief trips, a small group of companions made the decision to STAY, to find a community in Central America with whom they could create a long-term relationship; a community with whom they could wrestle and hope their way into something deeper, something truer, something more mutual; a community who wanted more than a charity project: they wanted a partner with them in the movement toward justice.

It took two years to find the right community. The elements important to the U.S. group were: (1) strong local leadership in place, willing to engage the North American group as partners, not patrons; (2) both the partner groups remaining open to the diversity of the other; (3) and a way for visiting partners to stay within, and engage with, the host community, rather than having to withdraw to hotels at night. Solidarity, they were learning, is about more than investing a week in one another's lives. It's about more, even, than knowing one another's names, and caring about one another's lives. Solidarity is about knowing what the real struggles and joys are in a partner's life, and making those struggles and joys your own in a way that has real, concrete effects on the priorities you set, the options you explore, and the decisions you make in your own day to day living. Solidarity means not only asking how will this vote will affect me and my neighborhood, but how will it affect Maria and her neighborhood. It means considering not only how the way you budget your money or your time will affect your family, but how it will affect Juan's family as well. Solidarity is a way of life, not just an occasional visit. The group's hope was that by risking partnership, they would find their way into solidarity.

Discovering Chacraseca

In 1998, just before Hurricane Mitch hit Central America, a small group of a dozen people or so made its first visit to Chacraseca, Nicaragua—a small farming community outside León with 1,500 households (eight thousand people) and an average income of $1 per person per day. And they stayed.

A pattern developed as one trip turned into two and then three; and two years turned into six and ten years; and visits to Nicaragua grew to visits from Nicaragua. Several of the original group stayed involved, including several who actually moved to other states, but continued to be involved in the Nicaraguan partnership. And every year new participants also got involved. Most years Leslie went, but some years she didn't—the dream and the passion had grown well beyond any single person to a shared vision and hope. Each team would meet with Chacraseca's community leadership team to discuss projects for the week and make financial decisions together. They would take walking tours around the community, visiting with residents, stopping by schools, going to church, and each group worked side by side with Nicaraguans on some jointly agreed upon project. At the end of each visit, those who had worked together all week co-hosted a fiesta for the community complete with piñatas and treats for everyone plus time for singing, and dancing, and sharing talents.

Growth and Continued Connections

Across the years, a number of the participants who had joined the group from other churches and organizations returned from their trips to begin working on getting their own churches or organizations involved in global partnerships. To date five additional active global partnerships in Oklahoma have started as a result of someone joining one of these trips and then returning to involve others. The original partnership with Chacraseca has generated over $200,000 in donations to its partnership projects, and the total donations to all five Nicaraguan partnerships have grown to well over $1,000,000.

But it was the "in between" work that proved most exciting. In between visits letters were written and phone calls made. A map of Chacraseca went up on the wall marking places that had become "holy ground" to the partners; and pictures of Nicaraguan people who had become "family" to other groups hung on their walls and bulletin boards. Three groups started small fair trade stores to sell Nicaraguan coffee and artisan pieces, and they all encourage "alternative gift giving"—giving family and friends gifts of charity to projects in Nicaragua rather than "things"—not only at Christmas, but on Valentine's Day and Easter and for birthdays. Groups started keeping up with how U.S. foreign policy affected Nicaragua and worked to understand the complexities of the World Bank and international foreign policy. Special worship celebrations were held on the same day at the same time in Nicaragua and in Oklahoma to honor the partnerships; and delegations from Nicaragua visited Oklahoma on a regular basis. Somewhere along the way, partnership had become solidarity.

The way of partnership wasn't easy for any of the groups, but it was enlightening and challenging and encouraging and rewarding. Groups discovered, with their partners, that when partnerships are truly striving for mutuality, details are critical—especially details concerning decision making and money: both symbols of power, both fundamental to almost every interaction.

Maintaining the Struggle

North American partners must be constantly vigilant about making decisions "for" rather than "with" their partners, often without even realizing it's happening. Experience revealed that often times the deep cultural sense of hospitality and grace of the Central American partners kept them from calling North Americans on our failures of mutuality. But slowly, the group that sustained that original partnership in Chacraseca struggled (and continues to struggle) to unlearn their tendencies toward colonialism. And slowly, the Nicaraguan partners struggled (and continue to struggle) to resist their tendencies to "be nice" rather than holding their North American partners accountable to the covenant of mutuality. Slowly trust grew, and solidarity infused hope—real hope, hope with legs- into lives and communities and relationships worn threadbare—some (on the U.S. side of the border) by "too much," and others (on the Central American side) by "not enough."

With each step in that long and sometimes painful process, trust deepened and the partnership strengthened. And with each step the same small group that ten years earlier had decided to "stay" in Nicaragua, began to imagine ways that other communities in the U.S. might be nurtured into global partnerships of solidarity and hope with people in Central America and around the globe. In June of 2007, a small, committed core group of people invested their hopes, their hearts, their hands, and their resources in birthing the dream that beyond paternalism, partnership is possible; that beyond colonialism, covenant can thrive; that beyond just hope for global solidarity is the dream of JustHope, the dream of a world interconnected by cross-cultural partnerships of mutuality and trust that are working cooperatively to inspire hope, increase justice, and nurture the common well-being of the world.

Making Hope

Vaclav Havel has written, "Hope is not the conviction that things will turn out well, but the confidence that what you are doing makes sense regardless of how it turns out." In a country dominated by an oppressive dictator, hope as the isolated wish of each individual farmer didn't make sense; it didn't "have legs." But partnering in the struggle for liberation and the work of social transformation did make sense, and it made Hope! Working together for common justice—not just for themselves, but for their neighbors, their children, their country—gave their hope legs. Partnering together to "be the change we want to see" does "have legs." It does make sense.

Bibliography

Alexander, M. Jacqui. *Pedagogies of Crossing: Meditations on Feminism, Sexual Politics, Memory, and the Sacred*. Perverse Modernities. Durham, NC: Duke University Press, 2005.
Althaus-Reid, Marcella. *Indecent Theology: Theological Perversions in Sex, Gender, and Politics*. New York: Routledge, 2000.
Anzaldúa, Gloria. *Borderlands/La Frontera: The New Mestiza*. 3rd ed. San Francisco: Aunt Lute, 2007.
Arellano, Luz Beatriz. "Women's Experience of God in Emerging Spirituality." In *Feminist Theology from the Third World*, 318–39. Maryknoll, NY: Orbis, 1994.
Armstrong, Karen. *Twelve Steps to a Compassionate Life*. New York: Anchor, 2010.
Bacon, David. *The Right to Stay Home: How US Policy Drives Mexican Migration*. Boston: Beacon, 2013.
Baker, Kendall Clark. *When Faith Storms the Public Square: Mixing Religion and Politics through Community Organizing to Enhance Our Democracy*. Cleveland: Circle, 2011.
Banfield, Edward C. *The Moral Basis of a Backward Society*. 3rd ed. New York: Free, 1968.
Besley, Tina, and Michael A Peters. *Interculturalism, Education, and Dialogue*. Global Studies in Education 13. New York: Lang, 2012.
Binford, Leigh, et al. *Fifty Years of Peasant Wars in Latin America*. New York: Berghahn, 2020.
Boff, Clodovis, and Leonardo Boff. *Introducing Liberation Theology*. Translated by Paul Burns. Maryknoll, NY: Orbis, 1987.
Boff, Leonardo. *Church: Charism and Power: Liberation Theology and the Institutional Church*. Translated by John W. Diercksmeier. New York: Crossroad, 1985.
———. *Ecclesiogenesis: The Base Communities Reinvent the Church*. Translated by Robert R. Barr. Maryknoll, NY: Orbis, 1986.
Borge, Tomás. *Christianity and Revolution: Tomás Borge's Theology of Life*. Translated by Andrew Reding. Maryknoll, NY: Orbis, 1987.
Bradbury, Ray. *Fahrenheit 451*. New York: Simon & Schuster, 1951.
Brazal, Agnes M. *A Theology of Southeast Asia: Liberation-Postcolonial Ethics in the Philippines*. New York: Orbis, 2019.

Brentlinger, John. *The Best of What We Are: Reflections on the Nicaraguan Revolution*. Amherst: University of Massachusetts Press, 1995.

Brown, Adrienne Maree. "Touching White Supremacy, Touching Beyond It (Strategy: Intimacy)." In *How We Fight White Supremacy*, edited by Akiba Solomon and Kenrya Rankin, 307–15. New York: Bold Type, 2019.

Camara, Dom Helder. *Essential Writings*. Edited by Francis McDonagh. New York: Orbis, 2009.

Camp, Elisabeth. "Perspectives and Frames in Pursuit of Ultimate Understanding." In *Varieties of Understanding: New Perspectives from Philosophy, Psychology, and Theology*, edited by Stephen R. Grimm, 17–45. New York: Oxford University Press, 2019.

Cardenal, Fernando. *Faith and Joy: Memoirs of a Revolutionary Priest*. Translated by Kathleen McBride and Mark Lester. Maryknoll, NY: Orbis, 2015.

Casaldáliga, Pedro, and José-María Vigil. *In Pursuit of the Kingdom*. Translated by Phillip Berryman. Maryknoll, NY: Orbis, 1990.

———. *Political Holiness: A Spirituality of Liberation*. Translated by Paul Burnes and Francis McDonagh. Theology and Liberation Series. Maryknoll, NY: Orbis, 1994.

Chavez, Daniel. *Nicaragua and the Politics of Utopia: Development and Culture in the Modern State*. Nashville: Vanderbilt University Press, 2015.

Chen, Martha Alter. *A Quiet Revolution: Women in Transition in Rural Bangladesh*. Cambridge: Schenkman, 1983.

Chhungi, Hrangthan, et al., eds. *Building Theologies of Solidarity: Interfacing Feminist Theology with Dalit Theology and Tribal/Adivasi Theologies*. Bangalore: St. Joseph's, 2012.

Chomsky, Noam. *On Power and Ideology: The Managua Lectures*. Cambridge: South End, 1987.

Chua, Amy. *World on Fire: How Exporting Free Market Democracy Breeds Ethnic Hatred and Global Instability*. New York: Doubleday, 2003.

Cobb, John B., Jr. *Sustainability: Economics, Ecology, and Justice*. Ecology and Justice Series. 1992. Reprint, Eugene, OR: Wipf & Stock, 2007.

Code, Lorraine. "Care, Concern, and Advocacy: Is There a Place for Epistemic Responsibility?" *Feminist Philosophy Quarterly* 1 (2015). https://doi.org/10.5206/fpq/2015.1.1.

———. "Epistemic Responsibility." In *The Routledge Handbook of Epistemic Injustice*, edited by Ian James Kidd et al., 89–99. London: Routledge, 2017.

———. "Who Cares? The Poverty of Objectivism for a Moral Epistemology." In *Rhetorical Spaces: Essays on Gendered Locations*, 103–19. New York: Routledge, 1995.

Collins, Patricia Hill. *Black Feminist Thought: Knowledge, Consciousness, and the Politics of Empowerment*. London: Taylor & Francis, 2002.

Cox, Keith. "Happiness and Unhappiness in the Developing World: Life Satisfaction among Sex Workers, Dump-Dwellers, Urban Poor, and Rural Peasants in Nicaragua." *Journal of Happiness Studies* 13 (2012) 103–28.

DeWitt, Richard. *Worldviews: An Introduction of the History and Philosophy of Science*. Chichester, UK: Wiley-Blackwell, 2010.

Dhawan, Nikita. "Can Non-Europeans Philosophize? Transnational Literacy and Planetary Ethics in a Global Age." *Hypatia* 32 (2017) 488–505.

Eisenstein, Charles. *Sacred Economics: Money, Gift, and Society in the Age of Transition*. Berkeley: Evolver Editions, 2011.

Eisenstein, Zillah. *Global Obscenities: Patriarchy, Capitalism, and the Lure of Cyberfantasy*. New York: New York University Press, 1998.
EIU ViewsWire. "Nicaragua: Briefing Sheet." April 15, 2021. http://www.proquest.com/docview/2512966005/citation/90D4B586C0254EA5PQ/1.
Elgin, Catherine Z. "Epistemic Agency." *Theory and Research in Education* 11 (2013) 135–52.
Farmer, Paul. *To Repair the World*. Berkeley: University of California Press, 2013.
Farmer, Paul, and Gustavo Gutiérrez. *In the Company of the Poor*. Maryknoll, NY: Orbis, 2013.
Firth, Raymond. *Human Types, by Raymond Firth*. Discussion Books 11. London: Nelson, 1938.
Foster, George M. "Interpersonal Relations in Peasant Society." *Human Organization* 19 (1960) 174–78.
Francis. *Evangelii Gaudium*. https://www.vatican.va/content/francesco/en/apost_exhortations/documents/papa-francesco_esortazione-ap_20131124_evangelii-gaudium.html.
Franklin, Jocelyn Sutton. "The Danger of the Extended Hand: A Critique of Humanitarian Aid in Makenzy Orcel's *L'Ombre Animale*." *Karib: Nordic Journal for Caribbean Studies* 4 (2018) 1–8.
Freire, Paulo, and Donaldo Macedo. *Pedagogy of the Oppressed*. Translated by Myra Bergman Ramos. 30th anniversary ed. New York: Bloomsbury Academic, 2000.
French, Jan Hoffman. *Legalizing Identities: Becoming Black or Indian in Brazil's Northeast*. Chapel Hill: University of North Carolina Press, 2009.
Fricker, Miranda. *Epistemic Injustice: Power and the Ethics of Knowing*. Oxford: Oxford University Press, 2007.
Girardi, Giulio. *Faith and Revolution in Nicaragua: Convergence and Contradictions*. Translated by Phillip Berryman. Maryknoll, NY: Orbis, 1989.
Godoy, Carlos Mejia. "Letra El Cristo de Palacagüina." Unpublished revolutionary folk song. https://www.musica.com/letras.asp?letra=1166208.
———. "Somos Hijos de Maíz." Unpublished revolutionary folk song. https://www.adncultura.org/somos-hijos-del-maiz-0.
González, Catherine, and Justo L. González. *The Pulpit and the Oppressed*. Nashville: Abingdon, 1984.
Gramsci, Antonio. *Selections from Cultural Writings*. Edited by David Forgacs. Translated by Geoffrey Nowell-Smith and William Boelhower. Cambridge: Harvard University Press, 1985.
Greider, William. *The Case against "Free Trade": GATT, NAFTA, and the Globalization of Corporate Power*. San Francisco: Earth Island, 1993.
———. *One World, Ready or Not: The Manic Logic of Global Capitalism*. New York: Touchstone, 1997.
Grimal, Henri. *Decolonization: The British, French, Dutch, and Belgian Empires, 1919–1963*. Translated by Stephan De Vos. Boulder, CO: Westview, 1978.
Gugelot, Frédéric. "A Jesuit Way of Being Global?" In *The Oxford Handbook of Jesuits*, edited by Ines G. Županov, 1036–53. Oxford: Oxford University Press, 2019.
Gutiérrez, Gustavo. *Las Casas: In Search of the Poor of Jesus Christ*. Maryknoll, NY: Orbis, 1993.
———. *A Theology of Liberation*. Translated by Sister Caridad Inda and John Eagleson. Maryknoll, NY: Orbis, 1988.

Hammer, Mitchell. "The Intercultural Conflict Style Inventory: A Conceptual Framework and Measure of Intercultural Conflict Resolution Approaches." *International Journal of Intercultural Relations* 29 (2005) 675–95.

Harrison, Beverly Widlung. *Justice in the Making: Feminist Social Ethics*. Louisville: Westminster John Knox, 2004.

Haslam, David. *Faith in Struggle: The Protestant Churches in Nicaragua and Their Response to the Revolution*. London: Epworth, 1987.

Hidalgo, Ann. "*Ponte A Nuestro Lado!* Be On Our Side! The Challenge of the Central American Liberation Theology Masses." In *Liturgy in Postcolonial Perspectives: Only One Is Holy*, edited by Cláudio Carvalhaes, 125–34. Postcolonism and Religions. New York: Palgrave Macmillan, 2015.

Holland, Dorothy, et al. *A Practice Theory of Self and Identity*. Cambridge: Harvard University Press, 1998.

hooks, bell. *Feminist Theory from Margin to Center*. Cambridge: South End, 2000.

Horton, Myles. *The Long Haul: An Autobiography*. New York: Teachers College Press, 1998.

Human Rights Watch. "Nicaragua: Doctors Fired for Covid-19 Comments." June 23, 2020. https://www.hrw.org/news/2020/06/23/nicaragua-doctors-fired-covid-19-comments/.

Hunt, Mary Elizabeth. *Feminist Liberation Theology: The Development of Method in Construction*. London: University Microfilms International, 1980.

———. *Fierce Tenderness: A Feminist Theology of Friendship*. New York: Crossroad, 1991.

Illich, Ivan. *Disabling Professions*. New York: Boyars, 2000.

Isasi-Díaz, María. *In the Struggle: A Hispanic Women's Liberation Theology*. Minneapolis: Fortress, 1993.

James, William. *The Correspondence of William James*. Vol. 12. Charlottesville: University of Virginia Press, 2004.

Jones, Lauren Ila. "Liberating Praxes of Latin American Women Educators in El Salvador, Nicaragua, Bolivia, and Argentina." *Journal of Feminist Studies in Religion* 28 (2012) 197–214.

Khader, Serene J. *Decolonizing Universalism: A Transnational Feminist Ethic*. Oxford: Oxford University Press, 2019.

Kontos, Pia C., and Gary Naglie. "Tacit Knowledge of Caring and Embodied Selfhood." *Sociology of Health & Illness* 31 (2009) 688–704. https://doi.org/10.1111/j.1467-9566.2009.01158.x.

Korgan, Jeffry Odell. *Solidarity Will Transform the World*. Maryknoll, NY: Orbis, 2007.

Kornbluh, Peter. *The Price of Intervention: Reagan's Wars against the Sandinistas*. Washington, DC: Institute for Policy Studies, 1987.

Korten, David C. *Agenda for a New Economy: From Phantom Wealth to Real Wealth*. San Francisco: Berrett-Koehler, 2009.

Kotsko, Adam. *Neoliberalism's Demons: On the Political Theology of Late Capital*. Stanford: Stanford University Press, 2018.

Kroeber, Alfred L. *Anthropology*. New York: Harcourt, Brace, 1923.

Kruks, Sonia. *Retrieving Experience: Subjectivity and Recognition in Feminist Politics*. Ithaca, NY: Cornell University Press, 2001.

Kwok, Pui-lan. *Postcolonial Imagination and Feminist Theology*. Louisville: Westminster John Knox, 2005.

Leach, Michael, and Susan Perry, eds. *A Maryknoll Book of Prayer*. Maryknoll, NY: Orbis, 2004.

Lewis, Oscar. *Life in a Mexican Village: Tepoztlán Restudied*. Urbana: University of Illinois Press, 1951.

Lloyd-Sidle, Patricia, and Bonnie Sue Lewis, eds. *Teaching Mission in a Global Context*. Louisville: Geneva, 2001.

Loorz, Victoria. *Church of the Wild: How Nature Invites Us into the Sacred*. Minneapolis: Broad Leaf, 2021.

Lopez, German. "In One Year, Drug Overdoses Killed More Americans Than the Entire Vietnam War Did." *Vox*, June 20, 2017. https://www.vox.com/policy-and-politics/2017/6/6/15743986/opioid-epidemic-overdose-deaths-2016.

Luna, Jessie K. "Peasant Essentialism in GMO Debates: Bt Cotton in Burkina Faso." *Journal of Agrarian Change* 20 (2020) 579–97. https://doi.org/10.1111/joac.12381.

Maldonado, Michelle Gonzalez. "Liberation Ecclesiologies with Special Reference to Latin America." In *Oxford Handbook of Ecclesiology*, edited by Paul Avis, 573–94. Oxford: Oxford University Press, 2018.

Marx, Karl. *Capital: A Critique of Political Economy*. Translated by Ben Fowker. New York: Penguin, 1990.

McCallie, Kathleen D. "Liberation and Liberal Freedom: A Critique of Rawl's Laws of People in Light of Positive Freedom." PhD diss., University of Oklahoma, 2006.

———. "Towards a Pedagogy of Privilege." *Sacred Spaces: The E-Journal of the American Association of Pastoral Counseling* 10 (2018) 56–74.

McFague, Sallie. *Blessed Are the Consumers: Climate Change and the Practice of Restraint*. Minneapolis: Fortress, 2013.

———. "God's Household: Christianity, Economics, and Planetary Living." In *Subverting Greed: Perspectives on the Global Economy*, edited by Paul Knitter and Chandra Muzaffar, 119–36. Faith Meets Faith Series. Maryknoll, NY: Orbis, 2002.

———. "The Loving Eye vs. the Arrogant Eye: Christian Critique of the Western Gaze on Nature and the Third World." *Ecumenical Review* 49 (1997) 185–93.

McGarrah Sharp, Melinda A. *Creating Resistances: Pastoral Care in a Postcolonial World*. Theology in Practice 7. Leiden: Brill, 2020.

———. *Misunderstanding Stories: Toward a Postcolonial Pastoral Theology*. Eugene, OR: Pickwick Publications, 2013.

Mendez, Jennifer Bickham. *From the Revolution to the Maquiladoras: Gender, Labor, and Globalization in Nicaragua*. Durham, NC: Duke University Press. 2005.

Merich, Diego de. "Empathy in Pursuit of a Caring Ethic in International Development." In *Ethics of Care: Critical Advances in International Perspective*, edited by Marian Barnes et al., 95–107. Chicago: Policy, 2015.

Metoyer, Cynthia Chavez. *Women and the State in Post-Sandinista Nicaragua*. Boulder, CO: Rienner, 1999.

Mies, Maria. *Patriarchy and Accumulation on a World Scale: Women in the International Division of Labour*. 5th ed. London: Zed, 1994.

Míguez, Néstor, et al. *Beyond the Spirit of Empire: Reclaiming Liberation Theology*. London: SCM, 2009.

Milani, Brian. *Designing the Green Economy: The Postindustrial Alternative to Corporate Globalization*. New York: Rowman & Littlefield, 2000.

Miller-McLemore, Bonnie J. "Disciplining: Academic Theology and Practical Knowledge." In *Christian Practical Wisdom: What It Is, Why It Matters*. Grand Rapids: Eerdmans, 2016.

Murphy, John W., and Manuel J. Caro. *Uriel Molina and the Sandinista Popular Movement in Nicaragua*. Jefferson, NC: McFarland, 2006.

Musgrave, Alan. *Common Sense, Science, and Scepticism: A Historical Introduction to the Theory of Knowledge*. New York: Cambridge University Press, 1993.

MZ.Many Names. "Attributing Words." *U.S. Against Equine Slaughter* (blog), November 3, 2008. http://unnecessaryevils.blogspot.com/2008/11/attributing-words.html.

Norris, Pippa. "Voters against Democracy: The Roots of Autocratic Insurgence." *Foreign Affairs*, May/June 2021. https://www.foreignaffairs.com/reviews/voters-against-democracy.

Nussbaum, Martha C. *Creating Capabilities: The Human Development Approach*. Cambridge: Harvard University Press, 2011.

———. "Human Functioning and Social Justice: In Defense of Aristotelian Essentialism." *Political Theory* 20 (1992) 202–46.

OAS. "Two Years into Nicaragua's Human Rights Crisis, the IACHR Stresses Its Permanent Commitment to Victims and Confirms the Consolidation of a Fifth Phase of Repression." April 18, 2020. https://www.oas.org/en/iachr/media_center/preleases/2020/080.asp.

Oliver, Mary. *House of Light*. Boston: Beacon, 1990.

Palmer, Parker J. *The Courage to Teach: Exploring the Inner Landscape of a Teacher's Life*. San Francisco: Jossey-Bass, 1998.

Peters, Rebecca Todd. *Solidarity Ethics: Transformation in a Globalized World*. Minneapolis: Fortress, 2014.

Peterson, V. Spike. "International/Global Political Economy." In *Gender Matters in Global Politics: A Feminist Introduction to International Relations*, edited by Laura J. Shepherd, 204–17. New York: Routledge, 2010.

Petrella, Ivan. *Beyond Liberation Theology: A Polemic*. Reclaiming Liberation Theology. London: SCM, 2008.

Pickrel, Lara Blackwood. "Not Yet Sisters: Friendship as Model for Mission and Ministry." DMin Project Report, Phillips Theological Seminary, 2019.

Primera, Alí. "No Basta Rezar." Unpublished revolutionary folk song. https://ali-primera.lyrics.com.br/letras/1904070/.

Probasco, LiErin. "More Good Than Harm: Moral Action and Evaluation in International Religious Volunteer Tourism." PhD diss., Princeton University, 2013.

———. "Prayer, Patronage, and Personal Agency in Nicaraguan Accounts of Receiving International Aid." *Journal for the Scientific Study of Religion* 55 (2016) 233–49. https://doi.org/10.1111/jssr.12263/.

Rajan, Hamsa. "The Ethics of Transnational Feminist Research and Activism: An Argument for a More Comprehensive View." *Signs: Journal of Women in Culture and Society* 43 (2018) 269–300. https://doi.org/10.1086/693885/.

Ramos, Alcida. "Pulp Fictions of Indigenism." In *Race, Nature, and the Politics of Difference*, edited by Donald S. Moore et al., 356–79. Durham, NC: Duke University Press, 2003.

Randall, Margaret. *Sandino's Daughters Revisited: Feminism in Nicaragua*. New Brunswick, NJ: Rutgers University Press, 1995.

———. *Sandino's Daughters: Testimonies of Nicaraguan Women in Struggle*. New Brunswick, NJ: Rutgers University Press, 1994.

Rawls, John. *The Law of Peoples*. 4th ed. Cambridge: Harvard University Press, 2002.

Recinos, Harold J. *Jesus Weeps: Global Encounters on Our Doorstep*. Nashville: Abingdon, 1992.

Redfield, Robert. *Tepoztlán: A Mexican Village: A Study of Folklife*. Chicago: University of Chicago Press, 1930.

Reuters. "Nicaragua Is on Road to Expulsion from OAS, U.S. Officials Say." February 2, 2022. https://www.reuters.com/article/nicaragua-usa-idINL1N2UE2AA/.

Riggs, Wayne. "Open-Mindedness." *Metaphilosophy* 41 (2010) 172–88.

Ruether, Rosemary Radford. *Becoming Human*. Philadelphia: Westminster, 1982.

———. *Christianity and Social Systems: Historical Constructions and Ethical Challenges*. New York: Rowman & Littlefield, 2009.

———. *Liberation Theology: Human Hope Confronts Christian History and American Power*. New York: Paulist, 1972.

———. *My Quest for Hope and Meaning: An Autobiography*. Eugene, OR: Cascade Books, 2013.

———. *To Change the World: Christology and Cultural Criticism*. New York: Crossroad, 1988.

Russell, Letty M. *Becoming Human*. Library of Living Faith. Philadelphia: Westminster, 1982.

Scott, James C. "Thin Simplifications and Practical Knowledge: Mētis." In *Seeing Like a State*, 309–41. New Haven: Yale University Press, 1998.

Scruggs, T. M. "'Let's Enjoy as Nicaraguans': The Use of Music in the Construction of a Nicaraguan National Consciousness." *Ethnomusicology* 43 (1999) 297–321. https://doi.org/10.2307/852736.

———. "(Re)Indigenization? Post-Vatican II Catholic Ritual and 'Folk Masses' in Nicaragua." *World of Music* 47 (2005) 91–123.

Segundo, Juan Luis. *The Liberation of Theology*. Translated by John Drury. Maryknoll, NY: Orbis, 1985.

Sengupta, Shuddhabrata. "I/Me/Mine—Intersectional Identities as Negotiated Minefields." *Signs: Journal of Women in Culture and Society* 31 (2006) 629–39. http://dx.doi.org/10.1086/499318.

Shepherd, Laura J., ed. *Gender Matters in Global Politics: A Feminist Introduction to International Relations*. New York: Routledge, 2010.

Shiva, Vandana. *Earth Democracy: Justice, Sustainability, Peace*. Cambridge: South End, 2005.

Singer, Peter. *The Life You Can Save*. New York: Random House, 2010.

Smith, Calvin L. *Revolution, Revival, and Religious Conflict in Sandinista Nicaragua*. Religion in the Americas Series 6. Leiden: Brill, 2007.

Smith, Christine M. *Risking the Terror: Resurrection in This Life*. Cleveland: Pilgrim, 2001.

Sobrino, Jon. *Companions of Jesus: The Jesuit Martyrs of El Salvador*. 2nd ed. Maryknoll, NY: Orbis, 1990.

———. *Spirituality of Liberation: Towards Political Holiness*. Translated by Robert R. Barr. Maryknoll, NY: Orbis, 1990.

———. *The True Church and the Poor*. Translated by Matthew J. O'Connell. Maryknoll, NY: Orbis, 1991.

Solis, Marco Antonio. "Cardboard Houses." Unpublished revolutionary folk song. https://www.songlyrics.com/marco-antonio-solis/casas-de-carton-lyrics/.

Spivak, Gayatri. "Can the Subaltern Speak?" In *Marxism and the Interpretation of Culture*, edited by Cary Nelson and Lawrence Grossberg, 271–316. Urbana: University of Illinois Press, 1998.

Stiglitz, Joseph E. *Globalization and Its Discontents.* New York: Norton, 2000.
Stimons, Henry L. *American Policy in Nicaragua: The Lasting Legacy.* New York: Wiener, 1991.
Stoltzfus, Kate. "Across Generations: Interview with Mary E. Hunt." *Journal of Feminist Studies in Religion* 33 (2017) 183–96.
Sumka, Shoshanna, et al. *Working Side by Side: Creating Alternative Breaks as Catalysts for Global Learning, Student Leadership, and Social Change.* Sterling, VA: Stylus, 2015.
Tarrow, Sidney. *The New Transnational Activism.* Cambridge: University of Cambridge Press, 2005.
Tinker, George. "Jesus, Corn Mother, and Conquest." In *American Indian Liberation: A Theology of Sovereignty,* 84–110. Maryknoll, NY: Orbis, 2008.
Townley, Cynthia. *A Defense of Ignorance: Its Value for Knowers and Roles in Feminist and Social Epistemologies.* New York: Rowman & Littlefield, 2011.
U.S. Embassy in Nicaragua. "Travel Advisory Level 3: Reconsider Travel." December 5, 2022. https://ni.usembassy.gov/travel-advisory-level-3-reconsider-travel/#:~:text=Reconsider%20travel%20to%20Nicaragua%20due,enforces%20laws%20for%20political%20purposes.
Wade, Christine J., and Thomas W. Walker. *Nicaragua: Living in the Shadow of the Eagle.* 5th ed. Boulder, CO: Westview, 2011.
Walker, Alice. *Possessing the Secret of Joy: A Novel.* New York: Simon & Schuster, 1992.
Weber, Clare. *Visions of Solidarity: U.S. Peace Activists in Nicaragua from War to Women's Activism and Globalization.* New York: Lexington, 2006.
Wolf, Eric R. *Peasant Wars of the Twentieth Century.* New York: Harper & Row, 1969.
Yunus, Muhammad. *Banker to the Poor: Micro-Credit Lending and the Battle against World Poverty.* 1999. Reprint, New York: Public Affairs, 2007.
Yuval-Davis, Nira. "Dialogical Epistemology—An Intersectional Resistance to the 'Oppression Olympics.'" *Gender & Society* 26 (2012) 46–54.
Zinn, Howard. *Declarations of Independence: Cross-Examining American Ideology.* New York: HarperCollins, 1990.

Index

ACOPADES, 48–49, 64, 67, 71, 95–96, 108–9, 111–14, 147, 170–71, 189, 191, 222–23, 263
Alexander, M. Jacqui, 26, 256
Althaus-Reid, Marcella, 7
anthropology, 177–78, 181
Anzaldúa, Gloria, 14
Arellano, Luz Beatriz, 197
Armstrong, Karen, 257

Bacon, David, 162
Baker, Kendall Clark, 58
Banfield, Edward C., 179
base communities, xx, 42–43, 48, 67, 215–20, 227–82, 237
beach, 125, 136, 148–51
Besley, Tina, 26, 213
Bible, 29, 177, 197, 212, 217
Binford, Leigh, 182
Boff, Leonardo, 6, 15, 245, 259
Borge, Tomás, 55
Bradbury, Ray, 152
Brazal, Agnes M., 177
Brentlinger, John, 6, 38, 60
Brown, Adrienne Maria, 141

CAFTA, 82
Camp, Elisabeth, 121
campesino, 165, 175, 183–84
capitalism, 3, 8, 83–84, 88–90, 90–93, 179, 181, 185, 232, 250
capitalist, 179–82, 190

Cardenal, Fernando, 56
Caro, Manuel, 13–14, 25, 185, 231–32, 260
Casas, Barolomé de las, 45, 184
Casaldáliga, Pedro, 5
Chomsky, Noam, 57, 261
christology, 7, 9, 11, 20–22, 59, 85, 112
Chua, Amy, 140–41
Cobb, John B., Jr., 90–91, 186
Code, Lorraine, 246, 249, 253–54
Collins, Patricia Hill, 141, 243, 254
colonialism, x, 12–14, 19, 40, 45, 167, 181–82, 210, 242–43, 249, 277–78; colonization, 270
communism, 28, 57, 214, 229, 243
Contra War; Nicaraguan War with the U.S., 10, 19, 28, 35, 118, 168, 215
cordobas; currency, 30, 35, 109, 201–2, 207
Corn Mother, 168
corporations, 90, 161, 199, 232
Cox, Keith, 167
cultural center in Chacraseca, 48, 50, 96, 108–9, 114, 164–65, 199, 262, 272

decolonization, 8, 181–82
deregulation, 89, 92–93
DeWitt, Richard, 121
Dhawan, Nikita, 255

ecclesiology, 11, 59
ecofeminism, 185
education, 50, 57, 95–119, 211, 215, 233–35, 241, 256; Christian, ix, 17, 25; popular, 117–19; theological, xviii, 3, 11, 16, 25
Eisenstein, Charles, 92–93
Eisenstein, Zillah, 89
Elgin, Catherine Z., 254
epistemology, xix, xxi, 7, 10, 20, 23, 246–59
ethics, ix, x, xv, xvii, xix, 7, 14, 238–39, 245, 254–55; care, 246; liberative, xx, 177, 246; solidarity, xi, 59–60. 190; transnational, xviii, 243, 254

farm; model in Chacraseca, 17, 30, 154–63, 175, 262–64
Farmer, Paul, 124, 213, 244
feminist liberation theology, xviii, 6–7, 15, 19, 55, 197, 243
feminist theory, 9, 120, 122, 246, 256
Firth, Raymond, 178
Foster, George M., 178–80
Francis, Pope, 240
Franklin, Jocelyn Sutton, 5
Freire, Paulo, xviii, 14–15
Fricker, Miranda, 249–54
FSLN, xxi, 56

gay, lesbian, bisexual, transgender, queer; LGBTIA identities, 219–20, 274
Gill, Leslie, 182
Girardi, Giulio, 243–44
Godoy, Carlos Mejia, xiii, xv, 12, 21, 53, 166, 184
Gonzaléz, Catherine, 6
Gonzaléz Justo L., 6
Gramsci, Antonio, 182
Greider, William, 25–26, 82, 88–89
Grimal, Henri, 181–82
Gugelot, Frédéric, 8
Gutiérrez, Gustavo, 6, 124, 184, 213, 244

Hammer, Mitchell, 249

Harrison, Beverly Widlung, 55, 58
Haslam, David, 56
health care, 55–58, 97, 124–53, 213, 234, 262
Hidalgo, Ann, 12
hooks, bell, 256
Horton, Myles, 256
housing, xx–xxi, 2, 35, 48, 54, 67, 111, 114, 125, 171, 187
Human Rights Watch, 265
Hunt, Mary Elizabeth, 6, 11, 197

Illich, Ivan, 5
imperialism, xi, 3, 6, 13, 19, 26, 56, 167, 179, 181, 196, 210–211, 243–44, 255
incarnation, 22, 197
intercultural, ix, xi, xv, xviii, xxi, 11, 24, 26, 137–38, 153, 177, 197, 237–49, 256
International Monetary Fund, 83
Isasi-Díaz, María, xix

Korgan, Jeffry Odell, 12
Korten, David C., 93
Kroeber, Alfred, 177–78
Kruks, Sonia, 120–21, 151, 255–56
Kwok, Pui-lan, 195
liberation theology, 7, 11, 14–15, 19, 43, 55, 185, 217, 227, 240, 243–45

Loorz, Victoria, 238
lucha, la; struggle, 216, 227, 233, 243–46, 262, 265, 277–78

Maldonado, Michelle Gonzalez, 243
Maria de los Angeles, 13, 39, 42, 232
Marx, Karl, 13, 59, 180–81, 232
marxism, 14, 89, 180–82, 232
Maryknoll, xiv, xx, 9, 50, 52, 61, 227, 228, 230, 234, 237, 265
mass, 113, 184, 228–29, 233–34, 265; folk mass, 12, 19–20, 53, 184
McFague, Sallie, 3, 90
Mendez, Jennifer Bickham, 91
Merich, Diego de, xviii
Metoyer, Cynthia Chavez, 176

microcredit, 72–76, 158, 171, 203, 262, 264
Mies, Maria, 14, 185–86
Milani, Brian, 91
Miller-McLemore, Bonnie J., xvii
Molina, Uriel, xxi, 3, 13, 15, 25, 42, 185, 227, 231–33, 260
murals, 13, 35, 39, 42–43, 199, 207, 215
Murphy, John W., 13, 15, 25, 185, 231–32, 260
music, folk, 12, 19–20, 41, 109, 118, 164–70, 183–84

NAFTA, 82, 89
nationality, xx, 8, 57, 239
neocolonial, x, xvii, 11, 14, 141, 153, 175, 177, 183, 241
neoliberalism, 7, 59, 90, 92, 178, 232
Norris, Pippa, 264
Nussbaum, Martha C., 246–51, 255

Ortega, Daniel, xxi, 83, 230, 260, 263

Palmer, Parker J., 252
patriarchy, 7, 14, 185–86
peasant, xxi, 155, 175–84, 242, 273; peasant mass, 20, 184
Penrose, Leslie, xxi, 3–5, 10, 16, 36, 60, 72, 187–88; oral history, 214–28
Peters, Michael A., 26, 213
Peters, Rebecca Todd, xi, 59–60
Petrella, Ivan, 7
postcolonial, xviii, xxi, 5, 10, 58, 93, 122, 177, 183, 195, 243
praxis, xviii–xix, 4, 6, 7, 10, 23, 60, 141, 239–46, 254–56
prayer, 9, 24, 29, 49, 51, 61–62, 66, 86–88, 97, 112, 114, 206, 221, 241, 253, 263
private property, 196
Probasco, LiErin, 5, 241

racism, xx, 137–42; white supremacy, 10–11, 14, 140
Rajan, Hamsa, 243, 254
Ramos, Alcida, x–xi
Randall, Margaret, 84

Rawls, John, 93
Recinos, Harold J., 12
Redfield, Robert, 179
resistance, 42–43, 54–55, 58–59, 77, 90, 167–69; mental resistance 107, 137, 151
Ruether, Rosemary Radford, ix, 15, 25, 90–91, 239, 243

sandinista, xxi, 14, 40, 43, 55–58, 104, 176, 183, 215, 228, 230–231, 235
Sandino, Augusto César, 19, 22, 41–43, 53, 57, 207, 219
scholarships, 50, 96, 108–9, 117, 165, 181–83, 243, 262
scripture, 7, 56, 217, 244–45. *See also* Bible
Scruggs, T. M., xv, 183–84
Segundo, Juan Luis, 244–45
sewing cooperative, 48, 50, 78–84, 114, 164. *See also* stitching hope
sexism, xx, 7: machismo, 23
Sharp, Melinda A. McGarrah, xiv, 11, 84
Shiva, Vandana, 246
Singer, Peter, 240
Sobrino, Jon, 6, 122–23, 212, 239
social enterprise, xx, 50, 76–78, 84, 91, 227, 273
socialism, 83, 89–93
Solis, Marco Antonio, 53
spiritual formation, ix, xiii, xvii, xx, 3, 10–11, 17, 19, 84, 123, 238, 240–241, 257
Spivak, Gayatri, 183, 247, 255
stitching hope. *See* sewing cooperative
Stiglitz, Joseph E., 92
Striffler, Steve, 182

Uhlen, Joan C., xx, 3, 8–9, 15, 90, 227, 265
United Church of Christ, xi, 3, 230
United Nations, 58, 230

volcano 31, 44, 70, 198, 208–9

Wade, Christine J., 40, 55, 176
wages, 89, 199, 274

Walker, Alice, 54
Walker, Thomas, 40, 55, 176
water, potable, 106, 110, 114, 194, 222, 263
Watson, Lilla, 1–2
Wolf, Eric R., 182
World Bank, 83, 88, 90–92, 277

yuca, 64, 74, 81, 132, 144, 154, 159, 190, 202
Yunus, Muhammad, 72, 76
Yuval-Davis, Nira, 247, 254–55

Zellya, Elmer, 5
Zinn, Howard, 57

Printed in the USA
CPSIA information can be obtained
at www.ICGtesting.com
LVHW021652160724
785289LV00002B/3

9 781666 782431